Praise for *Practice the Pause*
New Brain Science, and Wh

"What if a seven-second pause could transform your life? Caroline Oakes' warm-hearted *Practice the Pause* explores this question as a radically inclusive path for us all. Bringing together the wisdom of Jesus' ancient contemplative practice with the exciting, concrete discoveries of neuroscience, plus the sagest voices from all traditions, she takes us on an interspiritual journey to awaken—and keep awake—the spark of the divine within. A must-read!"

—Carmen Acevedo Butcher, PhD, translator of Brother Lawrence's *Practice of the Presence* and of *Cloud of Unknowing*

"I've been thinking that there needs to be a book that connects the dots between contemplative Christianity and neuroscience; I've also thought that we need a good book on Jesus' own spiritual practice. Caroline Oakes has written an excellent book that fills both of these needs. *Practice the Pause* is the type of book that you'll go back to again and again—and you'll recommend it to all your friends."

—Carl McColman, author of *Eternal Heart* and *The Big Book of Christian Mysticism*

"This book lives up to its title. When I first picked up a copy of Caroline Oakes' manuscript I was quite taken back by the title *Practice the Pause: Jesus' Contemplative Practice, New Brain Science and What It Means to Be Fully Human*—all in just 280 pages. But when I put the book down, all I could say was, "Yes! *Practice the Pause* is a WAKE UP call to see how Jesus' own practice, science, and being human indeed do dance together, and it is a call to STAY AWAKE to the ongoing intentional unfolding of my spiritual journey."

—Fr Carl J. Arico, founding member of Contemplative Outreach, author of *Taste of Silence*

"In this masterful piece of writing, Caroline Oakes artfully weaves together the depth, breadth, and wholeness of the contemplative journey around the unifying theme of the transformative power of the pause. Her remarkable achievement is that this weaving is accomplished in a straightforward and accessible form in which she gently leads the reader into both a brain-centered and a heart-centered understanding of the connection between even the simplest spiritual practices and our ability to transform our lives and the lives of others through contemplation *in action.* As an added gift, Ms. Oakes links the reader to the vast array of literary and biblical resources from which she abundantly draws."

—William Redfield, Episcopal priest and
founder of Wisdom's Work

"Viewing Jesus as a practitioner of contemplative prayer, Caroline Oakes takes readers on journeys through the bible which reveal the depth of Jesus' prayer life and its intimate connection with activist ministry. This re-framing, along with practical helps and explorations of contemplative neuroscience which show the healing efficacy of prayer, make for a great read for spiritual seekers and Christians who long for a fresh take on their faith tradition."

—The Rev. Jonathan Linman, Ph.D., Pastor of Faith Lutheran
Church, Phoenix, AR, and former director of General
Theological Seminary's Center for Christian Spirituality

"*Practice the Pause* provides a timely overview of Jesus' spirituality in the context of his first-century Judaism. The author guides readers from this foundation through the evolution of contemporary contemplative practices within modern Judaism and Christianity. The final chapters provide readers with practical advice, using Thomas Keating's unique insights from neuroscience on the transformative practice of centering prayer and meditation on the Bible.

Caroline Oakes' summary of Fr. Thomas' work, based on his writing, is the most substantive and accessible to readers I have ever seen. An excellent resource for group study and reflection."

—David G. R. Keller, Ed.D., Director of Thomas Keating's Contemplative Ministry Project and author of *Lord, Teach Us To Pray: One Hundred Daily Reflections on Jesus' Life of Prayer*

"A rich and desperately-needed Wisdom primer, *Practice the Pause* artfully bridges the gaps between neuroscience, contemplation, and contemporary Christianity to present anew the life, message, and prayer practice of our Master Teacher Jesus. Oakes is a trustworthy guide and her offering is a practical, enlightened course on living into the fullness of our Divine Potential through the recovery of the example of Jesus. If we have any interest in our personal or collective evolution into Love, we had best tune in for this one."

—Jane Savage Woods, Women's Wisdom Guide, Circle Facilitator, and Spiritual Companion at Waking House

"It's well known that meditation practices light up a brain scan and are proven to promote health and well-being. But how? Oakes focuses on the transformative moment in the millisecond pause between the fear stimulus and our ingrained fight-or-flight response. Then she shows us how to *practice that pause*, over and over, until a third neural path opens and our mind gradually expands in the Mind of Christ."

—David R. Anderson, author of *Breakfast Epiphanies* and *Losing Your Faith, Finding Your Soul*

"In the tradition of wisdom teachers, Oakes leads us on a rich spiritual pilgrimage out of our Western paradigm and into the East, where Jesus spent time in contemplation and prayer. Oakes explores the practices at the heart of Jesus' mission of 'metanoia' - true transformation - to be fully alive and explores these practices' extraordinary positive neurological impact. For anyone who seeks the intersection of science and faith and a new way of being, *Practice the Pause* is for you."

—Malika Cox, OnBeing Social Healing Fellow; Author of the *Flourish OKC Restorative Justice Learning Curriculum*; MA Practical Theology, MPhil Conflict Resolution & Reconciliation

"This remarkable book, the fruit of years of dedicated research and spiritual practice, draws upon Hebrew and Christian scripture as well as contemporary neuroscience to provide grounded and innovative guidance for ways of contemplative prayer. Don't miss the excellent guide for individual and group study and discussion as well!"

—Anne Silver, Director of General Theological Seminary's Center for Christian Spirituality

"In *Practice the Pause,* Caroline Oakes masterfully unlocks the 'hidden in plain sight' contemplative practice of Jesus, revealing Jesus as not only a fully realized spiritual teacher, but as one who is embodying a path of contemplation-in-action that we too can journey. Oakes weaves together ancient insight with modern neuroscience to give a complete picture of who and what we can all become by embodying the active, contemplative way of Jesus."

—Keith Kristich, founder of the *Closer Than Breath* contemplative community

"Through *Practice the Pause*, Caroline Oakes offers us a much-needed bridge—a bridge between Western and Eastern Christianity, and between contemplative spirituality and contemporary neuroscience. It is a bridge whose time has come. May it lead to greater unity, presence, compassion, and transformation in our world and in all of us."

—Christianne Squires, founder of the Light House community for contemplative women

"In *Practice the Pause,* Caroline Oakes adds a significant volume to the growing library of books reclaiming the ancient Christian Wisdom tradition. Jesus is revealed as a master wisdom teacher by the writers of the synoptic Gospels. Through realizing the mutual indwelling of the Divine within each of us and the intentional practice of contemplative presence, the followers of this contemplative way discover how to live from a deeper place revealed in the teaching and life of Jesus. The study guide makes *Practice the Pause* an ideal choice for spiritual journey groups of all sorts."

—Winston Charles, Director of the Clergy Spiritual Life and Leadership Program at the Shalem Institute for Spiritual Formation

PRACTICE THE PAUSE

PRACTICE THE PAUSE

Jesus' Contemplative Practice, New Brain Science, and What It Means to Be Fully Human

CAROLINE OAKES

Broadleaf Books
Minneapolis

PRACTICE THE PAUSE
Jesus' Contemplative Practice, New Brain Science, and What It Means to Be Fully Human

In all Scripture quotations, italics are the author's emphasis.

Cover design: Juicebox Design

Print ISBN: 978-1-5064-8307-8
eBook ISBN: 978-1-5064-8309-2

This book is dedicated to Allison, Cat, and Susie—
Together you opened my eyes to the magic, delight, and wonder
of practicing the pause.

CONTENTS

CONTENTS

INTRODUCTION

For millennia, spiritual teachers of every wisdom tradition have invited and encouraged and inspired us to "wake up" and to be "awake."

"Keep awake," says Jesus.

"Stay awake, my heart, stay awake," says Rumi.

"Now is the time to wake from sleep," says Paul of Tarsus.

"Arise, awake, and stop not until the goal is reached," says Swami Vivekananda.

"I am awake," says the Buddha.

"See beyond your mind," says Jesus.

"Be still and know that I am God," say the psalmists of Psalm 46:10.

"I am," says Jesus.

Even now, living our demanding and complex twenty-first-century lives, we can feel the tug of these ancient wisdom teachers calling us to wake up and imagine a profoundly more loving and perceptive way of understanding ourselves, our world, and the lives we are living.

But what would this way of being look like? What would it look like to be awake like Jesus?

A marvelous passage in one of Thomas Merton's journal entries may give us a clue.

Merton was a Trappist monk, a writer, and a social activist whose writing has inspired thousands of people of many faiths and religions. In this passage from his collection of journal entries, Merton describes a profound wake-up moment he experienced on one completely ordinary day while running errands for his monastery.

As Merton tells the story, he was standing on the corner of Fourth and Walnut Streets[1] in the heart of downtown Louisville, Kentucky, when he was suddenly overwhelmed with the realization that he *loved* all the people around him.

Merton said,

> This sense of liberation from an illusory difference was such a relief and such a joy to me that I almost laughed out loud. . . . It was as if I suddenly saw the secret beauty of their hearts, the depths of their hearts, where neither sin nor desire nor self-knowledge can reach, the core of their reality, the person that each one is in God's eyes. If only they could all see themselves as they really are. If only we could see each other that way all the time.[2]

Merton gives us a glimpse here of what it means to be truly awake. Having the kind of inclusive, unitive awareness that Merton experienced on Fourth and Walnut is the state of being Jesus calls us to throughout the gospels—"Wake up, do not be afraid—you can have eyes that see[3] beyond the fears and egoic constructs of your lives. Can you not see the divinity in yourselves,[4] in others, and in all that is around us? Watch how I do this."

~ ~ ~

Many of us as Western Christians will miss out on noticing this foundational gospel message and the potential personal transformation that it points to. If you have been taught to understand Jesus through a Western Christian "savior-oriented" lens,[5] it is easy to miss Jesus' clarion call[6] for us to wake up and recognize our *own* divinity, our *own* spark of the divine that dwells within us, and that spark of the divine indwelling in all others.

And so most of us as Western Christians then completely miss that the gospel writers reveal the way to answer that clarion call—Jesus' *own* profound contemplative practice of taking time to be in silence and solitude with God.

It turns out there is much more in the gospels than meets our Western Christian eye.

As Western Christians, we aren't taught, as many Eastern Christians are, to notice the role that Jesus plays as a master wisdom teacher who shows us the Way to *practice* waking up and having eyes that see beyond our unconscious, egoic reflex way of seeing. We don't notice that Jesus himself teaches and models the very path of spiritual awakening and personal transformation we are seeking. Despite Paul urging us to "let this mind be in you, which was also in Christ Jesus,"[7] many of us just have never been taught that it is the very practices of Jesus that get us there.

Thomas Merton himself, who some call a "Western explorer of the East,"[8] references his own practice of personal contemplation, his own time in solitude with God, as a precedent to his enlightened Fourth and Walnut moment. He says, "It is in fact the function of solitude to make one realize such things with a clarity that would be [otherwise] impossible."[9]

Because the lens through which Eastern Christians understand the life of Jesus is less savior-oriented and more "wisdom-oriented,"[10] many Christians in the East, including Eastern Orthodox and Eastern Catholics, are more able to recognize the wisdom of Jesus' wake-up call of transformation and then to more easily recognize the practices he demonstrates that make answering that call possible.

For Christians in the East, that path of spiritual awakening is not only modeled for us by Jesus; it is understood to be the very purpose of the spiritual life—*theosis*: Through the life practices of intentional silence and solitude, the divine indwelling within us can transform our minds and hearts. We are able to "put on the mind of Christ." Through Eastern Christian eyes, this is how we learn to see in the expansive and inclusive way that Jesus of Nazareth saw and to love in the way Jesus of Nazareth loved.

Shifting Eastward

Through the recent work of Richard Rohr, Cynthia Bourgeault, the late Thomas Keating, and other teachers of Christian contemplative practice and the wisdom tradition,[11] a growing number of Western Christians are now shifting a bit eastward, toward this more Eastern Christian wisdom orientation. With less focus on doctrinal systems and on what constitutes "belief" in Jesus, the emphasis of this wisdom movement is on experiencing the awakened way of *being* that Jesus embodied, particularly in the context of Jesus' own profound contemplative awareness *practice*. (We Westerners rarely notice Jesus even *having* an intentional contemplative practice; it is *that* hidden in plain sight for us.)

The power of Jesus' contemplative practice cannot be overemphasized. It is this transformative practice that became a model for Jesus' followers, for early Eastern Christians, for Christian monastics and mystics, and for followers of the Christian contemplative tradition for hundreds (even thousands) of years.

It is this transformative practice that is becoming a widely recognized contemplative model for both Christians and non-Christians today. With the surge of interest in the new field of *contemplative* neuroscience, and its studies of the power of contemplative practices being an antidote to the nonstop digital-age distractions that pull us from our center, there is now a parallel surge of interest in Jesus' own practice of contemplative awareness.

A growing number of people from all traditions are coming to realize that Jesus himself exemplifies what it is to be an engaged and active contemplative in a demanding and complex world.

As we take a slightly more Eastern view of Jesus here in *Practice the Pause*, and focus particularly on Jesus' transformative centering pause practice, I can almost imagine Jesus saying, "Yes, now do you see? *This* is the way to reconnect, to realign, and to remember your innermost self in God. *This* is the way to wake up and realize that we each embody God's radically inclusive, self-giving Love. So wake up, and stay awake! This Love that I embody is not an unattainable superpower. This Love that I embody is an innate and attainable state of being that is accessible to *everyone*. You can do this too—not only what I do but even greater things."[12]

So let's together try to refocus our Western lens just a little bit eastward for a while as we now begin our own wisdom journey, looking for markers of a path of transformation that may have been beckoning to us all along.

Waking Up

The first step on such a wake-up journey is realizing that we need to wake up at all. We in the West tend to think we already *are* awake (and doing just fine, thank you very much). After all, morning to night, we are busy getting things done, being where we're supposed to be, making things happen, meeting the incessant demands of our daily lives.

But if we pause for a fraction of a second, might we feel a gentle but insistent tug to stop and consider: Are we really as awake as we think we are? Don't many of us spend at least some of our day on automatic pilot, needing more time and space for our relationships, for ourselves, for true rest? Don't most of us find we push aside external and internal cues pointing to a need and to a real desire for a more balanced pace, more reflective responses, more of a sense of purpose in our lives, more insight—even wisdom?

What if we allowed ourselves to take that pause and listen to the still, small voice calling us to a more soul-nourishing rhythm of work and rest, of deeper connection, of space for quiet, and of living into our life's potential? What if Jesus' words "stay awake, pay attention, see beyond the mind"[13] are what the still, small voice in each of us is trying to say? And what if the very practices of Jesus, some hidden in plain view from our Western Christian eyes, have been showing us, all along, the *way* to wake up and live a life transformed—the way to *fully* live our "one wild and precious life"?[14]

Practice the Pause is an invitation to take that pause. It is an invitation to "come and see"[15] what it might look like to be truly awake and to be fully human like Jesus.

Surprise Research Revelations

When I began my graduate thesis research at The General Theological Seminary of the Episcopal Church, I wanted to engage in a deep study of the gospels, intentionally reading them as though for the first time. I was searching for clues to what it was that equipped Jesus of Nazareth to live so fully into his ministry of radical compassion, forgiveness, and speaking truth to power, day after day.

I intentionally had in mind a very human Jesus in my research, so I was searching for day-to-day practices and for particularly developed human capacities in Jesus, as opposed to signs of imbued divinity, that may have equipped him to calm the fight/flight, despair, and fatigue that are a part of being human and to "stay awake" and open to the promptings of the Divine. I wondered what equipped Jesus to see the world through an open and inclusive awareness, what he calls *metanoia*, and to be able to respond to life's rigor and challenges from a place of deep wisdom and divine indwelling.

My research was revelatory to me.

I became aware of the true meaning of two particularly errant (some say *tragic*) mistranslations in the gospels that, when read in their correct translation, actually break open for us what Richard Rohr and other wisdom teachers describe as "*the* central message of the Gospels." (A couple of spoiler alerts: gospel writers never intended the Greek word *metanoia* to mean "repent" in the way we understand it today, and Jesus' directive to "go into your inner room [to pray]" does not mean to go into a particular room in your house!)

Discovering the intended meaning of these and other key gospel passages, and then also becoming aware of three key Jewish concepts that were prevalent in Jesus' time, was like discovering a kind of Rosetta Stone code that revealed otherwise hidden meaning in Jesus' contemplative practice and way of being.

The Neuroscience Connection

Being simultaneously engaged in a Mindful Schools, Inc.[16] training program to teach the practice of mindfulness meditation, I became aware of the emerging new scientific field of contemplative neuroscience and of the very first groundbreaking studies proving that contemplative practices catalyze changes in the brain's neural pathways in ways that enhance focus, equanimity, compassion, and insight. Here was modern-day scientific confirmation of the link I was beginning to see between Jesus' own transformative practices and his way of living into his own human/divine potential, *a link the gospel writers may have been wanting us to see all along.*

Suddenly, the delightful "brainy" side of Jesus' practice became apparent. By showing us how to "stay awake" and "see beyond the mind" two thousand years ago, Jesus was modeling a practice that we now know literally rewires our brain to move past our fight/flight impulses, to release the confines of our own ego, and to equip us to live into being fully human.

Naming the Unnameable God

I notice that when modern-day wisdom masters such as Richard Rohr and the late Thomas Keating have spoken to large and diverse audiences, they have often described God as "Ultimate Reality, whom we call 'God' in the Judeo-Christian tradition."[17]

As a spiritual director, I have come to know individuals who are either reconstructing their faith or for other reasons may not be comfortable with simply the term *God* to describe what is, in so many respects, unnamable. Some people are more comfortable with other ways of capturing the living spiritual reality of All that is—Spirit, the Great Mystery, the Holy, Love, the Great Spirit, the Infinite.

I have enormous respect for all those who are on such a journey, and I have been honored to witness the many gifts this journey can bring. I invite all who are reading *Practice the Pause* to use a name of your choice to replace the ones I choose to use at any point to describe this Great Mystery.

Because I often think of God as being an active verb, you will find I also often refer to "that of God" or "the movement and flow of God" when speaking of the Unnameable Divine. Sometimes when we talk of God, the simple term *God* can seem overly conceptual, where "the spirit of God" seems to speak to a living reality, so you will see that occasionally I also refer to God in this way as well.[18]

Here We Go

So as we embark on this *Practice the Pause* journey together, discovering the core and ground of Jesus' own contemplative practice and how practices such as these can rewire our own brains, I invite you to "keep watch" to see if a subtle but profound revisioning might emerge—a revisioning of Jesus of Nazareth as a master wisdom teacher who shows us "the Way," a transformative path of practices we can follow that reins in the fight/flight reactions of our human psyche and attunes us to an innate, more expansive, attuned, and loving awareness of ourselves, others, God, and the world around us.

Just what were these practices of Jesus of Nazareth? And how can we take on similar practices that will equip us, as they apparently equipped Jesus, to move past the limiting fight/flight fears and impulses of everyday life controlled by the older regions of our brain and then live into our brain's human potential, controlled by the new parts of our brain? Might Jesus have been inviting us to "come and see" the potential of who we are in our core and essence and how we can "do good better" in our world?[19] Could it be that Jesus himself was showing us "the Way" to "put on the mind of Christ"?

These are the enlivening questions we will be living into as we journey through *Practice the Pause* together. My hope is that this book will help get us closer to what the answers to these questions might be for each one of us and that each of us might someday find ourselves caught up in our own Fourth-and-Walnut-Street moment.

I

AWAKENING THE HEART

CHAPTER 1

We Are Human, We Are Divine

Let the same mind be in you that
was in Christ Jesus.
—Philippians 2:5

Let's begin with a story.

My friend and fellow seminarian Oksana Lebidenko was seated next to me as the Metro North train headed up along the Hudson River toward Holy Cross Monastery, where we were to spend the weekend with fellow General Theological Seminary students. Holy Cross Monastery is a holy and welcoming retreat house hosted by Episcopalian monks who "pray the hours," chant psalms from the Book of Psalms at several allotted times throughout each day, and offer opportunities for silence and solitude in the Benedictine monastic tradition to their usually full house of retreat guests.

It was on that train ride that Oksana quietly described to me a very secret encounter she had as a young girl with her beloved Ukrainian grandmother. It was, Oksana told me, the moment she first learned about God. And it was a moment that has forever shaped Oksana's spiritual life and vision. I share her tender story here because, in it, Oksana is also describing both the power of the divine indwelling of God living within all of us and the transformative centering pause practice we will be exploring here in *Practice the Pause.*

Oksana is Ukrainian-born and was raised as a child in the 1950s in what was then the Soviet Union, when organized religion was suppressed and parents could even be deprived of their parental rights if they taught religion to their children.

Oksana told me that when she was a young girl, it was against the law in her country to believe in God or to assemble together in anything that might seem like a church gathering. She had been taught nothing at all about God or church in her very early years. But one day when she was five years old, her grandmother whispered to her that she wanted to tell her something very special. Oksana could tell that her grandmother was excited and nervous.

Oksana and her grandmother walked to a quiet place together, just the two of them. Oksana remembered that her grandmother knelt down so they could be very close. Then her grandmother began to whisper to her all about "this wonderful thing called God." Her grandmother's eyes were full and twinkling. She told Oksana that God loves her. She told Oksana that God is with her always. She told Oksana that "this loving God" is all around her, and in her, and in everyone, and in everything.

Oksana said she was captivated and enthralled with every word her grandmother was secretly sharing with her about this wonderful, loving God. She remembered she felt a "deep-inside excitement and even wonderment" because this God her grandmother was telling her about felt very, very familiar to her. This wonderful, loving God was something Oksana had already felt inside herself in her own way but did not yet have words for.

Then Oksana's grandmother told her that she must never, ever tell *anyone* this great secret. She said this was something that only she and Oksana could talk about with each other, no one else—no one. For many years, it was that way.

When I shared with Oksana how sorry I was that she could not talk to anyone about this great secret, she said, "Oh no, actually, this has been okay for me. Really. Because, you see, from that moment when my grandmother first told me about God, I knew I had a kind of 'monastery' right here, in my heart."

Oksana told me that in the years following, as she was growing up, she could turn her thoughts to her heart at any moment and know that God was there. And as she has grown older, Oksana said, coming back to her heart is how she comes back to her self and feels God close.

The Indwelling Presence of the Holy

Oksana's tender description of the holy, secret "monastery" within to which she returns for grounding and inner knowing is what I and other contemplatives might name as the divine indwelling, a place of quiet and stillness where we can connect to our deepest selves and to the Spirit within us.

As we begin *Practice the Pause*, I share this description of Oksana's experience of the indwelling presence of the Holy because her practice of intentionally returning to what she calls the "monastery in her heart" is the basis of contemplative practices of all major spiritual traditions and, as we will see, is the basis of the interior prayer taught and modeled by Jesus himself.[1] At the same time, Oksana's practice is also the basis for a large and fascinating body of revolutionary neuroscience research that now validates the benefits of contemplative practices of all kinds for emotional, psychological, and physical health.

Indeed, this movement of pausing, releasing, and returning is at the heart of the mindful, contemplative Judeo-Christian *way of being* taught and shown to us by Jesus of Nazareth in the gospel accounts of Christian scripture, which we will explore here in *Practice the Pause.*

Oksana's practice has equipped her to live fully "awake" in her life, and new scientific discoveries are now telling us what that means in the language of neuroscience.

In these next chapters, we will explore together how Oksana's simple practice, Jesus' own first-century centering pause practice (sometimes hidden in plain view), and even today's new brain science can all show us how we, too, might be renewed and transformed by the simple but powerful practice of pausing to return and rest in the wonder and power of the divine indwelling within us.

The Infinite Source

Modern theologians including Thomas Merton, Cynthia Bourgeault, and Richard Rohr have written with great clarity on the "divine indwelling," some in ways that can take our breath away.

In Thomas Merton's words, "At the center of our being is a point . . . of pure truth, a point or spark which belongs entirely to God [and] is the pure glory of God written in us."[2]

In the words of Cynthia Bourgeault, "As we move toward center, our own being and the divine being become more and more mysteriously interwoven. . . . The divine indwelling . . . reveals the Source of our own being. . . . It also reveals the direction in which our hearts must travel for a constantly renewed intimacy with this Source."[3]

This divine indwelling in each and every one of us is also described by Franciscan monk and priest Richard Rohr in heart-affirming, delightful ways: "You (and every other created thing) begin with your unique divine DNA, an inner destiny as it were, an absolute core that knows the truth about you . . . an *imago Dei* that begs to be allowed, to be fulfilled, and to show itself. Historically, it was often called 'the soul.' This is your True Self, the Divine Indwelling, the Holy Spirit within us." Rohr goes on to say he believes "the single and true purpose of mature religion is to allow you to experience your True Self—who you are in God and who God is in you—and to live a generous life from that Infinite Source."[4]

East and West

If you were brought up in a traditional Western Christian faith, that is, as experienced through a primarily Western worldview, this idea of following a spiritual *path* to fully "experience your Divine Indwelling, your True Self," and to "live from the Infinite Source" that is God, might not be familiar or anything like what you learned in Sunday school or even from the Sunday pulpit.

But for those who practice Christianity through a more open and inclusive Eastern Christian filter, pursuing an inner path of connecting with that divine indwelling is the very purpose and goal of the spiritual life.

Generally speaking, Christianity in the West puts a high priority on order, uniformity, and authority and is predominately savior-oriented, or *soteriological*,[5] with its theological emphasis on being saved, redeemed from sin, and reconciled with God by Jesus. (*Sōtērion* is the Greek word for "salvation," and *sōtēr* is Greek for "savior.")

Benedictine monk John Martin Sahajananda, OSB, points out Western Christianity's savior-oriented focus in his book *You Are the Light: Rediscovering the Eastern Jesus*. He writes:

> Jesus said, "I am the light of the world."[6] Jesus also said, "*You* are the light of the world."[7] . . . When Jesus discovered that the foundation of his being, God, was the light of the world, he also discovered that the foundation of every being, which is God,

> was also the light of the world. . . . Unfortunately, Christianity has concentrated on "I am the light of the world" and not "You are the light of the world," the statement that Jesus addressed to the whole of humanity. . . . We have to put the other wheel on the cart and embrace a vision of our full human potential.[8]

In contrast to the West, the Eastern part of the Christian world today (and earliest Christianity) is predominantly *sophiological*, meaning it is mostly wisdom-oriented (*sophia* being the Greek word for "wisdom"). Its theological emphasis is on pursuing a transformative wisdom path toward discovering the divine in ourselves and others, with Jesus as the "Life-Giver" showing us the way.[9]

As Cynthia Bourgeault explains in her groundbreaking book *The Wisdom Jesus: Transforming Heart and Mind—A New Perspective on Christ and His Message*, "A *sophiological* Christianity focuses on the path. It emphasizes how Jesus is like us, how what he did in himself is what we are called to do in ourselves."[10]

It is stunning to consider that every major world spiritual tradition today, with the exception of Christianity, has its own universally understood and nameable "path" of transformation. Buddhism has the Noble Eightfold Path, Hinduism has the Three Paths to Liberation, and Sufism has the Sufi Path of Love. Each spiritual path, or set of practices, is known to transform, over time, the way that followers see and act and relate in ways that equip them to move past their overreactive ego impulses and access their higher-functioning (calmer, less-stressed) impulses.

We do know that in the Book of Acts some of the earliest followers of Jesus referred to themselves as followers of "the Way." With Jesus' way of being as their guide, and with Jesus himself as their exemplar, it is said that "great grace was upon them all."[11] The Way was a movement as well as a named path of inner transformation that in many ways was a precursor to the earliest Christian contemplative wisdom tradition.

But with the fourth century's great creedal controversies and other debates and events in the centuries following, this wisdom tradition went underground, and as Episcopal priest Cynthia Bourgeault says in her book *Wisdom Way of Knowing*—

> Jesus was then repositioned from wisdom teacher to mediator, and the spiritual journey was reframed from a quest for divinization to a rescue operation. . . . This [quest] that in virtually every other spiritual tradition of the world is regarded as not only possible but the whole point of the undertaking—namely, the transformation of the person into the complete, full and whole image of the divine—[became] theologically off limits to Christians. It was a crushing defeat, the consequences of which are still being played out in the West.

Rediscovering "the Way"

So for centuries now we have heard little in the mainstream Christian West about following a universally recognized and named Christian *path* of self-transformation and *theosis*; however, current-day spiritual teachers like Cynthia Bourgeault and Episcopal priest Matthew Wright, Catholic priests Richard Rohr and Thomas Keating, writer Ken Wilber, and others are now capturing the imaginations of Biblical scholars and spiritual seekers alike by reclaiming many of the foundational spiritual practices of the Way and of the early Christian wisdom tradition.

It is notable that well-known *non-Christian* scholars of Eastern religion and culture recognize Jesus as a "spiritual revolutionary, an example of awakened humanity in action"[12] who discovered, *practiced*, and taught a transformative path of practices that can "wake us up" to the divine indwelling—and to the power of God *in us*.

As one recent example, spiritual teacher and author Adyashanti trained for twenty years under the tutelage of Zen Buddhism teachers and then wrote *Resurrecting Jesus: Embodying the Spirit of a Revolutionary Mystic*. Coming to understand Jesus as the "living embodiment of eternity, an embodiment of what exists within ourselves,"[13] Adyashanti describes what he calls "the Jesus story" as "a means of activating the living presence of our being, so that we realize that each one of us is the son or daughter of the living God." *Sounds True* writer Mitchell Clute wrote the foreword for *Resurrecting Jesus*, where he describes the gospel accounts as "a blueprint for the awakening process, a teaching that shows us how *we* might embody divine being in human form—just as Jesus did."[14]

The good news here is that with the current resurgence of interest in Christian contemplative practices, Christians in the West are rediscovering the revolutionary power of Jesus' *own* profound contemplative practices as the Christian *path of transformation* that it is. They are rediscovering the path of awakening experienced by Jesus' earliest followers, who followed this path that awakened them to who they are in Christ, the path they described as "the Way."

As we will see in these next chapters, Jesus' own practice is a profoundly contemplative *and active* path of transformation that can bring radical shifts to the way we understand ourselves, and can enable us to fully answer our inner divine call to "do for ourselves what Jesus did for himself."[15]

We, too, can practice the centering pause of Jesus and become truly awake and fully human.

We Are Human, We Are Divine

I invite you now to put aside for a moment your assumptions and beliefs about the humanity and divinity of Jesus of Nazareth so that we might explore with fresh eyes what gospel writers may have been telling us about this Jewish rabbi, this *moshel meshalim*,[16] this master of wisdom. Some of us may be overfamiliar with the life and teachings of Jesus, either through our years of experience in the church or simply by virtue of living in Western society in the twenty-first century. Some of us may have little or no real experience with the stories of Jesus at all.

So let us assume that the apparently divine characteristics of Jesus that have been generally attributed to him—his radical compassion, his keen insight, his wise and nonreactive response, his ability to perceive and see deeply, even his apparent and open channel to God—were not necessarily imbued in him or "thrust on him from above."[17] Let us assume for the moment that, like the rest of us, Jesus had to work at it.

This would mean that the transformational process of facing the very real psychological challenges we face as human beings—the fears and hurts and unconscious motivations and fight/flight reactions—and moving into an expanded awareness of the Divine within him and within all people actually took consistent and intentional effort on Jesus' part, effort that may have equipped him to live into the potential of what it means to be *fully* human—to grow into his divine nature.

In his essay "*The Humanity and Divinity of Jesus*," Martin Luther King, Jr. suggests an assumption similar to the one we are making here: being an exemplar of the fullness of humanity, even of the *divinity* of humanity, was something Jesus may have "achieved." King says, "The appearance of such a person, more divine and more human than any other, and standing in closest unity at once with God and man, is the most significant and hopeful event in human history. This divine quality or this unity with God was not something thrust upon Jesus from above . . . it was a definite achievement through the process of moral struggle and self-abnegation."[18]

We may want to consider this possibility even momentarily, no matter what our firm religious belief may be. Otherwise, were we to overemphasize the divinity of Jesus to the exclusion of his humanity, we could too easily convince ourselves that because Jesus may have had an imbued divine resolve and wisdom and inner strength, then *all* things were possible for him in his life and ministry simply by virtue of the superpower of his divinity.

But when we read gospel accounts of Jesus' life and ministry through new eyes, through the lens of Jesus also being truly, fully human and being transformed into the fullness of his humanity *in cooperation* with the Divine, we can then begin to notice the practices and disciplines Jesus may have been practicing himself that led to such spiritual awakening, that led him to "have the eyes to see and ears to hear" in a profoundly expanded field of awareness.

This assumption may, understandably, be a bit of a struggle for some of us. After all, many of us were taught to think of Jesus as God—and to think of God as omnipotent and omniscient. So it was natural for us to then think of Jesus as being completely on his own power, a kind of Western culture superhero, having the resolve and wisdom and inner strength to go it on his own, right to the end.

And then it was natural for us, when we were told by the Church to "follow" Jesus, to then be at a loss as to exactly *how* we were to do that, given the hurts and fears and obsessions and general fight/flight reactivity that always seem to get in our way and that are a very real part of our very human lives. So we figured maybe we were expected mostly just to do our best, do whatever we could, because since Jesus was God, it was easy to convince ourselves that we as mere humans could never be free of the confines of our ego and be able to attain to the inclusive and self-giving love of Jesus—and certainly could never come close to attaining his divinity.

But this is not the message of the writers of the Gospels of Matthew, Mark, and Luke, who inspired the fervent practice and teachings of early Christians for several centuries following the life and ministry of Jesus of Nazareth.

These gospel writers tell us that Jesus most definitely had an intentional and contemplative *practice*, an intentional way of being, and may have, all along, been showing us the Way to "stay awake" to practices that reveal our own inner divinity.

Jesus as Exemplar of Contemplation-in-Action

Now if we are used to reading the gospels through a more savior-oriented Western lens, it may not even occur to us that Jesus himself had or needed a consistent and intentionally grounding spiritual practice of his own. We were just never taught to look for it. But evidence of Jesus making time for intentional silence and solitude with God can be found throughout the gospels, especially in the synoptic Gospels of Matthew, Mark, and Luke.

Rereading the gospels through a more wisdom-oriented Eastern Christian filter, when we see Jesus as a Way-Shower to the Divine in ourselves and in others, then Jesus' *own contemplative practice* actually becomes front and center. The synoptic gospel writers were clearly purposeful in again and again and again showing Jesus' intentional and consistent effort to be *with* God, to rest in God, to intentionally be in the formative presence of God as an inner-life practice that apparently nourished and equipped him to meet the call and demands of his outer life.

Jesus embodies a pattern of seeking this time with God even in the midst of enormous daily challenges, and then moving forward into his active ministry, embodying the grace of his time apart. There is a definite rhythm to his practice as Jesus moves from time apart with God back into active ministry. Watch for it: Time with God, then action. Time with God, then action. Repeat. Repeat. Repeat.

Once we start looking, we realize references to Jesus' practice have been there all along, essentially hidden in plain sight exactly because we were never taught to look for them: In the Gospel of Luke, Jesus takes time for silence and solitude with God prior to each major event of his ministry. In the Gospels of Mark and Matthew, from Jesus' forty days in the desert to his Gethsemane prayers, the consistent backdrop of the accounts of his ministry is that "in the morning, while it was still very dark, [Jesus] got up and left the house and went off to a deserted place to pray,"[19] and again in Luke, "as was his custom"[20] and "in these days," Jesus retreated to the mountains to pray, sometimes through the night.[21]

It is important to notice and understand that the gospel writers did not *have* to include their many direct references to Jesus so fully engaging in the power of silence and solitude with God. So as we will see in chapter 10, we can easily assume the gospel writers intentionally *chose* to show Jesus following his own teachings on praying "in the inner room" through the many instances they include of Jesus taking time apart to be alone with God.[22]

And, significantly, as we will learn more comprehensively in chapter 8, Jesus was not departing to be alone for usual times for ritualized prayer. On the contrary, "as was his custom," Jesus was intentionally pausing to seek out time to be in solitude in particular places that were understood within first-century Jewish spirituality to be filled with, and symbolic of, the transformative Presence of the Divine, a presence that changes and shapes our psyche—indeed, our entire being.

That the gospel writers intentionally chose to include these references may reveal an awareness on their part that Jesus not only desired but may have needed this unusual (at the time) prayer practice and that this unique practice was somehow integral, foundational, and potentially formational to Jesus' character.

This interpretation, of course, again conveys a distinctly human character onto Jesus. And for some of us, it may initially seem incomprehensible that Jesus apparently desired or even needed these intentional and frequent encounters with God to equip him to meet the challenges of his ministry. But the gospel writers clearly point to a distinct and continuous pattern: Jesus engaged in this contemplative, rhythmic practice of pausing, seeking out, and being receptive to the power of spending time in silence and solitude with God. And then in his active, lived experience, Jesus has the ability to respond to demanding and confrontational situations, not with reflexive fight/flight overreactions but with intentional statements and actions of deep listening, compassion, and insight, apparently grounded in the presence and grace of God.

The pattern is there.

And so we begin to see what we had never been taught to see before: It is as though Jesus, the exemplar of contemplative-in-action, is saying, "Stay awake. Watch me. Watch how I live my life. Watch how I do this." Jesus shows us at every turn how a consistent pattern of pausing to return to God's presence again and again and again can ultimately change our awareness and perception, and can empower our capacity to awaken, so that (as Paul later says) "the eyes of [our] heart may be enlightened."[23]

Our Shared Divinity

As we explore further, we will come to understand this contemplative pause practice as revolutionary, as a way to come to see through Jesus' eyes and respond to the world with his insight and wisdom and healing love. We will see that by engaging in this profound practice of ceaseless interior prayer, Jesus was showing us how we, too, can live into our potential to push past our overly reactive ego and awaken to and align with a deeper, more intuitive, and expansive understanding of the world that changes the way we see, act, and relate, and ultimately connects us with our own divine nature.

This understanding does not deny the divinity of Jesus; rather, it affirms our shared divine nature with Jesus.

Richard Rohr offers a helpful perspective here:

> Jesus revealed and accepted a paradox in his entire being: Human and divine are not separate, but one, his life shouted! I wonder why we so resist our destiny? . . . Many clergy fight me on this, even though it is quite constant in the Tradition. Is it because we are afraid to bear the burden of divinity? Maybe we realize subconsciously that if we really recognized our True Self—which is the Divine Indwelling, the Holy Spirit within us—if we really believed that we are temples of God (see 1 Corinthians 3:16, 6:19; 2 Corinthians 6:16), then we would have to live up to this incredible dignity, freedom, and love.[24]

Might it be possible that the human, Jewish, powerfully contemplative Jesus of Nazareth cultivated a deep and profound and transformational centering pause practice that could, over time, transform human consciousness from being ego-led to one that ultimately could equip him (and us) to access the capacity to be fully human, with inseparable humanity and divinity?

Might it be possible that the focus and call of Jesus' three-year ministry traveling through Judea were to teach and show his followers (and, by extension, us) the Way to transform *our* consciousness, the Way to reach our own divine human potential, the Way to connect with and live through that part of us that has access to our own shared divinity with Jesus?

This is the message of the Gospels of Matthew, Mark, and Luke that inspired the intentional and consistent practice of Jesus' early followers, of the desert mothers and fathers, and of the deep and profound Christian contemplative tradition through the centuries. It is the message that to this day has inspired the practice of Eastern Christians, as well as the practice of thousands of Christians and non-Christians alike, modern contemplatives who are now flocking to wisdom practice schools springing up all across the United States and around the world today.

Living into the transformational centering pause practice of Jesus is the way we, too, can practice returning to the divine indwelling in ourselves and experience the powerful shift in consciousness that transformed the lives of Jesus' early followers and ultimately changed the world.

CHAPTER 2

It's Not "Repent," It's *Metanoia*

The whole mission [of Jesus] can fundamentally be seen as trying to push, tease, shock and wheedle people beyond their limited egoic operating system into metanoia. . . . This is the central message of Jesus.

—Cynthia Bourgeault[1]

Many Christians and non-Christians alike know well the verses in the Gospels of Mark and Matthew spoken by Jesus, "Repent: The Kingdom of God is at hand," and before Jesus, those words spoken by John the Baptist, "Repent! Make straight the path to the Lord." And when most of us hear the word *repent,* we tend to think about what we've done wrong in our life, where we have fallen short, or, worse, how we have really messed things up. For most of us, to repent means to show sincere regret or guilt or remorse about our wrongdoing. Because that's what Webster's tells us.

But this is not the meaning or the intent of the word *metanoia* in the original Greek, from which the Bible was translated. Far from it.

So how did this happen?

It was the Latin (Western) fathers of the early Christian church who originally translated the Greek *metanoia* of the gospels into the Latin word *paenitentia*, meaning "regret, repentance or penance," a decision that coincided with their teaching that eternal salvation could be obtained by performing acts of penance prescribed by one's confessor priest. This original (mis)translation was then established as authoritative when Jerome, the fourth-century Christian scholar known for his three-decades-long translation of the Bible into Latin, decided to maintain *paenitentia* as the translation of *metanoia*.[2]

But ever since Jerome's decision to retain "repent" as the translation of *metanoia*, scholars over the centuries and even in our modern time have not been happy about it.

One Greek and New Testament scholar cites the (mis)translation of *metanoia* into "repent" as "the worst translation in the entire New Testament."[3] Other scholars believe it to be "a linguistic and theological tragedy"[4] because, in their opinion, the true meaning of *metanoia* actually conveys *the very essence* of the Christian gospel and the central message of Jesus' ministry.[5]

(It is important to note here that "repent" is also a poor translation of what was the original Hebrew in these passages: *shoo-vog*. *Shoo-vog* conveys a sense of returning from exile, implying to hearers of the gospels an invitation, even a directive, to redirect their minds and hearts and "begin that journey of return from the separated self to a true self in the Divine."[6])

Awareness of this unfortunate mistranslation of "repent" is by no means a modern revelation. Visionary early church leaders, including Tertullian in the third century[7] and Martin Luther in the Reformation,[8] were among many others who spoke out against the word "repentance" being chosen as the translation of *metanoia*. Tertullian protested the unsuitable translation of the Greek *metanoia* into the Latin *paenitentia* by arguing that "in Greek, *metanoia* is not a confession of sins but a change of mind."[9] To John Staupitz, Catholic priest and spiritual counselor of Martin Luther, "*metanoia* seemed to indicate not only a change of the heart, but also a manner of changing it, i.e., by the grace of God."[10]

Metanoia: The Intended Message

So *metanoia* is actually not at all related to a feeling of remorse or contrition, or of deep regret for an action, or of needing penance, or of any of the other unhelpful and, at times, yes, tragic interpretations of *repentance* that we've adopted through church teachings (and that don't actually sound a whole lot like Jesus).

The concept of *metanoia* has a far more powerful meaning and intent than *repentance* does, and yet there is no English word that can fully capture its powerful and transcendent meaning. The Greek prefix *meta* of the Greek *metanoia* means "beyond" or "outside of," in the sense that something is beyond or outside the realm of a particular subject. (Think of the way metaphysics is beyond or outside the realm of knowledge contained in the subject of physics.) So with the suffix *noéo*, meaning "mind" or "thinking" or "perception," then *meta-noia* is "beyond the obstructions of one's mind, one's usual perceptions, or thoughts."

The *Merriam-Webster Dictionary* transliterates the Greek μετάνοια as "a transformative change of heart; *especially*: a spiritual conversion."[11] It is "a new way of loving others and God."[12] *Metanoia* is generally understood today to be a dramatic reorientation, a call to go beyond what we think we know, to go beyond the cluttered busyness of our egoic perceptions and attachments, both personal and cultural.

So we can see now that Jesus and John the Baptist are actually calling us into an altogether different reality than that of repentance.

They are calling us into a "cosmic shift in mind and heart,"[13] to higher and deeper levels of awareness and understanding, beyond our fight/flight mind, beyond the identities that each of us and our particular culture have created. They are calling us into a complete change of mind and heart, into the mind of Christ, the mind that sees through the eyes of God.

~ ~ ~

Hear the dramatic and meaningful difference between the message of the English "repent" mistranslation and the more original *metanoia* understandings:

- In the Gospel of Matthew, Jesus is not calling on the people to "Repent: The Kingdom of Heaven is at hand." Jesus is actually calling on the people to "*Metanoeite*[14]—See beyond your mind, your usual way of seeing: The Kingdom of Heaven is at hand" (Matthew 3:2 and 4:17).
- In Mark, when Jesus sent his disciples out two by two, the disciples did not "proclaim that all should repent" (Mark 6:7–12). Jesus' disciples actually "proclaimed that all should *metanoōsin*[15]—see with the eyes of their heart, with the deepest part of their being, with their true selves."
- In Acts, Paul is not telling the Athenians that "God now commands all people everywhere to repent" (Acts 17:30). Paul is actually telling the Athenians that "God now commands all people everywhere to *metanoein*[16]—see beyond their mind, to see through an entirely new field of awareness, to see through the eyes of their innermost selves in God."

Think of the impact of this teaching if we had learned this in Sunday school. What if, throughout our lives, every time we had heard the call to repent, we understood it to be an impassioned invitation to try to wake up and see beyond our mind's usual reflexive way of thinking, to see bigger, and to try to see with God's eyes?

We would hear an entirely different and very powerful call, the call the gospel writers intended for us to hear. We would hear a call to release ourselves from being captive to our small fight/flight minds, categorizing everything into good or bad, in crowd or out crowd, like or don't like, and move instead into an entirely new way of seeing the world, with the real insight and awareness we are innately capable of.

We would hear a call to embrace a more expansive and inclusive way of being and perceiving, to think both/and instead of either/or, to include the other rather than look for reasons to judge the other.

Now *this* sounds familiar.

Because, well, Jesus.

Metanoia: The Meta Perspective

I find it remarkable that, in the vernacular of today's popular culture, the concept of "going meta" actually comes quite close to the intended gospel meaning of *metanoia*. "Going meta" is a self-referential phrase meaning not only to be self-aware but to see from a higher and more expansive perspective. Imagine a movie camera pulling back to be able to see a bigger frame of what's happening in a given scene.

I remember giving a children's sermon, "Look How God Sees Bigger," to illustrate this idea for children and adults alike. Sitting on the steps to the altar and facing the children of the parish who were all sitting on the floor in front of me, I began talking about what it means to try to see with God's eyes of Love. I talked about how God's loving eyes see the big picture, whereas we often see a much smaller picture of what's happening in our lives. (I invite you now, as I did then to the adults in the congregation, to follow my step-by-step directions. You will see what I mean!)

I said,

> Okay, now try this: Touch the tip of your thumb with the tip of your forefinger to make an O and then bring your other fingers around so you make a kind of funnel, and then close one eye and look through the O the way you would look through a telescope. Look all around the room through that funnel. See how we see little parts of what's happening all around us? This shows how *we* see. Okay, keep looking through the hole, and now . . . open all your fingers, take away your hand, and see how much you see. Wow! Look how big! This is how God sees.

Rereading key gospel passages through the more accurate emphasis on *metanoia* rather than *repent* opens our eyes to an altogether new and fresh understanding of the gospel message: We are able to hear Jesus' call to go meta and imagine a more loving and inclusive state of being.

And in today's language of psychology, the gospel's call to go meta is a call to wake up and rewire our minds and reorient our hearts so we can stop living through the unconscious needs and reactions of our separated (false) self and instead live through our true self in the Divine.

It is the call to begin the journey of responding less from our reactive and fearful early, primal brain and respond more from our more human, higher-level thinking and loving brain.

William James used the term *metanoia* in his 1890 *Principles of Psychology* to describe a "fundamental and stable change in an individual's life-orientation."[17] Carl Gustav Jung used *metanoia* to indicate a spontaneous attempt of the psyche to heal itself[18] by radically shifting the balance of the personality from the persona toward the true self.[19]

Jung's *metanoia* work then influenced Scottish psychiatrist R. D. Laing's emphasis in his work on "the dissolution and replacement of everyday ego consciousness."[20] And certain current-day psychotherapy methods use the concept of *metanoia* to describe the experience of abandoning an old, scripted, and programmed perception of ourselves for a more open and true self.[21]

So we can see that through the *metanoia* lens, the central gospel message of Jesus is not about belief, or contrition, or salvation from punishment. The central message of Jesus' ministry is about shifting our focus and reorienting ourselves toward the Holy, away from the confines of our false/old self and toward the vision of our true/new self. It is about seeing beyond the limitations of our egos and transforming ourselves in ways that will transform the world around us.

Practicing *metanoia* is itself a powerful contemplative practice. Once we become aware of the gospels' intended *metanoia* message, we begin to see that Jesus himself is practicing *metanoia* over and over again throughout the gospels.

Metanoia: The Clarion Call

Cynthia Bourgeault describes *metanoia* as the "clarion call to a radical shift in consciousness that underlies all of Jesus' teaching"[22] and as *the central* message of Jesus:

> The whole mission [of Jesus] can fundamentally be seen as trying to push, tease, shock and wheedle people beyond their limited egoic operating system into *metanoia*, the "vast realm of mind" . . . which can see and live from the perspective of wholeness. This is the central message of Jesus. This is what the Kingdom of Heaven is all about. [It's as though Jesus is saying,] "Let's get into the larger mind. . . . I'll show you what it looks like. This is how you do it. Here, I'll help you."[23]

I love this delightful imagined moment that Bourgeault offers us here, with Jesus inviting us to move past the clutter of our egocentric perceptions and into the wholeness and expansiveness of *metanoia*.

And in fact, we hear Jesus' call to *metanoia* in his *first recorded words* in the gospels (in Mark 1:15): "The time is fulfilled, and the Kingdom of God has come near; [*metanoeite*] and believe the good news."

I am aware that it may feel like a significant shift for many of us to leave our lifelong experience of Jesus and John the Baptist telling us to repent, and to instead experience the invitation to embrace the actual, intended *metanoia* meaning of these central gospel passages. But can you feel this internal shift in yourself? When you hear "Repent, the Kingdom of Heaven is at hand," can you feel the way the initial directive to repent can bring a negative, inhibited, and guilty response, whereas the intended directive to "see beyond your mind" can bring an inner response that is more positive, proactive, and life-affirming?

Remarkably, dramatic shifts can happen when we reread the gospels through this ancient/new centrality of *metanoia*, looking for patterns and clues as to how Jesus himself was able to embody the *metanoia* way. We begin to notice important details that were otherwise hidden to us but in plain sight.

We are now more able to hear and experience Jesus' invitation to release ourselves from the hold of our overreactive fight/flight self, to change our mind and live into a transformed, more expansive, more inclusive way of being in the world. We may even be able to imagine the parallels between the way of *metanoia* and the practices that twenty-first-century neuroscientists have discovered actually rewire our brains to be less reactive, more insightful, and more compassionate.

And as our understanding of Jesus himself expands, Jesus can naturally become for us the *moshel meshalim*, the teacher of wisdom, one who taught the ancient traditions of the transformation of the human being,[24] one who practices *metanoia* so consistently that he actually embodies it.

Jesus becomes our Way-shower, not only "pushing, teasing, shocking and wheedling" us beyond our limited, egocentric way of seeing things and into *metanoia* but also—importantly—showing us a practice and a path that equip us to get there and to keep going, showing us how we, too, can be fully human.

CHAPTER 3

The Jesus Formula: The Centering Pause Practice

God offers us quiet, contemplative eyes . . . God also calls us to prophetic and critical involvement in the pain and sufferings of our world—both at the same time. This is so obvious in the life and ministry of Jesus that I wonder why it has not been taught as an essential part of Christianity.

—Richard Rohr

If you were to look at the gospels through a more Eastern lens, looking particularly for the wisdom *path or way* of Jesus, you would notice multiple references to Jesus' consistent "custom" of "rising before dawn to go out to a deserted place to pray," of "going to the mountain to pray," and even of "spending the night in prayer."[1] And you would most certainly notice the relevance and importance of his teaching on inner, wordless prayer.

The first-century gospel audience would have sat up and immediately noticed this particular practice of Jesus—of consistently making time to be in silence and solitude with God and often at unusual times and in unusual places. Master storytellers that they are, the gospel writers must have wanted their listeners to notice and take note of the ongoing contemplative pause/action rhythm of Jesus' life in God.

So, yes, it turns out there is a very practical how-to manual for going beyond our mind and seeing with the eyes of *metanoia.* The how-to instructions for accessing our own "in-sight" and tapping into our own human potential have always been sitting right here in our hands as we read the gospels. Jesus' very practical and lifesaving how-tos are available in his teachings *and* in his own lived practice.

In her book *Too Deep for Words,* spiritual director Thelma Hall says, "In Jesus' life his prayer and action follow one another in a rhythm which seems as constant as the inhaling and exhaling of breathing. . . . We cannot separate this prayer from [Jesus'] works, nor fail to see it is the very source of his teachings, his Gospel, and his mission."[2] So Jesus shows us a way—indeed, Jesus was showing us what earliest Christians called *the Way*—to "put on the mind of Christ."[3]

And this is good news.

Because as much as we Western Christians hear continuous exhortations from Sunday morning pulpits to "be like Jesus," the Church simply has not been very good at teaching us how we should attain to such a revolutionary call. Most of us were never taught about the call of *metanoia* or the practices that can *equip* us to shift our awareness and to see more expansively, beyond our usual way of seeing. So most of us were never shown a particular path or practice that would equip us to, like Jesus, react less, respond with compassion and equanimity, speak truth to power in love, and see with the eyes of our heart.

We have been left on our own to figure out *how* to be like Jesus.

And on our own, the journey for some of us has been more than daunting as we inevitably run into all the ways that we get in our own way and then begin to wonder if this call to be like Jesus is in fact even possible. We wonder: Is it really possible to bring down the chronic stress levels of our nonstop schedules and move past our egoic over-reactions? Is it really possible to move past our own ingrained unconscious bad habits and our good/bad, like/dislike dualistic thinking so that we might actually be able to attend to what is necessary to get us to slow down, to see bigger, and to transform our souls, our psyches, our relationships, and the health of our planet?

I have come to believe that the answer is a resounding yes and that the answer has come in the fullness of time.

At this inflection point, with many of us struggling to cope with the unending demands of our daily lives and at the same time yearning for deeper meaning and a sense of the Divine, religion and science are converging in profoundly hopeful ways: neuroscientists are discovering how contemplative practices rewire the brain toward calm and equanimity *at the same time* that well-known scholars of the Christian contemplative tradition are being sought out by growing numbers of Christians and non-Christians for their practical wisdom on the very real, transformative power of Jesus' hidden-in-plain-view contemplative practices.

But *which* practices, you may ask, and where are they in the gospels? Jesus gives us the first clue in his teachings on prayer beyond words.

Interior Prayer: Prayer Beyond Words

The mainstay of Jesus' teachings on the power of prayer beyond words is his "inner room" discourse in the Gospel of Matthew.[4] Scholars have pointed to this passage over the centuries as Jesus' primary directive to his followers to pray contemplatively, beyond words or thoughts or feelings, as the way to connect with, attune to, and be transformed by Divine Presence: "But whenever you pray, go into your room and shut the door and pray to your Father who is in secret; and your Father who sees in secret will reward you."[5]

At first glance, this passage does not appear to be a directive on quiet interior prayer. But I love how, once again, the original Greek brings clarity to the gospel writers' intention for us here: Matthew 6:5–6 is often called the *tameion* passage because *tameion* is the Greek word that has been translated here into the word "room." *Tameion* more precisely means an "inner chamber," a "secret chamber," a "private room," or, my favorite, "the inner room of you."[6]

Jesus is directing us to go into the inner room *of ourselves* to be with the Holy One.

For several reasons, most obviously because most first-century Galilean homes did not generally have inner rooms or private rooms in their residences, church scholars as early as the desert mothers and fathers understood that Jesus was not referring here to an actual physical place. They understood Jesus to be making a crucially important metaphorical statement here so that *tameion* is understood as an inner spiritual reality, our divine indwelling, what Oksana described as her "monastery of the heart," the continual return to which can cultivate our innate expansive and inclusive way of seeing and being to which Jesus calls us—*metanoia*.

At a time and a place where prescribed, routinized, verbal prayers were the norm, Jesus is directing his followers to spend intentional, undistracted time in interior prayer to connect with that of God in the deepest part of their being.

Centering Prayer founder Thomas Keating actually thought of Jesus' *tameion* directive as Jesus' "formula" for waking up to the essence of who we are:

> In Jesus' formula for waking up to who we are . . . he suggests entering this inner room. Then he says, "shut the door," meaning stop the interior dialogue. Get free or detached from our

> over-identifications with our thoughts, experiences, past life, future hopes. . . . [Here we are] in the process of awakening to the divine image within us, where faith, hope, charity, the divine indwelling are sitting, so to speak, in our unconscious, gathering dust, waiting to be used. And they can't come into full action until our over-identification with the false self and its programs for happiness have been reduced.[7]

Gospel accounts show us that Jesus himself lived this contemplative, prayer-beyond-words, "inner room" practice as he often ventures out alone for predawn "lonely prayer" or, "as is his custom," he retreats up the mountain or to the garden alone even in the busiest times of his ministry, sometimes being in prayer through the night. We can safely assume, as scholars have through the ages, that Jesus is not speaking out loud to God all night long.

The gospel writers' first-century audience would immediately understand that Jesus was intentionally and consistently making time to be "in" the powerful *and formative* Divine Presence as a way to become aware of, and attune to, the movement of the Divine within and all around.

Indeed, these *tameion* prayer-beyond-words practices point to Jesus' times apart as intentional times of restoration, refreshment, re-"membering," and re-attunement with the Divine, his source, his center, his ground of being. And critically important here is how these intentional times of spiritual renewal would then equip and inform his clear-eyed perception of the Divine in the *lived* prayer practice of his extraordinarily challenging day-to-day ministry. As Richard Rohr reminds us: "God offers us quiet, contemplative eyes; and God *also calls us to prophetic and critical involvement in the pain and sufferings of our world*—both at the same time. This is so obvious in the life and ministry of Jesus that I wonder why it has not been taught as an essential part of Christianity."[8]

Indeed, when we notice Jesus' times of spiritual renewal interspersed as they are throughout the arc of his ministry—from his teaching, healing, and feeding of the four and five thousand followers, to his last words at the Last Supper, in Gethsemane, and on the cross—we begin to notice the definitive pattern in Jesus' practice as a kind of flowing back-and-forth rhythm.

There is a continual pausing to let go (what scholars call *kenosis*, or emptying) of egoic attachments, fear, judgment, or expectations and then a returning to the Divine Presence again and again.

Let go.

Return.

Let go.

Return.

And the Divine is the one-pointed focus to which Jesus returns ceaselessly in this prayer rhythm of pause and release and return. This is Jesus' formula for waking up—his formula for himself and for his followers. It is what Keating calls "constant death and resurrection in every moment . . . we die to our own will and enter the present moment by consenting to whatever it is, either by accepting it or doing something that the Spirit suggests to improve the situation."[9] It is Jesus' practice for deepening the soul's awareness of and attunement with our innermost essence, the Divine within.

When we go into our inner room to be with God, we are pausing to release what our false self is attached to. We are returning to an awareness of God.

Release ego and agenda.

Return to awareness of God.

Release ego and agenda.

Return to awareness of God.

So we certainly are not talking about entering a physical inner room here. We are talking about the power of the practice of letting go of whatever is claiming the attention of our ego's false self and then reorienting to our deepest self in God.

Living from a Contemplative Center

This fundamental contemplative pause-release-return movement is *the* defining rhythm of Jesus' life and ministry. In most of his actions, you will see Jesus embodies this back-and-forth, flowing, release-and-return movement that is a kind of continual, contemplative, grounded-in-God prayer that changes minds, literally and grace-fully. It brings "an entirely new way of knowing the world"[10] that actually rewires our egocentric responses so we can get out of our own way and be more like Jesus—fully awake and fully human.

The gospel writers did not want us to miss this.

Jesus is "a perfect example . . . of human action from a contemplative center,"[11] living life with a one-pointed focus on the power and love of God, continually returning to the "monastery of the heart," both in his separate, formal times devoted to full engagement in interior prayer and prayer beyond words as well as in his full engagement with others in the remaining hours of his day.

As we have learned from Richard Rohr, living from such a contemplative center is "less about saying prayers than it is about *being* prayer." He says:

> It does not require life in a monastery; it requires questioning our "viewing platform." It requires asking ourselves, "How can I listen for God and learn God's voice? How can I use my words and actions to expand and not to contract? How can I keep my heart, mind, and soul open, even 'in hell'"?[12] (And for many of us, "hell" can be the nonstop busyness and crises of our day-to-day lives.)

I invite you to look back and notice that each of these questions that Rohr imagines here requires an intentional pause and release of ego and a contemplative and centering return to our awareness of God. To live from a contemplative center requires this movement of Jesus' practice, the movement from pause to release to return, the movement from *kenosis* to returning to the Divine and into *metanoia*. Each return to God deepens our attunement with that of God within us; and importantly, each return to God gradually transforms us into the likeness of that of God within us.

This deepening of our divine awareness is the goal and the heart of perennial wisdom from every faith. Rohr says, "This is how contemplatives 'know' things."[13]

This is how contemplatives "know" things!

We are able to see now the remarkable power of the contemplative arc of Jesus' centering pause practice. Like a glorious helix spiral, circling around and around and up and up: We pause, we release, we return, we deepen our ability to "know." We again pause, we release, we return, we deepen our ability to "know." It is a natural circling back around, each time to a more and more open and aware and inclusive sense of *metanoia*.

Recall now that this kind of practical and contemplative *knowing*, full of insight and deeper awareness, this *metanoia*, is Jesus' clarion call to his followers to "see beyond your mind." This is a natural circling back to the call that Jesus is "pushing and prodding" us into.

Indeed, the Christian wisdom contemplative tradition has been trying for centuries to teach us this transformative pattern of *kenosis*, this pause of self-emptying and return, that can cultivate in us the deep wisdom and deeper seeing of *metanoia*, bringing a radical compassion and ability to speak truth to power and a way to access and live through our essential nature.

Prelude to a Spiritual and Neurological Revolution

And this is revelatory.

We are seeing here why both spiritual leaders and neuroscientists believe the scientific discoveries of this era are a prelude to a spiritual and neurological revolution: The transformative pause-release-return movement of Jesus' practice, and of the contemplative practices of every spiritual tradition, is the same intrinsic movement that neuroscientists have proven reshapes the brain's neural wiring toward greater awareness and well-being. Science has shown that when we practice the pause in this profound way, we actually catalyze changes in the neural circuitry of our brain that enhance insight and compassion.

We are witnessing today the convergence, and the revolutionary potential of, the spiritual with the neurological.

As we will explore in more depth in the next chapter on the basics of neuroscience, what catalyzes the new neural firing, what literally rewires the brain in meditation (and in life), is the actual action of the pause to release the thought, to let go of the hold of the ego, and then to return to the present moment or to the Presence in the present moment. That nanosecond of pause is when neurons fire and wire together.[14]

So it is in the practice of Jesus.

There is a nanosecond of pause between the release of the ego's hold and returning to resting in the Presence of God within and all around. We've all felt the spacious and weighty effect of that pause at some point. We can feel it when we catch ourselves and stop for a moment to reconsider a situation. That simple movement of releasing the hold of the fight/flight ego response to then return to the Divine creates a pause, a space. That space is what Holocaust survivor and author Victor Frankl talks about when he says, "Between stimulus and response there is a space. In that space is our power to choose our response. In our response lies our growth and our freedom."[15]

It is this space, this *pause*, that makes room for the Divine, that opens us to the flow of what is. It is this space that makes room for a deeper, more intuitive and expansive awareness. The emptying makes room for the flow of the Divine within us, the divine indwelling, and sets us up for a more intuitive, thoughtful response.

And it is this space that holds the revolutionary potential of Jesus' centering pause practice to transform over time the way each of us sees and understands ourselves and the world and to bring meaningful shifts from our ordinary awareness into a dramatically expanded awareness that ultimately brings peace.

You may be familiar with the verse in Psalm 46 that says, "Be still and know that I am God." I found it delightful to discover that here the word "still" comes from a Hebrew word, *rapha*, meaning to "let go" or "release." So the Hebrew meaning of this verse would be best understood as, "Let go, and be aware of God."[16]

~ ~ ~

Ancient religious and spiritual traditions have taught us for millennia about the power of living from a contemplative center, of how letting go and returning to the Holy can fundamentally transform the way we perceive ourselves, others, and the world around us in ways that give us new eyes to see and new ears to hear. Living in this new way of being, of *metanoia*, changes the way we understand ourselves, changes the way we live our lives, changes the way our lives "live" us.

I marvel that we are now able to in some ways understand the science behind what we have been taught for millennia, the science behind what happens when we collaborate with God's call to us to awaken into our own divine potential.

We are living in a time when both the gospels and science are showing us the potential of finding short interludes of time to be still, to let go, and to create that nanosecond of pause that can open us to the power of God in us to transform our lives and the world around us.

II

AWAKENING THE MIND

CHAPTER 4

Wired for Transformation: Our Brain and Our Mind

One can argue that Abraham, Moses, Mohammed, Jesus, and the Buddha all reached spiritual enlightenment because they devoted years to intense meditation and prayer.[1]

—Andrew Newberg, MD, *How God Changes Your Brain*

When the mindfulness meditation instructor put up this beautiful slide of the drawing of a brain, I and two hundred other mindfulness meditation educators-in-training grew suddenly very quiet and fully attentive. The instructor noticed the sudden silence, looked up, smiled a broad smile, and said, "Oh, I *love* this part of this curriculum. This happens every time I put up this slide. The entire class goes completely silent like this, and I feel super smart!"

Everyone laughed, of course, and then immediately became silent again, in rapt attention. We were attending a standing-room-only

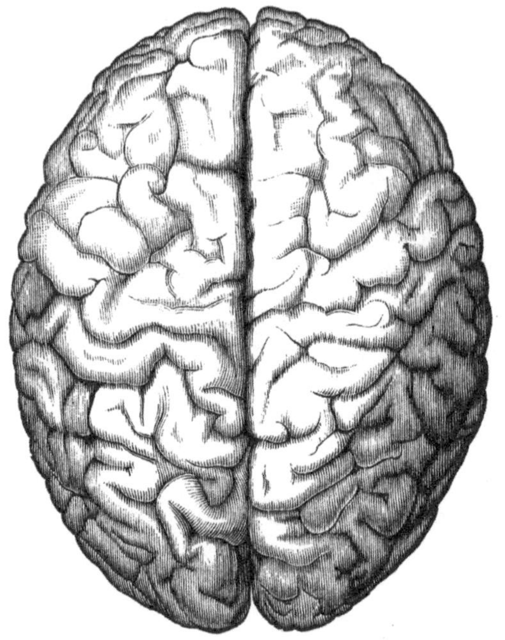

mindfulness meditation education training conference and were about to hear from one of the nation's top mindfulness instructors about the most recent neuroscience research studies confirming the connection between mindfulness meditation practices and positive, quantifiable changes in the human brain.

Much of our attentiveness was anticipatory awe: Some of us were future mindfulness instructors and school administrators. Some of us were spiritual directors and church leaders. The inner contemplative neuroscience geek in each one of us was ready to hear *more.*

Key Brain Basics

A certain kind of awe does take hold as we begin to catch scientific glimpses of how exquisitely we are created as human beings. With the advent of technological advances in functional magnetic resonance imaging (fMRI) and the new field of contemplative neuroscience that those advances ushered in, we are now able to learn in scientific detail the ways our brain circuitry is involved in our ability to become less reactive and more aware of the interplay between our ego and our essence, our deepest self. We can begin to comprehend how our human brains are wired for spiritual awakening and transformation.

And the brain science of transformation is as remarkable as the psychology and the spirituality of transformation are. One need not be a neuroscience nerd like me to be utterly captivated by the basic science behind Jesus' pause practice.

Even those who are more naturally drawn to religion and spirituality than to brain science often find themselves enthralled by the fascinating brainy side of contemplative practice, so I am excited to offer this practical synopsis here, especially in light of how the newest contemplative neuroscience discoveries on mindfulness meditation are so effective in explaining in scientific terms how the pause-release-return rhythm of contemplative practices like Jesus' centering pause practice not only calms our brain's fight/flight alarm center but gives us greater access to the higher functions of our brain, enabling us to expand our awareness and tap into deep reservoirs of love and inner wisdom.

We will be able to see from a *scientific* perspective how Jesus' pause practice actually catalyzes changes in our brain's neural wiring that equip us to release the confines of our own ego, to see more expansively, and to become more sensitive, aware, and compassionate toward others.

As I am not a neuroscientist, I rely on the work of several highly regarded neuroscientists, psychologists, and science writers for this short contemplative practice neuroscience primer, particularly the studies and the writing of Richard Davidson, Michael Spezio, Jeffrey Schwartz, Daniel Siegel, Andrew Newberg, Marsha Lucas, Daniel Goleman, and Sharon Begley.

So let's begin with a few key brain basics to ground us in the fundamentals.

Over the course of evolution, the three major regions of the human brain developed in layers, one over the other, and together are often referred to as the triune brain, after a well-known brain theory developed by physician and neuroscientist Paul MacLean in the 1960s.[2] MacLean referred to these regions as the brainstem/reptilian system, the limbic system, and the cortical system. (I would like to note that while MacLean named the brainstem system the "reptilian" brain, many neuroscientists today call this system the "primal" system, as I will here.) Each of these three major brain systems can be understood visually as being separate entities, but in reality these regions and their functions are profoundly integrated, with functions in each region constantly informing and receiving from the other.[3]

According to MacLean, the primal brain, the oldest of the three brain systems, controls the body's vital functions such as the heart rate, body temperature, breathing, and balance.

The second brain system, the limbic, "mammalian" brain, evolved with the first small mammals and works with the primal brain to control our basic drives of safety, security, and pleasure. This system also participates in creating our emotions and the often unconscious like/dislike, good/bad value judgments[4] that so strongly influence our everyday behavior.

It is in this limbic system that the amygdala is located, which, among its other functions, is best known for its role in controlling our fight/flight stress response: when something happens in our environment or in ourselves that is in any way a fearful stimulus, signals are immediately sent to the amygdala, which then signals parts of the brain, including the hypothalamus, to trigger a fight/flight response and activate the sympathetic nervous system to prepare for action.

The third brain system, the cortical system, is called the thinking brain, the neocortex, or the "new mammalian" brain because it expanded with primates and especially in humans. This outer layer of the brain, located just under our foreheads, is the brain region that makes us human. Indeed, neurological evolution of the brain suggests that empathy and social awareness are the most recently developed parts of our psychological anatomy.[5]

Fight and Flight and the Human Plight

Whether a person is Jesus of Nazareth or the Buddha or Mahatma Gandhi or you or me, the circuitry of our human brains is wired with millions of neural pathways in the prefrontal cortex. This uniquely human part of our brain gives each one of us the potential to live into the fullness of our humanity and to exemplify the loftiest of virtues—compassion, wisdom, love, curiosity, patience, empathy, imagination, self-control, generosity of spirit, and insight into our inner world.

Of course, also as human beings, the circuitry of our human brains is wired with millions of neural pathways in the limbic brain, giving us the remarkable ability to perceive danger even before we become cognitively aware of the threat. We are very easily triggered away from our prefrontal cortex, back into our limbic brain, and into fight/flight survival mode.

And that's where life gets tricky for us.

When the lower, more original part of our brain (specifically the amygdala) perceives any kind of threat to our survival, either real or imagined, the amygdala sends signals to areas of the brain like the hypothalamus to trigger our fight/flight stress response to take over the higher, thinking part of our brain (the prefrontal cortex) so our body can fight or flee as quickly as possible from the perceived danger.

We all know this moment well: Our brain is initiating a series of electrochemical reactions that increase our heart rate, raise our blood pressure, constrict our muscles, tighten our chest, dilate our pupils, and limit our ability to focus on anything but the perceived danger. This phenomenon essentially allows us to react without thinking.

This is fine and good if we are, indeed, in a life-threatening situation. But when our fight/flight reaction is activated, our ability to reason or to *see the bigger picture* goes offline. So if the perceived "threat" is not, say, a poisonous snake crossing our path but simply the dismissive facial expression of a colleague or someone cutting us off in traffic, our bodies nonetheless may move into immediate and full fight/flight mode, and then it is next to impossible to catch ourselves before we do or say something we will later regret.

Encounters that trigger our fight/flight reflex are something each of us experiences every day, often then getting us stuck in obsessive loops of anxiety, hurtful conversations, and old conflicts. In fact, neuroscientists today maintain that many of us have developed *overreactive* fight/flight reflexes due to our current hyper-stressed lifestyles. From the time our alarm clocks wake us in the morning, we are in full *on* mode, commuting to and from our jobs, scheduling back-to-back Zoom meetings, checking our phones, sending texts and emails well into the night before we fall into bed, often exhausted. We spend some days in *constant* overreactive fight/flight mode.

From a brain science perspective, when we live full days, even weeks, in chronic fight/flight reactive mode, we are making decisions primarily from the survival/animal parts of our brain. We are limiting our days to making survival decisions with our brainstem and our alarm centers—the amygdala and hypothalamus. We are shutting off access to our higher-functioning prefrontal cortex's deep wisdom and the means to enact our deepest desires and ambitions.

We are essentially holding ourselves back from becoming who we are called to be and from the grace of accessing our full human potential. We are getting in our own way.

But the good news here is that breakthrough neuroscience studies are now confirming scientifically what ancient spiritual traditions have been telling us for millennia: There is a way to get out of our own way. Self-transformation is possible.

The Contemplative Neuroscience Revolution

It is hard to imagine that it was just over two decades ago that even some of the world's most highly regarded neuroscientists believed our brain's emotional wiring was set and unchangeable from a relatively young age.[6] Which meant that if you were, say, caught in an obsessive loop of anger or anxiety—a kind of hamster wheel of reactivity or obsessive looping in anxious, ruminating thoughts—much of the medical community would have believed there was little hope in changing your brain's already set wiring and emotional overreactivity. These age-old theories shifted dramatically in the 1990s with advances in fMRI technology, which enabled neuroscientists to investigate detailed physical changes taking place in our brain in real time.

These fMRI studies eventually confirmed what neuroscientists themselves now describe as the "revolutionary" phenomenon of *neuroplasticity*—the ability of the brain's neural circuitry to change as a result of behavior and environment.[7] Following this discovery, several now-prominent neuroscientists who for decades had been "closet meditators," eagerly went to work conducting neuroscience studies that soon produced conclusive and compelling evidence that meditation and other contemplative practices can change the brain and ultimately bring significant, and even transformative, shifts in awareness and consciousness.[8]

The new field of contemplative neuroscience was born.

Now dozens of studies at university research centers worldwide have shown that an intentional contemplative practice *of even short duration* can significantly rewire the brain in ways that develop new prefrontal cortex neural patterns,[9] which slow down the mechanisms that cause the amygdala to fully activate the fight/flight response. In essence, they've proven that in a remarkably short amount of time, the inherent pause and release of meditation and other contemplative practices rewires the brain in ways that calm our limbic system and enables our prefrontal cortex to have time to come on board to regulate our fight/flight stress responses.

Dr. Britta Hölzel's groundbreaking 2008 study of the effects of an eight-week mindfulness meditation program, for example, revealed a significant increase in neuron density, or gray matter, in the prefrontal regions of the brain related to self-awareness.[10] In related studies by Dr. Sara Lazar, these same "release-and-return" meditation practices were found to decrease density of certain collections of neurons in the amygdala, which activates the fight/flight reflex.[11]

The Way This Works

The basic science behind how our day-to-day contemplative practices can actually change our brain's neural patterns is fascinating (and is actually fairly straightforward and easy to understand).

The human brain has more than one hundred billion (billion!) *neurons*, which are nerve cells that transmit information, both incoming and outgoing. Each neuron has thousands of *synapses*, which are the connections between neurons. A series of synapses forms a *neural pathway*. By the age of three years old, we have an unfathomable number of synapses *per neuron*: fifteen thousand. That fifteen thousand is roughly double the number of synapses in an adult brain.[12]

Current neuroplasticity studies are showing that neurons that are frequently used develop stronger connections, and those that are rarely or never used atrophy and eventually die. This is a key component to the pliable, plastic nature of the brain's neurons.

In simplest terms, this happens because the brain commits resources to whatever actions it is doing most. Neuroscientists cite Hebb's law to describe this process: "Neurons that fire together, wire together."[13] Activity in certain parts of the brain creates increased new connections and density, also called gray matter,[14] in those regions.

And this is key: As we are meditating, when we notice a thought and then pause, release the thought, and return to a sense of Presence, or to present-moment awareness, areas of our brain involved in attention and awareness are fully activated, bringing more blood flow to those areas. If this activity continues for even a very short amount of time, the highly efficient brain will wire new neural pathways with the firing neurons in the area that is lit up. This new neural circuitry acts as a series of new pathways or bridges connecting entire regions of the brain.[15]

The implications of these studies are that certain contemplative practices activate the brain in a way that can enable us to calm our own egoic fight/flight responses, to change our overreactive behavior patterns, and to cultivate the capacity to choose how to respond to stressful situations through a fuller awareness of what is happening in our inner and outer worlds.[16]

These and other breakthrough brain studies are indeed validating in scientific terms what spiritual contemplative traditions have maintained through the centuries, namely that consistent effort in sustaining certain contemplative practices actually creates optimal conditions for the *formation* and transformation of the person engaging in the practice. Transcending our self-preserving fight and flight instincts, being better able to respond from a place of no fear, and over time, literally "changing our own neurochemistry,"[17] is the result. Certain methods of meditation and contemplative prayer indeed can radically transform the way we think and behave, can shift our perspective, and can ultimately bring cognitive, even transformative, shifts in our awareness and consciousness.[18]

Becoming More Human to Help Heal the World

And today, engaging in contemplative practices in order to change our brain has gone mainstream. Neuroscientists are being joined by psychologists, schoolteachers, and corporate executives in recommending a steady, intentional practice of a few minutes a day of meditation as a kind of mental training to build the "muscle of attention" in the brain, much like repetitions in a gym workout build the muscles of the body. The fact that science is now validating the physical, psychological, and social benefits of meditation and other focused awareness exercises[19] is convincing many who might otherwise be skeptical to begin their own contemplative practice.

Neuroscientist Richard Davidson, PhD, believes that by 2050, a few minutes of mental exercise every morning, in the form of meditation or other contemplative practices, will be as commonplace as running is now for physical exercise and brushing our teeth is for overall health.[20] "In this historical era," he says, "I think we have a moral obligation to bring these practices to as many people as we can, to heal the world and cultivate a more collective kind of warm-heartedness, which I think most people would agree the world could use more of."[21]

In language that is at once psychological, religious, and scientific, these practices equip us to release our inner drives and motivations, to make room for the movement of the divine indwelling within us, and to access a higher level of intelligence, insight, and response.

Andrew Newberg, MD, says it this way: contemplative practices "make us more human."[22]

Indeed, we are becoming aware of the potential for us as human beings to be transformed in a "continuing evolution to higher states of consciousness." Thomas Keating believes we are experiencing a spiritual evolution that is "a prelude to a *divine-human way of functioning*, to all the virtues of which humans are capable but which we have not yet learned to put into practice."[23]

CHAPTER 5

Flipping Your Lid: A Close-Up Look

Between stimulus and response
there is a space. In that space is our power
to choose our response. In our response
lies our growth and our freedom.

—Victor Frankl

"I flipped my lid."

"I blew a fuse."

"I was triggered."

"I lost it."

The idioms we use to describe high-stress moments when we lose control of our anger were suddenly making more literal sense to me.

I was participating in a study cohort, taking a course on neuroscientist Daniel Seigel's book *Mindsight: The New Science of Transformation* under the tutelage of Dr. Seigel himself, who was demonstrating his popular, easy-to-understand hand/brain model to explain what happens inside the brain when the human brain's fight/flight reflex is fully engaged in times of stress. The intent of Dr. Siegel's demonstration was to set the stage for the rest of his course on the revolutionary neuroscience behind the practice of meditation.

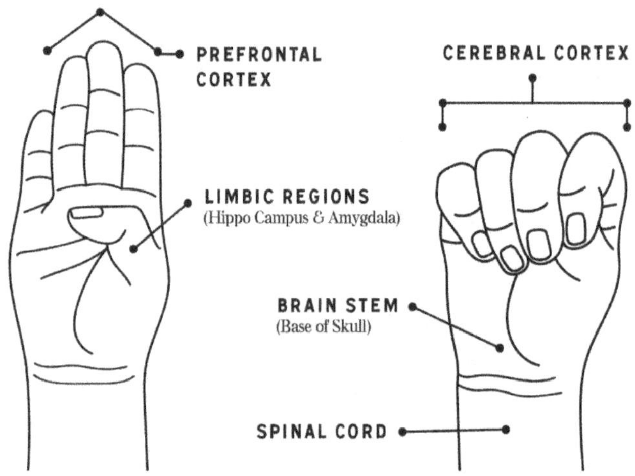

Hand Model of the Human Brain[1]

To directly experience Dr. Siegel's enlightening explanation, I invite you to use your own hand as a "brain model":

Begin by holding your hand up with a closed fist. Imagine the back of your hand is the back of someone's head. From the knuckles just over your fingernails down to the front of your wrist is their face. In your wrist is the spinal cord, rising from the backbone, represented by your arm. When you open your hand, your palm represents the inner brainstem, the primal brain. When you put your thumb in the middle of your palm, your thumb is in the approximate location of the limbic system, the brain's emotional network, in which lies the almond-shaped and critically important amygdala, which is known for, among other things, its role in processing our fear.

There are actually two amygdalae, one on either side of the brain in the region closest to each ear. Each amygdala is a collection of *nuclei*—a group of neurons performing certain functions—that are part of the brain's alarm system where many of our emotions, including fear, anger, and aggression, are registered and interpreted.

When you bring your fingers back down around your thumb into a fist, your fingers all together represent the cortex. Further down the fingers, the area from your first knuckles to your fingertips (which would be located just behind the forehead) is the prefrontal cortex, which, as Siegel points out, has evolved to the extent it has only in human beings.[2]

Your middle two fingernail areas represent the middle prefrontal cortex, which is the most integrative region of the entire brain. It is easy to see why this is so: when you lift your fingers up and put them back down, you will see how the middle prefrontal cortex (your two middle fingertips) rests on top of the limbic system (the hand model thumb), *also* touches the brainstem (the palm), and *also* links directly to the side cortex (the outside fingers).

We can see what Siegel means when he points out the "anatomical uniqueness" of this middle prefrontal region, being "one synapse away" from neurons in the cortex, the limbic area, and the brainstem.[3] Because this part of the cortex is connected to the other two primary regions of the brain (the original/primal brainstem and the limbic system), this middle prefrontal area of the brain plays a key role in managing our reactivity level in a typical stress response.

The Stress Response in Action

Continuing to use your own hand-brain model, you will now be able to visualize what transpires during a highly emotional encounter when the functions of an otherwise integrated brain disintegrate and cannot remain optimally engaged.

Siegel explained that as soon as the amygdala gets the alert signal from the brainstem that there is danger of any kind, it makes an immediate assessment of its own as to whether the situation is safe or dangerous. The amygdala responds in about fifty milliseconds (about half an eye blink), while the more complex and "thinking" cortex takes about ten times as long (500–550 milliseconds) to develop conscious awareness of what the amygdala has already reacted to.[4] This means that information about potential threats to us can reach the amygdala before we are consciously aware there is something to be afraid of.

If the thinking cortex is not able to calm down the amygdala, the amygdala sends out the alarm to the rest of the brain to send chemical and electric messages throughout the body. Cortisol is released to put the body's metabolism on high alert to meet the challenge. Our heart rate goes up, our belly tightens, our jaws clench. In highly emotional encounters, *if the thinking cortex is still not able to fully engage* and regulate all the energy coming from the amygdala, the entire limbic system goes on high alert, bursting with fiery activity just below the prefrontal cortex.[5]

Holding your hand up as a hand-brain model, imagine the amygdala-thumb of your hand model with neurons firing out of control. When the amygdala is this fired up, the fight/flight reflex triggers the amygdala to override the higher, "thinking" part of our brain in order for our body to fight or flee as quickly as possible from the perceived danger.

Now pull the prefrontal cortex fingers away from the thumb-amygdala. The amygdala-thumb is activating in such an out-of-control manner that the cortex at this point goes offline completely and is literally disengaged, no longer connected with either the limbic system or the brainstem. It is easy to see that at this point in a stress response, the brain is operating solely through limbic and primal brain impulses, with no access to the thinking cortex, as the coordination and balance of the brain are completely disrupted.

This is what Siegel calls "flipping our lid."[6]

Our uniquely human prefrontal cortex is "flipped" away from the other brain regions. This is why we overreact in these situations, sometimes not even recognizing ourselves or the words we are saying. We are in survival mode, speaking and acting through inflexible and reactive survival impulses, without integrated access to our thinking brain.

Even without access to fMRI brain scan images (the latest neuroscientific technology to measure brain activity), Dr. Siegel's hand/brain demonstration gave my study cohort a remarkably straightforward and simple way to visualize why we as humans feel completely unmoored at this point in highly charged, emotionally stressful situations: the primary structures of our brain become disconnected from one another, or what Dan Siegel calls *disintegrated.*

Calming the Fight/Flight Reflex

Understanding the mechanics of the fight/flight stress response at such a basic level made it clear to each of us in Dr. Siegel's study cohort how vitally important it is to find ways to slow down the brain's hair-trigger fight/flight reflex and cultivate the sometimes even lifesaving capacity to be able to pause between stimulus and reaction. *This is where meditation has become the superhero of new brain science.*

New brain science in the past decade has confirmed that the intentional and consistent practice of meditation can move our thinking prefrontal cortex into action as a kind of amygdala circuit breaker that enables us to pause and reconnect not only during emotional outbursts, as illustrated above, but during daily challenges in general.

So we can see why neuroscientists describe this new era in their field of science as *revolutionary*: the groundbreaking scientific confirmation of the self-neuroplasticity of the human brain (its ability to change form in response to our own practices) means that we ourselves can engage in practices that change our own brain.

By the end of Dr. Siegel's hand/brain demonstration, even the idioms that we use to describe what it feels like to regain our sense of equilibrium after an angry outburst were suddenly spot on:

"I got my head on straight."

"I plugged back in."

"I reengaged."

"I came back to my senses."

Seeing "inside" the brain with Siegel's simple, clear model, we can now understand the very direct connection between making time for a few minutes of contemplative practice every day and keeping our head on straight.

Careful Not to Demonize the Amygdala

It is important for me to note here that as the knowledge of basic neuroscience has become more mainstream in recent years, the amygdala has received far more than its fair share of negative press for its role in initiating the fear response. It is all too easy for those of us who are laypeople in the field of neuroscience to make the mistake of mislabeling or even demonizing the amygdala when we learn how easily its alarm system is tripped and how our overreactions soon follow. (I've even seen YouTube classes for *kindergarteners* on the basic brain science of the fight/flight response where the instructors overdramatically (and incorrectly) characterize the prefrontal cortex as "the hero" and the amygdala as "the bad guy.")

To counter this trend, as concepts in brain science increasingly become common, everyday household language, some neuroscientists are urging laypeople to resist joining in with what they call the anti-amygdala camp. Indeed, just as we need to be careful to not demonize the *ego* in our psychological discussions of our true self and false self, it is important to be careful not to demonize the *amygdala* by falling into easy labeling and oversimplifications. Just as we can honor the ego and attempt to rebalance its influence, we can honor the amygdala and attempt to rebalance its influence.

In a discussion I recently had with neuroscientist Michael Spezio, he said that, "In general, any attempt to portray the amygdala as "reptilian" or as a "primitive fear center" is "outdated and does not reflect the best understandings of the brain in the twenty-first century." As a neuroscientist whose Scripps College laboratory has done rigorous studies on the effect of contemplative practice on the brain, Dr. Spezio points to the growing body of evidence that suggests the amygdala plays a far more complex role in our emotions and behavior than neuroscientists previously realized, a positive role that goes well beyond its ability to detect environmental threats and to generate fear responses.

Neuroscientists are currently discovering and making known a number of positive attributes of the amygdala that we can honor and become aware of. Researchers are presently investigating the amygdala's role in evaluating and prioritizing what is going on around us, both positive and negative, and then generating emotional responses to what is important. They are also finding evidence of the amygdala's role in the consolidation of memories that have a strong emotional component, both pleasant and unpleasant, positive and negative.[7]

As Spezio pointed out,

> In fact, connectomics—the study of replicable networks in the brain—shows us that the amygdala in adult humans is widely connected to the prefrontal cortex and to other cortical areas, and participates in our being able to value our health and relationships with other persons, among its other roles.

The Critical Cortical Override

The superhero role that meditation and other contemplative practices play in *calming* our brain's alarm centers is also fascinating. Meditative contemplative practices can move our prefrontal cortex into action as a kind of circuit breaker so that we don't end up flipping our lid.

Here is how that works:

Research is showing that by developing more neural pathways (which means stronger connections and clearer communication of messages) to and from the amygdala and the neocortex, a steady practice of meditation and other contemplative practices recruit the higher, "thinking" areas of the brains to create a "cortical override"[8] of the amygdala's overreactivity. This means the prefrontal cortex can come online a few crucial microseconds sooner in emotional situations; it notices the fight/flight response has been activated, and then short-circuits the firing of an overactive amygdala.

Thanks to the stronger neural pathways developed through a steady contemplative practice, that (relatively) early awareness of our fear response gives us a crucial momentary meta perspective. We are able to *pause and see a bigger picture.* We can more easily realize that our initial fear or potential threat was perhaps not as dangerous as it seemed, possibly was even a normal event or just a misunderstanding. We are able to offer more reflective, reasoned responses, and can be more receptive to others' perspectives.[9]

If this is sounding a lot like *metanoia* to you, you are not alone.

Pausing, seeing the bigger picture, being reflective of and receptive to others' perspectives—we are talking about the exquisite neuroscience of our human brain, and at the same time we are hearing clear and vibrant echoes here of *metanoia,* Jesus' clarion call[10] and the central message of the gospels. Even in these simple and basic explanations of recent breakthrough neuroscience discoveries of the power of contemplative practice, we are able to see and to some extent grasp the actual brain mechanisms behind the expanded awareness and the new way of seeing to which Jesus calls each one of us.

Got Eight Weeks (or Even Just Five Days)?

One of the primary brain mechanisms responsible for communicating these internal and external awareness messages from the limbic brain system to the cortex is the anterior insula. In your hand-brain model, the insula lines part of the underside of your fingers and is connected with the cortex and the limbic region (which you may remember is the emotional network of the brain in which lie the two amygdalae). The insula is generally understood to be a kind of superhighway of information, the primary connector between the cortex and amygdala.[11]

As neuropsychologist Marsha Lucas explains, "To be able to reduce your hair-trigger, 'not-thought' body reactivity, you need the areas of your brain that respond to a threat (most of the limbic brain) to have a fast and reliable conduit running back and forth to the more 'reasonable' part of your brain."[12] Having such a fast and reliable connection between the limbic alarm centers of our brain and the prefrontal cortex means we can have a few more milliseconds to evaluate what we had first sensed as a potential threat.

This means that beefing up the insula is key if we are to develop the capacity to *see the bigger picture* and more expediently put the emotional brakes on our overreactive fight/flight reflexes.

Neuroscientists have been conducting breakthrough studies on this phenomenon since the very early 2000s: when Sara Lazar and her colleagues at Harvard compared the brains of meditators with nonmeditators in a 2005 study, the primary difference between the two groups was that those who meditated had significantly larger anterior insulae than those who did not meditate.[13]

This group of neuroscientists then announced another breakthrough in 2011, which proved that the differences found in previous studies were not due to preexisting conditions in the brains of those who had previously meditated, as participants in this newer study had never meditated before. This study showed that, even in beginning meditators, as little as *eight weeks* of training in mindfulness meditation practice increases the neural circuitry, or "gray matter density of the insula."[14]

And, notably, in 2015, the very short-term mindfulness meditation training of *five days, thirty minutes per day*, conducted by Yi-Yuan Tang and his colleagues, was shown in brain-imaging investigations to increase insula thickness in a relatively large sample of forty undergraduates[15] and make a "noticeable difference" in the well-being of its participants. Tang himself noted that participants in certain body-mind meditation practices had lower stress, higher immunity, and improved cognitive performance in areas like attention, memory, creativity, and problem-solving.

"Five sessions can improve brain activity in the tension area, emotion area, reward area, and the self-control area, usually in the middle of our brain," Tang said. "After 10 sessions, we find this area becomes bigger."[16]

As we learned in the earlier discussion of neuroplasticity, this increase in size is a result of increased neural firing in that area of the brain. It is believed that *each time we pause and release a thought and return to a present-moment awareness* rather than get caught up emotionally in the thought, the insula is activated to inform the cortex of what is happening in our body.

With the increase in neurons firing in this part of the brain, new neural connections are made, and the insula grows in size. As the insula increases in size with more gray matter, there are more neural bridges of communication between the cortex and the amygdala. These neural connections act as all-important bridges to integrate the communications functions of the cortex and the amygdala.[17] Important information reaches the cortex more quickly, giving the cortex a wider, more flexible attention span and a few crucial milliseconds of space to pause and send calming signals to the amygdala.

Remember, the pause-release-return movement of meditation is the basis of the contemplative practices of every world spiritual tradition. Here we may be catching a glimpse of the exquisite science that *underlies* the transformative and universally freeing gesture of letting go of egoic demands and agendas.

The actual physical anterior insula may be in some way related to the more metaphysical *kenotic* "muscle of surrender" Cynthia Bourgeault speaks of in *Centering Prayer and Inner Awakening* when she describes the effect of the repeated gesture of letting go of thoughts in our contemplative practice:

> In this way, the repeated returning [in Centering Prayer] gives the "muscle of surrender" a good aerobic workout. . . . Contemplative prayer or meditation offers a consistent and reliable way of practicing the passage from small self to greater Self, from the tunnel vision of ordinary awareness to the larger and more spacious presence that resonates in one's spiritual awareness, i.e. the way to transformation.[18]

As Tang says, when "you distance your thoughts or emotions and realize they are *not* you, then you see the reality in an insightful and different way."[19]

As either a spiritual or purely scientific gesture, the gesture of pausing, letting go of thoughts, and returning to present-moment awareness does catalyze the neural circuitry of the insula. But these gestures *also* offer that way to transformation that both Bourgeault and Tang speak of here and that appear to be a factor in the physiological shifts that beginning meditators report anecdotally—particularly the sense of being calmer and less reactive after even a short time spent practicing meditation.[20]

Practice the Pause and Stay Calm

It makes sense, then, that studies also show that with just eight weeks of mindfulness meditation, the amygdala is smaller in size.[21] Each time we release a thought and return to present-moment awareness, the prefrontal cortex projects a neurochemical substance called gamma aminobutyric acid (GABA) to soothe the overactive amygdala.[22] GABA signals the amygdala to stay calm and not get alarmed. The amygdala is less activated, there is less firing of neurons in this part of the brain, and over time, neural connections begin to atrophy.

Researchers have found that gentle forms of yoga that emphasize breathing and stretching have been shown to increase GABA levels in the brain by as much as 27 percent, and are associated with lower levels of depression and anxiety. (No wonder we feel somehow lighter and freer after even one gentle yoga session.)[23]

Thus, by regularly practicing meditation and other contemplative practices, we equip the brain to be more optimally integrated and synchronized. These are all ways we can release the hold of our overactive fight/flight reflex and enable our prefrontal cortex, the most human function of our brain, to do its work and to work with the limbic system, providing us the means to respond from a place of wisdom and insight rather than react defensively and often reflexively.

Freeing Ourselves from the Prison of Fight/Flight

As groundbreaking and exciting as these neuroscience studies are, they can sound oh-so-technical next to the actual life experiences of how significantly contemplative practice can actually change real lives.

When I was tutoring a young woman who was incarcerated at the local correctional facility in my hometown, I saw firsthand the phenomenon that has been confirmed in these neuroscientific studies—that a person can feel calmer and less reactive after only a few short weeks of meditation practice. The young woman (whom

I will call Alisha here) had been incarcerated for the possession of cocaine. During one of our weekly life skills tutoring sessions, I introduced her to the life-skill practice of meditation.

Several weeks of tutoring sessions later, Alisha shared with me that during the week prior, she had been put in three-day solitary confinement for sneaking in some cigarettes given to her by a friend during one of the prison's weekend visitation hours. As Alisha was telling me her story, she expressed her gratitude to me for teaching her how to meditate. She said she had been practicing off and on since the week I had first taught her and that she had meditated often during her three days in solitary confinement.

Alisha said that when she entered the prison cafeteria on the day of her release from the solitary cell, she immediately sensed that her perspective had shifted in a way that she said was hard to describe. She said it was as though she had "a kind of soft, protective veil around her, like a cocoon" that shielded her from "the hard places." She no longer felt a need or desire to argue with or even react to a particular person whom she said had been her enemy, a fellow prisoner who lived in the same wing of the prison that she did. And she no longer "hated" the female prison guard in the way she had so hated her before.

Alisha said, "I don't know, I just suddenly got that, hey, that girl has young kids, too, like I do."

~ ~ ~

I have had the honor of teaching meditation and other contemplative practices to young and older individuals in various church settings, in spiritual direction, and in a local county correctional facility. Hearing these individuals' life stories helped me to see how the fight/flight overreactions of our ego can not only complicate our already chronically stressed lives, and disconnect us from our awareness of God, they can finally imprison us, both figuratively and literally.

But seeing the nascent and powerful movement of the Spirit in the lives of so many who have begun a discipline of contemplative practice as an answer to their yearning for ways to be more aware of the Divine within or, in some cases, as an answer to their need for ways to survive the painful vicissitudes of their lives, I have witnessed the power of contemplative practice to set us free.

The Insula Connection as a Highway Works Project

Some neuroscientists imagine the gradual and freeing process of the brain being rewired through meditation as a kind of highway works project, and the insula is the superhighway that is being developed. The smoother the highway is, the more quickly that necessary and even crucial information will travel from one place to the other.[24]

Using this metaphor, even our very beginning attempts to pause and return again and again to present-moment awareness begin to clear the way for a bit of a path in the insula so that a road can be laid. As we continue a steady meditation practice, the path gradually becomes a narrow road and then becomes a wider, two-lane highway. As we become more aware of our thoughts and our internal state through a steady meditation practice, the insula finally is able to serve as a "super highway of information between the limbic and prefrontal cortex systems of our brain."[25] And now here is the science of being set free.

In an emotionally charged encounter, the insula is then more able to communicate important information about the body to the cortex, so the cortex can pick up on emotional cues and know when to deliver GABA to the amygdala and effectively regulate and direct necessary messages to the rest of the body system.[26]

Because there is roughly a quarter-of-a-second gap between the time an event occurs and the time it takes the amygdala to react, those who maintain an intentional and consistent contemplative centering pause practice are more able to intervene before a fight/flight response takes over and then respond from a centered, thoughtful place—more fully aware, creative, curious, and expansive.

Neuroscientist Jill Bolte Taylor, who authored *Stroke of Insight* after her eight-year recovery from a debilitating hemorrhagic stroke, explains what she calls the "90-second rule" to describe the potential of communication between our insula and cortex region. She points out that the chemicals that flood through us during a high-stress situation actually are flushed completely out of our bloodstream in less than ninety seconds. She says this means that for those ninety seconds, we have a choice: we can either choose to feel the chemicals wash through us and let them "dissipate after 90 seconds, or we can act it out for 90 seconds, or we can rerun that circuit into a loop of emotion that goes on and on and on for 90 minutes or 90 years."[27]

By maintaining an intentional and consistent contemplative centering pause practice, we lay down a communications superhighway that enables our brain to be more integrated and more equipped to intervene in those sometimes crucial ninety seconds before a fight/flight response completely takes over. By practicing the pause in our intentional practice, we are more able to practice the pause in highly stressful situations rather than overreact or even flip our lid.

Think of young Alisha in the prison, who had only just begun to clear away the brush of her brain's neural pathways, just enough to see a bit of a dirt road in front of her. Even at this very beginning of her own highway works project, Alisha could see a slightly bigger picture of her life and could even begin to recognize the humanity in a person toward whom she had previously felt fear and resentment.

While Alisha (and probably many of us) has a long way to go before her insula is a well-traveled superhighway, and before her *metanoia* is more fully developed, she already had access to the few microseconds she needed for her prefrontal cortex to move into action so that she could respond more thoughtfully and even compassionately.

Contemplative Neuroscience Studies: A Deeper Look

Readers who are interested in learning the hard science behind the benefits of meditation in even more detail may want to join me in this section in investigating one of the neuroscientist community's most important and groundbreaking studies, still touted today for its strong evidence that practicing meditation changes the brain, specifically in ways that directly impact physical and mental health and well-being.

The monumental study, called "Mindfulness practice leads to increases in regional brain gray matter density,"[28] was led by Drs. Sara Lazar, Britta Hölzel, and a team of researchers in the Massachusetts General Hospital Psychiatric Neuroimaging Research Program. It was the first neuroscience study to document meditation-produced changes over time in the brain's gray matter.

The specific focus of this 2011 study was to identify changes in specific brain regions that would be associated with participation in an eight-week mindfulness-based stress reduction (MBSR) program, which has become one of the most widely used mindfulness meditation training programs worldwide. The program focuses on the effect of formal meditation practices on the capacity for contemplative awareness, or present-moment awareness, or what the study's authors formally call "mindfulness," which is now universally well known for its positive effects on psychological well-being.[29]

Particularly, the study was focused on measuring positive cognitive and psychological shifts that persisted following formal mindfulness meditation practice sessions. The results of Lazar and Hölzel's groundbreaking study, as published in *Psychiatry Research: Neuroimaging*, showed that participating in an eight-week MBSR program appears to make measurable changes in brain regions associated with memory, sense of self, empathy, and stress.

In the introduction of this Massachusetts General study, the authors offer helpful background on the power of neuroplasticity:

> A large body of research has confirmed that meditation and other present-moment awareness-based practices have been found to reduce symptoms of a number of disorders, including anxiety, depression, substance abuse, eating disorders, and chronic pain, as well as improving well-being and quality of life. It has been suggested that this process is associated with a perceptual shift in which one's thoughts and feelings are recognized as events occurring in the broader field of awareness.[30]

The study incorporated the standardized program of MBSR, which consists of eight weekly group meetings lasting two and a half hours each. During classes, formal meditation training exercises were demonstrated and practiced to assist in developing the capacity for contemplative awareness/mindfulness.

Exercises included sitting meditations of gradual duration, up to twenty minutes in length. Participants were encouraged to always gently return to the "simple awareness of one's presence in the here and now" whenever thoughts, feelings, and sensations appeared in consciousness. To facilitate the integration of mindfulness meditation into daily life, participants were instructed to practice contemplative awareness informally during everyday activities such as eating, walking, washing the dishes, and taking a shower. At the end of the study, meditation group participants reported spending an average of twenty-seven minutes each day practicing mindfulness meditation exercises.

To investigate changes in brain gray matter concentration attributable to participation in the MBSR program, MRI images were taken of the brain structure of sixteen study participants two weeks before and two weeks following their participation in the program. Exploratory analyses were then performed on the entire brain. Changes in gray matter concentration were investigated and compared with a control group of seventeen nonmeditators who had MRI images taken over a similar time interval.

Two weeks after the conclusion of the MBSR program, results of the study's questionnaire indicated significant cognitive and psychological differences when compared with preprogram responses. MBSR participants significantly increased their mindfulness scores in three mindfulness subscales: acting with awareness, observing, and nonjudging. The control group did not experience increases in these mindfulness subscales.

The MRI image analyses taken of the study participants two weeks after the program specifically confirmed increases in gray matter density within

(1) the hippocampus, involved in learning, memory, and modulation of emotional control
(2) the posterior cingulate cortex, involved in attentional focus and self-awareness, particularly in autobiographical contexts
(3) the temporo-parietal junction, involved in empathy and self-awareness
(4) the cerebellum, involved in the regulation of the speed, capacity, consistency, and appropriateness of cognitive and emotional processes.

No increases in gray matter concentration were reported in the study's control group, suggesting that participation in an MBSR course causes structural changes in brain regions involved in learning and memory processes, emotion regulation, self-referential processing, and perspective-taking.

Previous studies from the Lazar/Hölzel group and other laboratories had observed thickening of the cerebral cortex in areas associated with attention and emotional integration in the brains of *experienced* meditation practitioners. The results of the Lazar/Hölzel 2011 study documented that this cerebral cortex thickening *was produced by the meditation practice itself.*

In the study's summary comments, Britta Hölzel, PhD, a primary author of the paper and then a research fellow at Massachusetts General, said, "It is fascinating to see the brain's plasticity and that, by practicing meditation, we can play an active role in changing the brain and can increase our well-being and quality of life."

The Science Is in: Meditation Is a "Must-Have"

The field of *contemplative* neuroscience has come into its own and is now well established, with neuroscience laboratories around the world conducting new studies on how meditation changes the brain. These ongoing studies continue to confirm that meditation and other contemplative practices directly and significantly affect the parts of the human brain that are related to emotional regulation, complex thinking, a sense of self, empathy, pain tolerance, perception, and body awareness.

It is hard to believe that just two decades ago, mainstream neuroscience would not have accepted the premises that are now the very basis of thousands of neuroscience studies being conducted worldwide. And now evidence is conclusive: our brain changes both functionally and structurally as a result of stressful experiences *and* of positive experiences, and our brain changes in revolutionary ways as a result of meditation.

Prominent researchers in the field agree that "the converging evidence is compelling—meditation should no longer be considered simply something 'nice-to-have' as your daily practice. Meditation is a 'must-have,' a way to 'train' our brains to improve mental, emotional, and physical health, to support self-regulation and effective decision-making capabilities, and to protect ourselves from toxic stress."[31]

As psychologist Christina Congleton and neuroscientists Britta Hölzel and Sara Lazar said in their study presented in *Harvard Business Review*, when we "take a seat, take a breath, and commit to being mindful, particularly when we gather with others who are doing the same, we have the potential to be changed."[32]

CHAPTER 6

Contemplative Neuroscience: Confessions of a Closet Meditator

We are the beneficiaries of a revolution in the understanding of the brain and of human potential. . . . Yes, the brain can change. And that means we can change.

—Sharon Begley

I was reading the transcript of a recent interview with Dr. Richard Davidson, one of the world's top neuroscientists, when these words jumped off the page: "I was a closet meditator."

I had to read the quote twice to make sure I had read it correctly. I couldn't imagine how someone who is considered a pioneer in the revolutionary new field of contemplative neuroscience would have ever needed to keep his own meditation practice "underground," as he said. After all, this former "closet meditator" has for the past three decades conducted groundbreaking, well-funded lab studies on exactly that—the practice of meditation.

But Davidson was describing what it was like for him during his early career as a Harvard doctoral student of psychology in the early 1970s. At that point, he was studying meditation on his own and was meditating daily. He said he had noticed "a different quality of being" in the people he knew who meditated, and also in himself, and was eager to see if it were possible to assess scientifically quantifiable differences between meditators' and nonmeditators' brains.

Davidson's hopes were stalled at that time by multiple barriers: fMRI technology was not well developed, and neuroplasticity was an unknown concept then,[1] so there was no funding support or real interest in meditation research. Even Davidson's senior colleagues discouraged him from his academic pursuit, believing meditation research to be a likely "dead-end career." Instead, in his early career, Davidson played a vitally important role in the field of emotion and the brain.

But twenty years later, in a kind of fullness-of-time moment—when the concept of neuroplasticity had been newly proven, and significant advances had just been made in fMRI imagery—Davidson was invited to meet with the Dalai Lama in his home in Dharamshala, India.

In what Davidson describes as an "absolutely pivotal meeting," the Dalai Lama posed a hopeful question to Davidson: "You scientists are using the sophisticated tools of modern neuroscience to mostly study anxiety, depression, and fear, all these negative feelings. Why not use those same tools to study positive human qualities like the human capacity for kindness and compassion and equanimity?"[2]

His Holiness had posed his question to the right person at the right time.

Richardson said the Dalai Lama's question was a "total wakeup call" and a "pivotal catalyst" to him then deciding to dedicate his life to researching the effect of meditation on the brain. It was at that meeting that Davidson said he "made a commitment to myself and to His Holiness that 'now is the time to come out of the closet' with my interest in this area, which we've been calling contemplative neuroscience, to begin to talk publicly about it, and to begin to actively do research in it."[3]

The Dalai Lama assisted Davidson's research efforts, recruiting Buddhist monks to travel thousands of miles to Davidson's lab at the University of Wisconsin-Madison to participate in his fMRI brain-imaging studies investigating the long-term effects of meditation on the brain's ability to, in Davidson's words, "cultivate the qualities of mind that promote a positive outlook."[4]

Davidson's studies began to show the power of the mind to change the brain.[5]

A few years later, in October of 2004, a group of world leaders in the then-newly emerging field of neuroplasticity traveled to the home of the Dalai Lama, wanting also to learn more about the long-term effects of the practice of meditation on the brain. Daniel Goleman, PhD, renowned science journalist and author of the internationally bestselling book *Emotional Intelligence*, was included in this gathering, and said he noted then how such a meeting of minds would have been "unthinkable" one or two decades earlier, when the century-old neuroscience doctrine still held that the brain takes its shape for life during childhood, with no structural change expected in later life.

Yet here were the world's top neuroscientists actually discussing how *the mind* can change the brain, a phenomenon that Goleman describes as "a second revolution in thinking in the field: It's not just that the brain changes its structure throughout life, but that we can become active, conscious participants in that process."[6] In his fascinating chronicling of this landmark event in the preface of Sharon Begley's *The Plastic Mind: New Science Reveals Our Extraordinary Potential to Transform Ourselves*, Goleman reminds readers that, for thousands of years, practitioners of meditation "have been exploring the potentials of brain plasticity . . . and passing them on as instruction for future generations, down to our day."

And now these ages-old meditation practices are demonstrating what Goleman calls "one of our day's most exciting scientific revolutions."[7]

A Seed of Hope

Now hundreds of gifted neuroscientists, neuropsychologists, psychiatrists, and pastoral counselors are devoting their lives to the work of the continually emerging discoveries of *contemplative* neuroscience. They have published hundreds of peer-reviewed studies and journal research articles investigating and confirming that certain kinds of mindfulness meditation and contemplative practices can induce significant, long-lasting positive changes in the brain[8] that actually train the brain, enabling even short-term practitioners to be less reactive, more aware, and consequentially more focused, more productive, and more empathetic.[9, 10]

These scientific studies point to the past, to what humans have achieved for millennia through a steady contemplative practice, and they point to the future, to what we as humans can now achieve with this new scientific awareness. These studies are responses to the seed of hope the Dalai Lama planted thirty years ago—that scientific knowledge of the power of meditation and other contemplative practices might enable these practices to finally go mainstream and reach a worldwide audience looking for ways to manage stress and to cultivate compassion and well-being.

As if right on cue, just a decade after the Dalai Lama's "fullness of time" question to Davidson and the neuroscience revolutions that followed, new smartphone technological advances ushered in the digital age worldwide, along with its new normal of having infinity in our back pockets and being personally available 24/7. Both the conveniences and the trappings of the digital age have collectively stressed and stretched us beyond what we thought was possible.

So today's revolutions in neuroscience, and its revelations about the power of meditation to rewire our brain and reorient our hearts, may conceivably become *a kind of antidote* to the stress and strain of our modern digital age. The new field of neuroscience may be offering the same good news that wisdom spiritual traditions have taught through the ages, the same good news we heard from the master storytellers of the gospels, the same good news that Jesus of Nazareth, the wisdom master, was showing us all along: there is a way of being, accessible through an intentional and consistent centering pause practice, that can carry us through today's morass of busyness and nonstop demands into a divine/human way of relating to ourselves, to others, and to our world.

Even now.

~ ~ ~

Richard Davidson has now been meditating for forty-five years. His advice for those who want to start meditating is to commit to a daily practice for at least thirty days. While noting the published studies that show as little as eight minutes of meditation can actually produce a measurable objective change, he says, "it doesn't matter how small that number is, just do it every day."[11]

Davidson says he still sits for a period of meditation every morning, and then afterward, for just a few minutes, he scans his calendar to check on the day's upcoming meetings. He says he then *pauses* "to reflect on how I can bring the right stuff to be present and most helpful . . . [Then] I can go through a day where I have ten straight hours of meetings, and at the end of that period I feel still nourished and refreshed."[12]

Contemplatives of ancient times and meditation practitioners of our modern era are, each and all, conveying the message to us that we can, in essence, live a profoundly meaningful, engaged, and active outer life that is continually supported by our inner contemplative life, even in the midst of this digital age we are living in. When we find a way to regularly take a pause from the emotional turmoil of our lives and incorporate some time apart in meditation and contemplation, we connect with the deepest, truest aspect of ourselves. We become more self-aware. We become more God-aware. We are able to manage our own distressing emotions. We are able to recognize and thoughtfully respond to feelings in other people. We transform our day-to-day way of being and move toward reaching our human and divine potential.

In Sharon Begley's words, "As these discoveries of neuroplasticity, of self-directed neuroplasticity, trickle down to clinics and schools and plain old living rooms, the ability to willfully change the brain will become a central part of our lives—and of our understanding of what it means to be human."[13]

Through the new scientific awareness of the extraordinary power of an intentional and steady meditation practice to improve our capacity for the innate human virtues of compassion, empathy, kindness, and awareness, we are realizing the possibility that engaging in our own steady, transformative contemplative practice may even bring about what Begley calls the *exceptional states* of each of these virtues in ourselves.

Sounds a bit like the Jesus practice.

And even more promising discoveries in contemplative brain science are on the horizon in regard to the scientific study of specifically *spiritually oriented* contemplative practice.

What Makes Contemplative Awareness Exercises a *Spiritual* Practice?

At this point, you may be wondering to what extent the meditation techniques being used in contemplative neuroscience studies have a *spiritual* component or if the practices are entirely secular. And what constitutes one practice being described as *spiritual* when another is secular?

Until recently, neuroscientists have been predominantly using nonreligious, secular meditation practices in their investigation of the effect of contemplative practices on the neuroplasticity of our brain. Despite the Dalai Lama's Buddhist roots, even Richard Davidson and the Dalai Lama remained intentionally secular in their collaborative studies and refrained from incorporating the tenets of any particular spiritual or religious tradition into the focused-attention exercises they used in their contemplative awareness studies.

Some neuroscientists have described the nonreligious focused-attention contemplative practices that are used in their neuroscience studies as being tacitly Buddhist-inspired, but these practices could just as easily be described as Sufi-inspired, Christian-inspired, or Wisdom-inspired. The pause-release-return method of the basic meditation practice that neuroscientists are using is actually the bare-bones basic contemplative awareness method that is fundamental to the core contemplative dimension of all religious or spiritual wisdom traditions:

(1) Stilling the body and mind for a period of quiet
(2) Pausing to release thoughts when they arise throughout the period of quiet
(3) Returning to the present-moment stillness

This basic method is not tied to a particular spiritual or religious tradition. Neuroscientists have been using this basic contemplative awareness practice for their scientific study of nonreligious contemplative practice for decades now. The method is free from spiritual teachings or spiritual intention. Practitioners continually pause to release distracting thoughts or sensations that occur in the period of quiet, and then each time the practitioners return to the present-moment stillness, they again *focus their attention* on their breath, or on an image, or on the present moment.

But when this method is set within the context, orientation, teachings, and *intention* of a spiritual or religious tradition, this basic meditation method shifts in a subtle but nonetheless quite profound way. I can speak anecdotally to this profound shift from a particularly Christian experience (though it is possible my personal experience may be similar to practitioners of other contemplative wisdom practices).

Once rooted in a religious or spiritual tradition, this basic method of meditation is no longer about focusing attention at all. At the point in the meditation process when we release a thought that arises and then we return to the present-moment stillness—be it our breath, an image, the present moment, or even a sacred word—we do not then *focus* attention on any of these, or even on the stillness, so much as we release and *open into a profound intention.*

In Christian practice, our intention is to open into an awareness of the presence and action of God, the Holy, the Divine, whatever we experience that presence to be within our innermost self and within all. But this practice of the presence of God is not limited to a simple acknowledgment of the presence of God. It is a transformative practice that, over time, equips the practitioner to become what in the Jesuit tradition is called a "'discerning person' *(anthropos diakritikos)* . . . someone perpetually mindful or watchful of God working in all things and at all times."[14]

So then when thoughts arise, the breath, image, present moment, or word to which one returns is simply a symbol of the practitioner's intention to consent to, and to *open to*, an awareness of the natural flow and presence of the Divine all around and within us—what I call "What Is." There is a sense of connection and a natural oneness with God in that "opening into" movement. (In scientific terms, there is a sense of relationality.)

The movement is one of release: it is less a movement of doing in order to *get hold of* something; it is more a movement of *giving oneself over to* being in something. Practiced in this way, this basic method becomes foundational to profoundly transformative contemplative wisdom practices of many spiritual traditions, including Centering Prayer in the Christian tradition.

New Studies of Spiritually Oriented Meditation

Because the initial movement of the pause to release thoughts is the same between a secular and spiritual practice, this means contemplative practitioners from Christian, Sufi, Buddhist, and other wisdom traditions can experience similar physiological benefits as practitioners of secular meditation—less fight/flight stress, more calm and focus, more awareness. But because of the difference in the second movement, toward opening into the presence and action of the Divine rather than toward focused attention, practitioners of spiritual wisdom traditions speak to a life-changing, relational, and deeply rooted attunement and *connection* to themselves, to others, and to God that they experience through their practice. They testify to the power of their spiritual practice to *transform* their way of being in their day-to-day lives by the new awareness their spiritual practice brings. There is an understanding that one transforms into the likeness of what one holds within our hearts.

Scientists and spiritual leaders have recently been collaboratively investigating these relational and transformational aspects of spiritually oriented contemplative practice, specifically Christian practices, along with the *transcendent* quality they have also observed in their preliminary scientific studies. And because the basic movement of Centering Prayer so closely resembles that of secular focused-attention mindfulness meditation (despite differences in intention and outcome), there has been particular neuroscientific interest in investigating the ways that the practice of Centering Prayer changes the mind, our heart center, and our actions, *as well as* the brain.

Being a cognitive scientist and a Presbyterian minister, Dr. Michael Spezio works in the interdisciplinary area of theology and science and advocates for "the scientific acknowledgment and study of the '*mindfulness of God*'[15] that is inherent in the rich historical traditions of biblically based, contemplative Christianity."

~ ~ ~

From the Dalai Lama's first offer to assist Western science in its investigation of the transformative potential of the human brain to the latest neuropsychological and neuroscience studies investigating the transformative potential of the practice of Centering Prayer, we are on the crest of a wave of new neuroscientific and religious research and convergence.

As this next wave embraces a decidedly *spiritual* component in the already revolutionary neuroscientific research, we are witnessing an intersection of science and religion that magnifies the revolutionary potential of Jesus' own practice to rewire our brain and reorient our heart in ways that make it possible to live into our full human potential.

CHAPTER 7

The Spiritual and the Secular: It's about Connection

The soul is not in the body. The body is in the soul.

—Hildegard of Bingen

With the growing prevalence of spiritually based therapies in pastoral counseling and psychotherapy settings, a number of neuroscientists and neuropsychologists are working to catch up on their scientific evidence-gathering, anticipating yet another new frontier emerging in contemplative neuroscience studies: the effect of Christian centering meditation practices on the brain and behavior.[1]

In one landmark peer-reviewed study, neuropsychologist Jesse Fox and his colleagues investigated the "lived experience" of Centering Prayer practitioners who have had at least five years of steady Centering Prayer practice experience in order to provide neuroscientists a solid foundation for designing studies to identify and test the "causal mechanism of Centering Prayer and the benefits that can be derived from the practice."[2]

Participants in this Fox study and others reported an "acute, experiential awareness of the divine at the center of their being, which filtered out into their perception of the exterior world and the people they met."[3]

Addressing the participants' emotional mental health experience in their practice of Centering Prayer, the Fox study noted the practitioners' responses that their "anxiety and stress were all but extinguished through their experience in Centering Prayer." In the words of the participants, they no longer responded to stressors "in a frantic manner" or felt "determined by their circumstances."[4]

In their well-recognized 2018-published paper, renowned neuroscience scholars Denis Larrivee and Luis Echarte underscore the "relational and affective transformation of the meditator engaging in Christian meditation . . . [noting how] Christian meditation adopts de facto a relational praxis . . . to a higher and universal order." Given this relational emphasis, the study points to Christian meditation being likely to "secure additional benefits not readily secured through mindfulness meditation or Eastern religious spiritual exercise."

As such, they suggest, Christian meditation is "uniquely poised to extend the range of mental health benefits beyond those of mindfulness, warranting future scientific investigation for its psychotherapeutic potential."[5]

~ ~ ~

With these current as well as upcoming studies in the field of contemplative neuroscience, we are on the cusp of incorporating an understanding of particularly spiritually oriented meditation practices into recent secular scientific revolutions and revelations about the power of meditation to catalyze new neural pathways in the brain.

These investigations are going beyond exploring the *brain* and our *mental* well-being; they are taking into consideration *the mind* and our *spiritual* well-being.

As Hildegard of Bingen has said, "The soul is not in the body. The body is in the soul."

The Convergence of Scientific Analysis with "Simply Wanting a Cup of Tea"

A growing number of scientists and theologians, along with historically well-known luminaries in the field of science including Pierre Teilhard de Chardin, Albert Einstein, and John Polkinghorne, believe such dialogue between science and religion can be mutually enriching to both fields of interest and inquiry.

Despite the fact that they conduct their craft from a secular scientific perspective, numerous contemplative neuroscientists and neuropsychologists speak openly about being personally connected to Jewish, Christian, Buddhist, and other spiritual teachings.

Richard Davidson, Daniel Goleman, and Jon Kabat-Zinn speak of the *dharma* teachings they themselves try to live by.[6] Neuroscientist Jeff Schwartz, PhD, who is another pioneer in neuroplasticity studies and is the scientist who coined the phrase *self-directed neuroplasticity*, speaks openly of the movement of the Holy Spirit in his life.[7] Michael Spezio is a cognitive scientist and an ordained Presbyterian minister. Dan Seigel points to the ground-breaking self-directed neuroplasticity discoveries of our modern era as being confirmation of what ancient spiritual traditions have been telling us for centuries about the power of spiritually grounded contemplative practices to shift our perspective and transform our way of being.

The Rev. Dr. John Polkinghorne, renowned former Cambridge professor of physics, is a particularly delightful example of a scientist/theologian who fully embraced the mutuality of both religion and science. When Polkinghorne resigned his chair at Cambridge in 1979 to pursue his call to the Anglican priesthood, he told his colleagues, "I like to say that I am 'two-eyed,' viewing the world through the lenses of science *and* religion, a binocular vision that enables me to see further and deeper than I could with just a single eye. I need to take science and religion with an equal seriousness."[8]

Some scientists, like Dr. Polkinghorne, recount moments of beauty, awe, and wonder in their research that led them to believe there is "something beyond science." For some, this "other reality" motivated them in their research, in their teaching, and in their lives outside of the lab. Their experience reminds me of a famous quote by Dr. Polkinghorne himself that exemplifies the convergence of the scientific and the spiritual: "Yes, the water boils because the fire under the pot is hot. However, the water also boils because I happen to want a cup of tea."[9]

The Role of Our Inner "Wise Advocate"

The ability of these scientists to embrace the mutuality of science and religion stands in contrast to materialist scientists who claim that the brain rules the mind, that all of our actions are solely the result of the mechanisms of our brain. On the contrary, says scientists like Daniel Goleman, neuroplasticity is proving there is a "two-way street" between the mind and the brain.[10] Goleman and other scientists in the field of contemplative neuroscience speak of how their neuroplasticity research is proving that *the willful effort and intention of the meditators' minds* are integrally involved in the process of laying down new neurocircuitry.

Neuroscientist Jeffrey Schwartz has spoken directly of how what he calls "the spiritual aspect" of contemplative awareness practices is essential to our human development. He says,

> Using the mind to change how the brain works by rewiring the brain function is the "practical key . . . that leads to the development of the human mind's full potential"[11] . . . [and] it is an action that, beyond doubt, has *true spiritual content.* When examining the entire process, it becomes obvious that the *spiritual* aspect is not separate, but an integral and essential element to be acknowledged and considered.[12]

Schwartz goes a step further in his 2011 book *You Are Not Your Brain.* (I love the irony here—that an acclaimed brain scientist has written a book titled *You Are Not Your Brain*).

The premise of Schwartz' book is that having an intentional and consistent contemplative practice deepens our connection with what he calls our own inner "Wise Advocate"—that aspect of ourselves that knows our inner truths and aspirations, that calls us out on our own "deceptive brain messages" and steers us toward our truest aspirations.[13]

Schwartz has explained that when he speaks of connecting with our Wise Advocate in *You Are Not Your Brain,* he is referring to deepening our connection with our own spark of the divine within us. He is speaking of the Holy Spirit as understood in Christian terms.

At the same time, Schwartz makes the point that the term Wise Advocate can and is used in both religious *and secular* meditation contexts. His primary example is Rebecca Gladding, MD, Schwartz's cowriter of *You Are Not Your Brain*: Dr. Gladding enthusiastically endorses Wise Advocate as *her* secular term of choice for the inner wisdom that is a universally human aspect of all of us,[14] an inner wisdom that can transform our lives.

As we will explore further in the next chapter on first-century Jewish spirituality, this relational concept of the Holy Spirit is actually pre-Christian: Sufis and Jews incorporate a very similar intention and relationality in their contemplative practice as Christians do; the *shekinah* in the Hebrew tradition is understood to be the *indwelling and active spirit of God.* And as biblical scholar Karen Armstrong notes, "the *Sakina* seems to be related to the Hebrew *shekinah,* the term for God's presence in the world."[15] In the Sufi Islam tradition, the *Sakina* is the Spirit of Tranquility or the Peace of Reassurance—a lovely description that seems to fit each of the Abrahamic spiritual traditions.

III

AWAKENING IN THE WISDOM TRADITION

CHAPTER 8

Jesus the Rabbi: First-Century Jewish Spirituality

The first title given to Jesus by his immediate band of followers was a moshel meshalim, *"master of Wisdom." In the Near Eastern culture into which he was born, the category was well known, and his methods were immediately recognizable as part of it.*[1]

—Cynthia Bourgeault

Story after story, page after page, the gospel writers are telling us a great deal more about the fabric of Jesus' everyday world and the transformative power of his contemplative practice than meets our Western eye. So while much is being revealed to us in Western science about the revolutionary potential of contemplative practices, we still need a particularly Eastern and Jewish wisdom orientation to reveal key insights into the contemplative life and ministry of Jesus that might otherwise go missing:

- Jesus' practice of silence and solitude with God is rooted in the venerated, centuries-old prayers and spirituality that are embedded in Jewish literature and spiritual practice.
- The "wilderness" places to which Jesus departed were each profoundly symbolic in the Jewish tradition of the *transforming* power and even the "conversation" of the indwelling spirit of God.
- The concept of the "indwelling spirit of God" is pre-Christian.

If we are to realize the exciting depth and details of Jesus' profound spiritual practices, we as Western Christians first need a better sense of the remarkably rich and theologically vibrant spirituality of first-century Judaism in which Jesus, the gospel writers, and the gospel audience were all immersed.

Jesus' first-century audience lived in Jesus' world. They lived in the time in which Jesus did. They lived in the same spiritual and cultural context.

As modern Western twenty-first-century readers, we will want to know, as much as is possible, what it was like for the gospel writers' first-century audience when *they* first heard the vibrant gospel accounts of this man from Nazareth whose lived message of transformation changed the hearts of all who heard him.

Crossing the Threshold

We want to enter this first-century world as humble guests, with open eyes and curiosity.

And we want to enter this world knowing that we ourselves may discover new ways of understanding God and prayer that may enliven *our own* spiritual lives in our own modern time. By engaging ourselves with the world of first-century Jewish spirituality, we will be enabling that world to shine its spotlight on revelatory, otherwise hidden, and potentially transformative messages of both Jesus and the gospel writers that we may otherwise miss.

Also, and importantly, when modern readers are able to understand the gospels through the additional lens of early Judaism (rather than simply through a purely New Testament lens), the significant influence of prophetic Jewish spirituality on Jesus' own teachings moves to the foreground and cannot be merely glossed over (or overlooked entirely).

Cultivating this greater awareness is vital for this time in Christian and Jewish relations.

Amy-Jill Levine, Jewish scholar and Christian divinity school professor, makes the important point that "I have very much worried about the anti-Jewish views that frequently surface in studies about Jesus. A number of Christian commentators feel the need to make Judaism look bad in order to make Jesus look good. Instead of portraying Jesus as a Jew talking to other Jews, he becomes in their view the first Christian, the one who invented divine grace, mercy, and love."[2]

This lack of awareness (or, in some unfortunate cases, intentional disregard) of the profound influence of Jewish spirituality on Jesus' own teachings and practice has had tragic and ongoing consequences for Jewish/Christian relations in all these centuries since Jesus' time.

So we will begin this journey into first-century Judaism with our sights on a deep and broad understanding of the vibrant Jewish roots of Jesus' own practice of prayer, as well as some nuances of first-century Jewish spirituality that give us the ears to hear Jesus' transformative message and the eyes to see his active/contemplative way of being.

Recitation of the *Sh'ma*

Some Christians are surprised to learn that when Jesus said the most important commandment is "You shall love the Lord your God with all your heart, with all your soul, with all your mind, and with all your strength"[3] (what Christians call the Greatest Commandment), he was actually paraphrasing the soaring centerpiece of Jewish prayer called the *Sh'ma*. All five verses of the full *Sh'ma* are found in the Book of Deuteronomy from Hebrew scripture (which some Christians still refer to as the Old Testament and Jews refer to as the *Tanakh*).

The centrality of the *Sh'ma* in Judaism is impossible to overstate. In Jewish prayer practice, the *Sh'ma* is both a credal declaration of faith and a heartfelt connection to God. Observant Jews have recited the *Sh'ma* at the beginning and at the end of each day since biblical times, as directed in Deuteronomy 6:7, "when you lie down and when you rise."

As author Rabbi Wayne Dosick says, "The *Sh'ma* was and remains for Jews the journey into the highest and deepest realms of the place where God dwells, the way to touch and be touched by God."[4]

~ ~ ~

The word *sh-ma* means "hear" or "listen" in English and is taken from the first word of the full prayer commandment. Here is the full text of the *Sh'ma* (You may want to take a moment to say the words out loud slowly and intentionally, savoring them, to get a full sense of their spiritual power and what it may have been like for Jesus to recite them, morning and night.):

> Hear, O Israel: The Lord is our God, the Lord is One. You shall love the Lord your God with all your heart, and with all your

> soul, and with all your might. Keep these words that I am commanding you today in your heart. Recite them to your children and talk about them when you are at home and when you are away, when you lie down and when you rise. Bind them as a sign on your hand, fix them as an emblem on your forehead, and write them on the doorposts of your house and on your gates.[5]

We know the (at least) twice-daily recitation of the *Sh'ma* was of pre-Christian origin in Jewish tradition. There are references to the recitation of the *Sh'ma* in the works of first-century historian Josephus, as well as of first-century scholars Hillel and Shammai.[6] As a Galilean Jew living in Israel in the first century, we can assume the *Sh'ma* was unquestionably central to Jesus' character through its daily recitation.

The Second Commandment, Like the First

The commandment that Jesus then declared, unprompted, to be the second most important and to be "like the first"—you shall love your neighbor as yourself[7]—is also a paraphrase of Hebrew scripture; specifically, it is a paraphrase of Leviticus 19:18: "You shall not take vengeance or bear a grudge against any of your people, but you shall love your neighbor as yourself . . ."

As background, it is interesting to know that in Jesus' time, there was ongoing debate among scholars in regard to which commandment was primary, or the greatest, in the Law (meaning the Law of Moses, which usually refers to the Torah, the first five books of the Hebrew Bible). Some were defending the Law of Sacrifices to be the Greatest Commandment, others the Law of the Sabbath, others the Law of Circumcision.[8]

By declaring that the commandment to love your neighbor as yourself "is like the first," meaning it "is like" the Greatest

Commandment, and that "all the law and the prophets *hang on these two commandments*,"[9] Jesus is not only dramatically stating the priority of these commandments as a universal credo over other commandments; he was *integrating* the two commandments in a way that points to his consistent unitive message throughout his ministry: Loving your neighbor as yourself *is like* loving God with all your heart, with all your soul, with all your mind, and with all your strength. They are one and the same. God's love is in all and through all.

With even this brief glimpse into how all-encompassing the *Sh'ma* is in the Jewish world, and how all-encompassing the *Sh'ma* was in Jesus' ethos, we can see that Jesus not only fully embraced and prioritized the *Sh'ma* as the paramount principle for society to live by; we can see that Jesus *himself* was living into the essence of the *Sh'ma* in the way he so consistently and intentionally turned to God in both his inner life and in his active life of engagement with others.

Actively loving God and others with his entire being, with all his heart, with all his soul, with all his mind, and with all his strength, we could say Jesus was living his life *through* the prayer of the *Sh'ma*. Jesus was *incorporating* the *Sh'ma* into himself. Notice the word *corp*, meaning "body," is the root of *incorporate*.

The *Sh'ma* was *in the body* of Jesus.

This idea of living into the *Sh'ma* is reminiscent of what I have heard when mystics and other teachers of mine describe their experience of praying a mantra or a breath prayer so consistently, continually, and intentionally that they begin to feel "prayed in" themselves. The prayer becomes in*corp*orated in them. They are one with the prayer.

As far-off and mystical as this may sound, we are also catching a glimpse here of what emerging brain science is telling us about how exquisitely our brains can be rewired, how new neural pathways are catalyzed in ways that give us access to the most developed parts of the human brain. Jesus showed us in real time that intentionally releasing our egoic demands and returning again and again to the power of God's love in our prayer practice and in our actions can equip us to live through God's divine love, *to be incorporated* in God's love.

Divine love was being in*corp*orated into Jesus. This "incorporation" of divine love was what Julian of Norwich called "oneing,"[10] an old English word she uses to describe the encounter between God and the soul. Jesus was actively living the Oneness of God.

And he was showing us how to do the same.

Recitation of the *Amidah*

In addition to the one-pointed focus and devotion of the *Sh'ma* being recited twice a day, observant Jews have prayed the deeply felt, hallowed petitions and thanksgivings of the *Amidah*[11] at least three times daily every day since before Jesus' time through today. (The traditional Jewish practice of praying three times a day is a practice some Jews attribute to the patriarchs: in the Torah, it is said that Abraham was praying to God in the morning, Isaac in the afternoon, and Jacob at nightfall.)[12]

The *Amidah* is comprised of beautiful, poetic blessings, three of which are blessings of praise, thirteen of petition, and three of thanksgiving. The literal translation of the word *Amidah*[13] is "standing," as the blessings of this prayer are meant to be spoken while standing with feet firmly together and without any material thoughts in mind, with complete focus and attention on the words of the prayers.

The *Amidah* typically ends with a blessing that is familiar to us today. This blessing is understood to be words ordained by God and given to the priests by Moses: "The Lord bless you and keep you; the Lord make his face to shine upon you and be gracious to you; the Lord lift up his countenance upon you and grant you peace."[14]

The basic text of the *Amidah* is thought by most scholars to have been composed in the fifth-century BCE[15] and to have been in existence at the time of Jesus' ministry.[16] Some scholars have noted the similarity between the petitions of the *Amidah* and those of what is traditionally known as the Lord's Prayer.

Imagine the power of remembrance in stopping three times a day to say words similar to the Lord's Prayer and the Moses blessing.

Prayer at Meals

While the synoptic gospels are clear in their portrayal of Jesus having a prayer life in some ways independent of the prayer customs of his day, we can make the assumption Jesus was influenced by the ancient culture in which he grew up, immersed as that culture was in the biblical tradition of prayer—"in the air of the Psalter, the confession of the *Sh'ma*, and the deeply felt, hallowed petitions and thanksgivings contained in the older parts of the *Amidah*."[17]

Prayers of blessing were also offered by the host before the meal in first-century Judaism, following ancient custom.[18] (In Hebrew, the word *grace* literally means "blessing.") The blessing before meals is specific: derived from Psalm 104:14, it is ideally recited over a whole loaf of bread—"Blessed art Thou, O Lord our God, King of the Universe, who has brought forth bread from the earth."[19]

It is notable that specific thanksgiving is not a part of the recitation of that grace/blessing said before a meal. We will note this custom and its alteration in Jesus' feeding of the 5,000.[20]

Kavanah as Even More than Intention

In first-century Judaism, it was understood that prayer *begins* with intention.

The act of prayer itself has been described since ancient times in the Hebrew tradition as a "service of the heart." Prayers must be endowed with a proper intent, allowing the innermost self to be expressed and experienced. This quality of mindful, Holy-directed intention was and is today called *kavanah*, a word that implies "straighten," or "point to," and is understood to mean "direction of the heart."

In the Jewish rabbinical tradition, "he who prays must direct his heart to heaven."[21] Praying with *kavanah* is praying with your heart directed to God.

~ ~ ~

There is an old Jewish tale of a beloved rabbi coming to a synagogue and turning back at the door, unable to enter.

"Too many prayers inside," he said.

"But, Master," asked his disciples, "surely a room full of prayer is a good thing?"

"But these prayers have no wings," the rabbi answered. "They are stuck there in the building. None of them are going up to heaven."

~ ~ ~

A service of spoken prayer or even the private recitation of the *Sh'ma* is "true" prayer only if the words spoken are in harmony with the inner thought of the one praying.[22] (Think back to your experience just now of saying the words of the *Sh'ma* slowly and intentionally.) And this distinctly meditative quality of prayer was not limited to spoken prayers. Any *mitzvah* (a Godly commandment or a good deed) was complete or valid only if made with holy intent, with *kavanah*.[23]

At first, *kavanah* may sound a bit like mindfulness, living in the moment. But I've come to see that the profound meaning of *kavanah* is more than being intentionally aware of the present moment. Our prayers or actions have *kavanah* when we intentionally align our inner and outer awareness with our heart and soul and redirect our entire being toward God's love.

As a current-day example, *kavanah* would be when we focus fully, with all our heart, on someone who may be asking for our attention: We put our phone down. We look in their eyes. And we give them our full and undistracted attention and love.

Kavanah would be when we stop what we're doing and send loving kindness with all of our heart to someone who we know is having a rough time of it these days. *Kavanah* is when we sit down for our own prayer or meditation time, as we do in the practice of Centering Prayer, and release our scattered thoughts, set our intention on fully opening to and resting in the movement and Love of God within us and through us, and then as our attention wanes, we return to our intention.

Jesus exemplifies *kavanah* not only in his intentional time apart to be with God. We see him continually releasing his own egoic demands and challenges and intentionally redirecting himself toward the transformative power and presence of God.

And in our own practice, following Jesus' lead, here again is that place where transformation can happen, where we can participate in the exciting intersection of science and spirituality. The science: we know that every time we intentionally release a distracting thought (and the egoic demands it represents), we are laying down new neural pathways in areas of our brain responsible for compassion and emotion regulation. The spirituality: every time we intentionally return to our openness to the love of God/Divine/the Holy, our own being and the Divine become what Cynthia Bourgeault describes as "more and more mysteriously interwoven."[24]

Both ancient spiritual traditions and the new science of contemplation point to how intentional contemplative practice lifts us into greater awareness. We are moved to see beyond the mind, beyond our usual way of thinking. We find God in places we hadn't expected. We find wonder in the everyday.[25] Indeed, we experience the "hallowing of the everyday"[26] that *kavanah* brings.

Jewish Meditation

While not as prevalent as prescribed daily prayer, contemplative practice has always had a place in the Jewish tradition. Some Jews even trace the practice of meditation in the Jewish tradition to one of the patriarchs. In Genesis 24:63, when Jacob went out to walk in the fields, according to a classical Jewish translation,[27] the verb in this passage is interpreted as "meditate." In her essay on Jewish meditation, Rabbi Rachel Baranblat says, "So one could make the case that from the patriarchs on, Jewish prayer has always had a meditative component."

Anecdotally, several Jewish friends of mine have spoken of the surprisingly meditative quality of their liturgical prayer, known in Hebrew as *tefilah*. These are the prayers spoken during their Shabbat and holy day services. While at first glance, one would not imagine many spoken words said in succession as having a meditative quality, some Jews know their Hebrew so well they find they occasionally move into a meditative state during these prayers. Others choose particular lines of the prayers to recite while putting their focused attention and intention (*kavanah*) on each word of the prayer.

Barenblat points out that with the root of *tefilah* being *l'hitpalel*, which means to "judge oneself," we can see how liturgical prayer carries with it the invitation not only to connect us outward toward others and toward God but also to connect us inward, into our deepest selves.

In *tefilah*, Barenblat says, we are invited "to take a long deep look inside ourselves, to see who we most truly are, to become aware of our consciousness and our thought processes, and to guide ourselves toward becoming the people we most intend to be."[28] Like Christian contemplative prayer, *tefilah* is meant to "move our hearts in both directions, as it is itself a contemplative practice."

Rabbinic literature also speaks of "saints of former times," pious Jews from ancient Judaism known as *Hasidim ha-Rishonim*, as those who would meditate inwardly for an hour before prayer to bring full *kavanah* to the words of their prayers and then would meditate for one hour to allow the meaning of the prayers to be incorporated into their hearts and souls.[29]

Later, in the eleventh century, the Jewish mystical tradition of Kabbalah introduced contemplative and meditative visualization practices with the goal of connecting with God and having access to a higher consciousness. Other Hasidic practices to achieve communion with God then developed over time, including *hitbodedut*, which means "self-seclusion"—walking alone in the woods and communing with God—and *hitbonenut*, meaning contemplation of divinity.

While some of these practices are current, most are as old as the earliest Jewish prayers and were likely practiced in the first century by the gospel writers, the gospel writers' audience, or by Jesus himself.

CHAPTER 9

The Call of the Natural World in Jesus' Time and Now

The Sacred calls us into the Wild, and the Wild calls us into the Sacred.
—Victoria Loorz, *Church of the Wild*

I remember as I was leaving the hospital with my newborn twin daughters, and my two-and-a-half-year-old daughter at home, my doctor pulled me aside to offer me some sage advice that has been remarkably sustaining to me in all these years since. He said, "You may have a few challenging nights and days and even months ahead, caring for three little ones under the age of three years old. I have found it always helpful to remember—when things get difficult, go out and *be under the sky.*"

Be under the sky.

While I didn't realize it at the time, my doctor was inviting me to enter into what author Victoria Loorz calls the "Great Conversation,"[1] the conversation between the voice of the human heart and the voice of the natural world. This dynamic, life-giving conversation between God and the people of God is prevalent throughout Hebrew scripture—in the Torah, the psalms, and the prophets. Many of us in this twenty-first century have lost touch with the sustaining and transformative power of this Great Conversation, but to those living in the time and culture of Jesus, they knew that divine power to be an integral part of their faith history.

So when I became aware of the pre-Christian Jewish understanding of the spirit of God as a formative presence not only *within* each person, transforming all of humanity,[2] but also immanent and present in the *natural* world, I felt a quickening of my own memory and then of my curiosity. I wanted to know more.

This multifaceted Jewish expression of the formative *spirit* of God, well established in pre-Christian Judaism, was one of the most enlivening concepts I discovered in my research of first-century Judaism.

The Sacred Call of the Wilderness

First-century Jews were very aware of the presence of God in the natural world. In the Hebrew culture, it was understood that one could connect with, and be transformed by, the mystery of God *by being in and a part of* the natural world.

Mountains, rivers, and the forest or desert, wilderness in general—all isolated places that in the Greek is the *erémos*—are cited throughout Hebrew scripture as places of privileged sacred encounter with the presence of God: Each one of the patriarchs and many of the prophets were called by the spirit of God to venture out of their day-to-day lives and into the wilderness. The Jewish people themselves were led into the wilderness and came to know God there. Jesus, for forty days, and Paul, for three years, were both led by the Spirit into the wilderness before key turning points in their call. And Jesus continued following the call of the spirit of God into the *erémos* throughout his ministry.

The word *wilderness* appears in the Bible more than three hundred times; nonetheless, both the visuals and the transformative power of this biblical wilderness eluded me—until I read Victoria Loorz's compelling insights on early Hebrew culture, language, and understanding of the natural world in her book *Church of the Wild: How Nature Invites Us into the Sacred.*

Through my research, I had known that areas in the natural world like mountains, rivers, lakeshores, gardens, and other places of wilderness were assumed by first-century Jews to be filled with the formative presence of God. But I didn't know why this was so easily assumed.

The role of the Hebrew culture and language is key: both are *relational* and *verb-based* and focus on relationship. Loorz says, "Many cultures, including Judaism and most Indigenous nations, consider the divine a verb, a relationship, rather than a noun . . . suggesting that God is the dynamic intimacy of relationship, a verb of back-and-forth connection, of Love that created everything and connects everything and moves everything forward."[3] She notes that the Jewish people were less interested in defining the substance of God and more interested in how to relate to and please God: "Yahweh, for them, was not a noun entity. God was a verb: God was *being* rather than *a* being."[4]

God was *being* itself rather than an entity, rather than a separate being. Immediately, there is a shift here from our traditional modern-day "noun" theology into an active, moving, and *relational* verb orientation toward the Divine.

Conversation in the *Erémos*

This *beingness* of God was, and is, an intrinsic part of the life and vibrancy and dynamic conversation of the natural world. Loorz lets us know that for people in Jesus' time, the wilderness, the *erémos*, in the Mediterranean was a place where one was isolated and apart from crowds, away from other humans, yes, but the *erémos* was also "alive with growing plants, trees, rivers, a place where shepherds could bring their sheep"—a place filled with the life and vibrancy and dynamic *conversation* of the natural world.

The *erémos* was a living world that God *speaks through.*

In the biblical tradition, it is understood that all people are called into the mountains, rivers, lakeshores, and gardens of the wild to be in "animate relationship with the living world," Loorz says, pointing to the eleventh-century BCE Psalm 19—

> The heavens declare the abundance of God,
> the skies reveal God's hands.
> Day after day their speech flows out;
> night after night they reveal knowledge.
> There is no speech, and no language
> where their voice is not heard.

I am struck by how cut off we are in our modern time to this way of understanding ourselves and the Sacred, particularly in relation to the natural world. We go to church to be with God, and we go into the natural world to be with nature. And never really connect the two.

Loorz tells us more about how conversation with nature is embedded in the Hebrew language. She points out that the Hebrew word *midbar*, usually translated as "wilderness," is rooted in the verb *dabar*, which means "speaking." *Ba-midvar*, translated in most cases as "*the wilderness*," also means "the organ which speaks."[5]

Think of the wilderness in which the Jews wandered after being led out of Egypt; think of the wilderness into which the Spirit led Jesus, where "the angels ministered to him." Understanding the wilderness of the "living Earth" to be a place that *speaks through* the wind, the rain, the birds, and the animals "transforms it from a harsh place of difficulty to a tender place of intimacy."[6] Even in our modern time, many of us can recall when we ourselves have experienced a kind of conversation in the wild that somehow includes a deeper silence that invites us to pause and "listen to the voice of the sacred . . . a voice that is deeply your own and also the trees and also God."[7]

Gifted spiritual director that she is, Victoria Loorz reminds us that "the Sacred invites us into the Wild, and the Wild invites us into the Sacred," and she offers us questions we can "live into": "Have you experienced a mystical connection with God, with Mystery, with the soul of the world by listening and responding to the creatures and places around you? What if we really did belong to this beloved community that expands beyond our species?"[8]

The "Thin Places" between Heaven and Earth

I have come to think that certain places of *erémos* in the first century must have been what "thin places" are to many of us today. The term *thin places* may seem to be an odd expression for what is a rather transcendent phenomenon, but the name makes sense: Thin places is an ancient Celtic description of those locales where the veil we generally experience between heaven and earth suddenly becomes more permeable and porous—it feels thin to us in ways that enable us to better sense the "holy oneness of heaven and Earth. We become lost in wonder and held in Love."[9] In these thin places, even we ourselves seem to become more open and porous to the movement of the Divine in our midst.

A favorite writer of mine describes thin places as those places that "beguile and inspire, sedate and stir."[10] They jolt us out of our usual way of seeing and understanding the world. We move into a different sense of time in thin places, a *kairos* time rather than our usual *chronos* time. *Chronos* time is chronological time we spend our day-to-day lives living. *Kairos* is a Greek word and a Greek understanding of a sense of time beyond time, a time that touches on the eternal.

Thin places are often outdoors where water and land meet or where the land and sky meet. But they are also indoors: certain cathedrals are found to be thin places where there is a felt sense of the Divine. "Heaven and Earth," the Celtic saying goes, "are only three feet apart, but in a thin place that distance is even shorter."[11]

In the Biblical tradition, it is understood that the people of God are transformed by contact with the presence of God,[12] particularly in natural-world locales like mountains, gardens, and other places having sacral quality in the biblical tradition, so it is likely the gospel writers were conveying that dynamic by portraying Jesus as "turning to prayer" in these locations. The gospel writers' continual references to Jesus in prayer "on the mountain" would likely influence the early gospel audiences' understanding of the character of Jesus as being formed and transformed by his dialogue and communion with God in the midst of his call to serve God.

So we can see now how Jesus going to the *erémos*—to the mountain, or garden, or other isolated place to pray, "as was his custom"—would immediately catch the attention of the gospel audience. These were thin places. Something important and transformative was going to happen there.

The gospel writers were letting everyone know that Jesus was regularly (one gospel uses the word "forever") going to places where everyone knew one goes to be in the presence and action of the spirit of God. This would be like us today hearing that someone was going on a retreat to the Isle of Iona in Scotland, or to Rumi's tomb in Turkey, or to Lourdes in France, or even to a favorite magical bookshop to linger for a while for rest and restoration.

Notice how even imagining such a spot settles the soul.

With the exception of Jesus' prayers in Gethsemane, in all the synoptic gospel accounts there are no actual recorded words when Jesus is in these places of *erémos*, so Jesus' "prayer" in these accounts can be understood at least in part as times of *being in wordless conversation with the formative "beingness" of God there.*[13]

Shekinah as the Formative Presence of God Within

The Jewish tradition stresses both God's transcendence (God beyond us) and God's immanence (God with us). God is transcendent, the Holy One, and at the same time, everyone understood that the spirit of God is also an immanent Divine Presence that is all around us as well as in human personality, creating and giving life to the spirit of the people—inspiring, renewing, and making human beings whole.[14,15]

A powerful word evolved through the ages in the Jewish tradition to express the essence of this divine aspect of God in our very midst—that word is *shekinah* (from *shakan*, "to dwell, inhabit, or abide in").

While the centrality of the *Sh'ma*, the *kavanah*, and the daily recitation of prayer blessings give us valuable insights into the richness of the prayer culture Jesus was immersed in, it is the *shekinah* that becomes a kind of Rosetta Stone for us, revealing first-century clues to an even deeper understanding of Jesus' own prayer practice and his transformative path of awakening.

In the biblical tradition, it is understood that the *shekinah* was the Holy Spirit of God that accompanied the Jews in the desert. After the conquest of Canaan, the *shekinah* moved wherever the "tent of meeting," or the tabernacle, went (the tabernacle is the portable earthly dwelling place of God that Jews traveled with in the desert), finally abiding in the temple built by David and Solomon in 957 BCE until the destruction of the temple in 586 BCE, when it is believed the *shekinah* then disseminated and became "a divine power capable of transforming the human being and the world."[16]

In pre-Christian Judaism and in early Rabbinic literature of the first and second centuries, the term *shekinah* suggested not simply Divine Presence and activity throughout the world but particularly an *indwelling* presence, a nearness to, and even an intimacy.[17] Even with the temple destroyed, the immanent activity of the *shekinah* in the world nevertheless did not cease, so that such first-century scholars as Ishmael ben Elisha could say that "the *shekinah* is in every place."[18]

The Breath of God and the Christian Holy Spirit

The words *shekinah, ruach,* and *pneuma* each functioned as references to God's immanent presence at various times in Jewish history. Immediately prior to the emergence of Christianity, the *shekinah* gradually became the dominant way of speaking about the Divine Presence, replacing *ruach* and *pneuma*.

In the Biblical tradition, the *ruach* is the breath of God that formed humanity; in pre-Christian Hebrew understanding, the locus of the *pneuma* is in places of holiness—mountaintops and the wilderness, in the ark and the temple of Solomon; and then after the destruction of the first temple, the *shekinah* is understood in the Hebrew tradition to be the immanent and abiding presence of God in and through all things, including the people of Israel.

If this description of the *shekinah* is sounding to you a lot like the Christian understanding of the Holy Spirit, this is because the *roots of the Christian Holy Spirit are Jewish.*

In the past few decades, the Vatican itself has published several documents on the need for clarity and awareness on the "common heritage" of Christians and Jews, particularly regarding the Jewish roots of the Christian Holy Spirit.[19]

As these Vatican documents make clear, the underlying connections and main aspects between the Jewish *shekinah* and the

Christian Holy Spirit are numerous. Both are attributed with "guiding power, healing power, ordering power, and vivifying power," and each of these attributes is outlined in detail in the Vatican document, with corresponding biblical passages to support each one.

The Vatican also acknowledges the term "Spirit" itself as being rooted in the biblical *ruah* ("the breath of God" in Genesis) and the Christian feast of Pentecost as being rooted in the Hebrew feast of Pentecost, saying, "The out-pouring of the Spirit by the Risen Lord coincides with the Hebrew feast of Pentecost, which celebrates the gift to Israel of the Covenant and the Torah. The Spirit of the Risen Lord is not the cancellation but the renewal of the Mount Sinai covenant."[20]

~ ~ ~

Equipped with this basic introduction to first-century Jewish worship, prayer, and spirituality, we are able now to interpret gospel passages from a closer perspective of the gospel writers' audience.

Here is a people who experienced God as both "out there" and "in here," as well as in all of creation, particularly in thin places of awe and wonder and *conversation.* God is the Holy One, beyond all, and God is also immanent, with a universal and yet intimate inner presence and power that can *transform humanity.* Here is a people who connect with that transforming spirit of God through prayers and practices several times each day, with their hearts intentionally open to and directed toward God. Here is a people who understood God as "being" itself that speaks through the wildness of the natural world.

Here is a tradition that includes a fully developed acknowledgment and acceptance of this transformative and even intimate presence of the spirit of God—*the shekinah*—that has animated and transformed the world since the beginning of creation.

Our glimpse into first-century Judaism also sheds light on the person of Jesus and enables us to see more deeply into the gospel writers' messages to us about Jesus' own prayer practices, his own ways of being with that of God within and with that of God in all. We now see Jesus in fuller dimension, immersed in the oral Hebrew tradition of the centrality of the *Sh'ma* and daily benedictions, and the intention, the *kavanah*, that sustained and buoyed them.

Here is a Jesus who, through his propensity for intentional time apart with God, not bound by conventional prayer times, spent time in thin places in the natural world, where *everyone knew the spirit of God in creation can meet the spirit of God within.* Here is a Jesus with evident intention and awareness of the transforming power and presence of the spirit of God in both his inner and outer lives, showing us what it means to live as a true contemplative and one who is fully human.

~ ~ ~

> The apostles gathered around Jesus, and told him all that they had done and taught. He said to them, "Come away to a deserted place all by yourselves and rest a while." For many were coming and going, and they had no leisure even to eat. And they went away in the boat to a deserted place [like Iona!] by themselves.[21]

We cannot know if Jesus' constant return to prayer in his innermost self and in the Wild, is made out of deep need or desire or both. We know only that the synoptic gospel writers portray Jesus as being continually and intentionally returning to God in possibly a kind of ceaseless interior prayer. It is this continual intentional prayer to which Jesus calls his disciples (and each one of us who might have "ears to hear"), both through his example and even his very direct invitation: "Seek ye first the kingdom of God."[22]

CHAPTER 10

Time Alone with God: Jesus Practicing the Pause

Come away by yourselves to a
deserted place and rest a while.
—Jesus of Nazareth

In her book *The Luminous Web: Essays on Science and Religion*, Episcopal priest Barbara Brown Taylor describes how the new physics of today is showing us that our universe is one of unity, of *undivided wholeness*, in which all of life is held together, connected, from the subatomic level to the most distant star in our universe.

She asks, "Is this physics or theology, science or religion?"[1]

We feel it and we see it when look with awe through a microscope at the relationship of microscopic objects, when we look with awe through a telescope at the relationship of the stars and the planets, when we look with awe at the tiny, precise veins on the inside of a tulip petal opening into full bloom.

Taylor says, "We live in an infinite, luminous web of *relationship* that animates everything that is. . . . It is not enough for me to proclaim that God is *responsible* for all this unity. Instead, I want to proclaim that God IS the unity—the very energy, the very intelligence, the very elegance and passion that makes it all go . . . the I AM that Moses heard when he asked for the name of God."[2]

Taylor's description here reminds me of an epiphany I had in an orthopedic doctor's waiting room, of all places, after one of my daughters fractured her arm when she fell off the school's jungle gym. We were waiting there for what seemed like a long time, so finally I got up and started reading those posters we see in offices such as these—the various stages of broken bones being set and healed.

One poster showed a drawing of a completely broken bone. The next-stage frame was the bone set just right but with the break still visible. And the progression of the next set of frames showed the intricate weaving of the bones' cells that eventually completely connected the two bones, one to the other.

It was a moment I will never forget. I was suddenly in awe. I thought, *This* is what God is!

This is God *as a verb.*

This is what Carl Jung meant when he talked about our "innate push toward wholeness" that is within each of us. What I was looking at here was the miraculous force, the energy, the *love*, really, that heals and reconciles all things. From scraped knees, to broken relationships, to even our own brokenness, the world is rigged for healing love and for connection. I suddenly got that.

And I realized that this is the same transformation, the same *push toward wholeness* we experience in intentional and consistent spiritual practice. Two thousand years ago, Jesus showed us how to step right into this awareness, into this consciousness that Taylor speaks of. He showed us how to attune and align ourselves with this flow of oneness, this flow of all-connected life that is always pushing toward wholeness—wholeness of ourselves, of our relationships, and of this planet we live on.

Jesus shows us how to get there.

Setting Things Right

Jesus shows us what can happen when things are "set right," just like the doctor's office drawings. He shows us what can happen when *we* are set right, when *we* are fully awake and aware that we are one, and all are one, in this luminous web of God's love.

Notice how it seems Jesus can't help but serve and feed and heal and love and connect and listen and see and transform, making the blind see and making the deaf hear (and even making some pretty good jokes when he is speaking truth to power to the authorities).

It's as though Jesus is saying to all of us, "*This* is what it looks like to live in this force and movement of the love that is God, to fully live into the fullness of our humanity."

And when we pull the "whoa, wait, hey, but I'm only *human*" card, Jesus just deals us in anyway. He deals us in and says, "Yes, you are *human*. You are *exquisitely* human. And you will not only do the works that I do, but, in fact, you'll do greater works than these."[3]

We don't like that so much. Because it is sooooo much easier just to follow Jesus.

So how do we, like Jesus, stay in connection with God, and with each other, and with ourselves? How do we engage in this awesome, constant web of sustaining and always healing love? With so much going on in our lives, we are so often living on a kind of autopilot as we make our way through the busyness of our day.

Jesus shows us not only what it *looks like* when things are set right, he shows us *how* to set things right. We don't see it at first because it was never pointed out to us, but you can see it in every gospel: Jesus takes time in silence and solitude to rest and restore in that flow of the love of God. He takes time to rest and attune and align in the power and presence of the spirit of God. Watch for it: the disciples are forever looking for him, and he's off somewhere—for an hour or so in the morning sometimes, for an entire overnight retreat at other times—off and away for some silence and solitude alone with God before getting back to the day-to-day demands of his life and mission.

In today's vernacular, Jesus again and again takes time to unplug from the emotional day-to-day surface turmoil of ordinary awareness. In her inimitable way, Annie Lamott offers her own wisdom on how important this is when she says, "Almost everything will work again if you unplug it for a few minutes, including you."[4]

And of course, in a circular kind of logic, here we know that when Jesus unplugs, he is actually plugging into full awareness of the presence of God and showing us how we, too, can work the dial and tune in to the frequency of the love of God.

Time to Unplug and Tune In

Taking a fresh look at the gospels, trying to see through a more Eastern lens, and knowing Jesus is showing us the path for transformation, we may be able to now notice how frequently the gospel writers refer to Jesus' steady practice of heading out to deserted places to be in silence and solitude in the presence of God. Equipped now with a deeper understanding of first-century Jewish spirituality, it makes sense to us that the gospel writers are intentionally calling our attention to Jesus' undistracted times alone with God as a possibly sustaining and transformative inner practice of attuning with God. And that this inner contemplative awareness equipped Jesus in his outer practice of remaining ceaselessly attuned to this awareness of the Divine in his everyday life engaged with others.

These intentional times apart with God that Jesus consistently made time for and turned to in the midst of everyday demands, distractions, and fight/flight challenges were clearly a high priority for him and were interwoven throughout his ministry from the very beginning:

Deserted Places

> In the morning, while it was still very dark, he got up and went out to *a deserted place*, and there he prayed. (Mark 1:35)
>
> When Jesus heard this [the news of the death of John the Baptist], he withdrew by boat *privately to a solitary place.* (Matthew 14:13, NIV)
>
> Instead he went out and began to talk freely, spreading the news. As a result, Jesus could no longer enter a town openly but *stayed outside in lonely places.* Yet the people still came to him from everywhere. (Mark 1:45, NIV)
>
> At daybreak *he departed and went into a deserted place.* (Luke 4:42)
>
> But now more than ever the word about Jesus spread abroad; many crowds would gather to hear him and to be cured of their diseases. But he would *withdraw to deserted places and pray.* (Luke 5:15–16)
>
> The apostles gathered around Jesus, and told him all that they had done and taught. He said to them, "*Come away to a deserted place all by yourselves* and rest a while." For many were coming and going, and they had no leisure even to eat. And they went away in the boat to a deserted place by themselves. (Mark 6:30–34)

Mountains

Immediately he made his disciples get into the boat and go ahead to the other side, to Bethsaida while he dismissed the crowd. After saying farewell to them, *he went up on the mountain to pray.* (Mark 6:45–46)

Immediately, he made the disciples get into the boat and go on ahead to the other side, while he dismissed the crowds. And after he had dismissed the crowds, *he went up the mountain by himself to pray.* When evening came, *he was there alone* . . . (Matthew 14:22–23)

When *he was sitting on the Mount of Olives*, the disciples came to him privately . . . (Matthew 24:3)

But now more than ever the word about Jesus spread abroad; many crowds would gather to hear him and to be cured of their diseases. But *he would withdraw to deserted places and pray.* (Luke 5:15–16)

Now during those days *he went out to the mountain to pray*, and was passing the night *in* the prayer of God. And when day came, he called his disciples and chose twelve of them, whom he also named apostles. (Luke 6:12–13)

Now about eight days after these sayings Jesus took with him Peter and John and James, and *went up on the mountain to pray*. And while he was praying, the appearance of his face changed, and his clothes became dazzling white. (Luke 9:28–29)

Every day he was teaching in the temple, and at night *he would go out and spend the night on the Mount of*

> *Olives*, as it was called. And all the people would get up early in the morning to listen to him in the temple. (Luke 21:37–38)
>
> *He came out and went, as was his custom, to the Mount of Olives*; and the disciples followed him. When he reached *the place*, he said to them, "Pray that you may not come into the time of trial." (Luke 22:39–40)

In each of these accounts of Jesus taking time apart with God, we can see now that the gospel writers' first-century audience would have immediately been alerted to something important and unusual happening: First of all, Jesus was praying alone at unprescribed times and in unprescribed places that were outside the expected multiple daily rituals of *Sh'ma* and *Avidah* prayer. Secondly, in each of these passages, Jesus is intentionally finding time to go to the *erémos*, to a deserted place to pray, to be in solitude and silence with God. Remember, to first-century Jews, the *erémos* is a solitary place where humans don't live. *Erémos* places are what we usually envision when we think of getting out in nature. There is time and space there; there is the chance to be refreshed in the rhythms of nature. It was understood that the *erémos* was a place providing "needed quiet where God richly grants holy presence and provision for those seeking God."[5]

Reading the gospels through this new lens, we can see that Jesus' custom of taking time to be in prayer with God is actually one of the main features in the synoptic gospels. The gospel writers begin pointing out his practice from the beginning of Jesus' ministry.

In fact, Jesus taking time apart to be with God in deserted places is reiterated so often that the scenes become almost comically easy to imagine, with the less-than-enlightened disciples so often looking around for where Jesus might have gone off to and then realizing, once again, exactly where he is likely to be, of course.

From Mark's View

Each synoptic gospel writer treats Jesus' contemplative time alone with God in a slightly different way. Let's begin with Mark.

Almost immediately in the Gospel of Mark, we are told that Jesus takes time to be in prayer in the beginning of his ministry. This gospel is the first recorded gospel, also the shortest, and the writer of Mark is thought to be in a huge rush to proclaim his gospel, using the words "immediately" and "at once" a remarkable thirty-nine times throughout.

Mark omits the birth narrative of Jesus that Luke includes, and he omits the "begats" and "begots" of Matthew. So in Mark, we "immediately" learn that even before Jesus officially begins his ministry, "at once the Spirit sent him out into the wilderness"—which was a forty-day desert wilderness encounter—where he was "tempted by the accuser . . . and was with the wild animals and the angels were ministering to him."

Here is the powerful *erémos* imagery again.

As we saw in the last chapter on first-century Jewish spirituality, author Victoria Loorz's clear-sighted reimagination of this *erémos* as a place of animated relationship with the natural world can help us understand that

> rather than a punishment, being sent to the wilderness becomes a provision, an opportunity for listening and deepening relationship . . . [Jesus] needed this [wilderness] support as he faced his accuser, *diabolos* in Greek. You know the one—that inner critic, accuser, adversary—intent on keeping us distracted and safe from the dangers of prophetic leadership."[6]

We begin to better understand why Jesus so often chose excursions into the natural world for his time of silence and solitude with God.

Loorz says, "[Jesus'] prayer place was the wilderness, yes. But he went there to enter *into* a union with the sacred, speaking through the wild elements there."[7] We are able to reframe the mountains and other deserted places of *erémos* to which Jesus is called as places in which he was in *conversation* with the "beingness" of the Sacred, a *conversation* to which we are all called.

We can now understand that this forty-day encounter in the transforming and powerful presence of the *shekinah* in the *erémos* could have actually *equipped* Jesus for the temptations he encounters both there in the desert and in his ministry.

(Note here, too, that the temptations Jesus resists are the very temptations that are the unconscious vulnerabilities of the human condition: Jesus resists the temptations of esteem, security, and control.)

Mark then tells us that Jesus goes straight to Galilee to proclaim his message of *metanoia* there. Remember—the first message of his entire ministry was to tell us to see in new ways—*metanoia*—and know the kingdom of God is "at hand."[8]

Jesus then calls his disciples, they go to Capernaum, and that first Sabbath day is packed: Jesus teaches at the synagogue, teaches "with authority," and drives away an unclean spirit, after which "at once" his fame began to spread throughout Galilee. He and his disciples leave the synagogue and go directly to Simon and Andrew's house, where Jesus cures Simon's mother-in-law's fever, after which, at sundown, "they brought to him all who were sick or possessed with demons and the whole city was gathered around the door."[9]

The momentum is palpable here.

After such an eventful day, and before the next big day begins, everyone is waking up to continue on their new mission, but where is Jesus? The disciples can't find him. Mark tells us the disciples had to "hunt" for him. Once, again, Jesus has left to go out and pray in the *erémos*. He had gotten up early, left before dawn—long before everyone else's *Sh'ma* and *Amidah* morning prayers began—to go out on his own once again to be alone in the presence of God.

So from the outset, "immediately" (at this point, we are still in *the very first chapter* of Mark's gospel), Mark's audience is told that Jesus seeks out places apart from the demands of his daily life, and from the constraints of his own ego, to be in silence and solitude with God. The disciples told Jesus, "Everyone is searching for you," but Jesus resists egoic impulses to go back and revel in his newfound fame with the crowds of Capernaum. He is able to move on from Capernaum and continue in the purpose of his mission throughout Galilee.

It is remarkable how Greek translations offer enlightened nuances to the meaning of certain scriptural passages such as these. When we become aware of the original Greek, we can better appreciate how vigorously the writer of Mark emphasizes the very deliberate intention with which Jesus takes time to pray.

In English, Mark 1:35 reads: "In the morning, while it was still very dark, he got up and went out to a solitary place, and there he prayed." But in the Greek translation, we get more of a sense of the timing in the writer's double emphasis on how *unusually* early it was: The word *proi* means "the day-break watch, sometime between 3 o'clock in the morning until 6 approximately"[10] and is underscored by the inclusion of the word *ennuchon*, meaning "by night, a great while before day,"[11] highlighting the fact that Jesus is up before anyone else to find a quiet place to be with God.

With Mark's unnecessary but intentional double emphasis here, we can sense the gospel writer's desire to ensure that his audience is made *fully aware* of Jesus' clear intent and determination to pray alone with God.

It is also ironic and meaningful that in Mark, of all the gospels, being the shortest and most rushed, the writer himself makes it a priority to *pause* and slow down his own account to share the detail that Jesus invites his disciples to *pause* and slow down and join him in time apart with God, saying, "Come away by yourselves to a desolate place and rest a while." As Mark explains, "For many were coming and going, and they had no leisure even to eat. And they went away in the boat to a solitary place by themselves."

Here again, Mark tells us the crowds recognized Jesus and the disciples, so Jesus "had compassion on them," taught them, healed them, and fed them. (This was the feeding of the five thousand.) But notice: Jesus then made his disciples go ahead of him on a boat; he dismissed the crowds, and "after saying farewell to them," he withdrew *on his own* to the mountain to be in the *erémos*, in God.

From Matthew's View

The same unmistakable pattern of retreating into silence and solitude with God in the natural world can be seen in the Gospel of Matthew. Within just ten quick-paced verses of this gospel, Jesus "withdrew from there in a boat to a *solitary* place by himself"[12] (after hearing of the death of John the Baptist).

It is at this point in Matthew that the writer recounts the same Markan story of the feeding of the five thousand. The writer implies Jesus stayed there afterward for some time, when he then says, "When evening came, he was there alone." The mountain may be referring to the Mount of Olives, as Matthew again depicts Jesus being there alone later in his gospel.

Likewise, Jesus addresses the importance of finding a private place for intentional and undistracted prayer with his "inner room" teaching in Matthew's gospel: "But whenever you pray, go into your room and shut the door and pray to your Father who is in secret; and your Father who sees in secret will reward you."[13] We now know that prayers in the first century were spoken throughout the day in all places, which would make impossible Jesus' directive to go to an actual room "whenever you pray."

Knowing that constant, routinized prayer was everyday practice in Jesus' time, we notice it is unusual, then, that Jesus departs at unprescribed times to pray in unprescribed places, to what we now recognize in virtually every case are places known in biblical tradition as a place of *shekinah*, God's presence. Having more of a sense of the first-century Jewish perspective has given us insight into the ancient Jewish understanding of *shekinah* as the formative, indwelling presence of God residing within the people of Israel as well as in the temple and other holy places, so that Jesus' directive to go to pray in your *tameion*, in your inner room, can now likely be understood as a reference to an inner spiritual reality, a divine indwelling.

From Luke's View

The writer of the Gospel of Luke brings us several new insights into Jesus' practice of taking time for silence and solitude with God.

It is in the Gospel of Luke that we learn that Jesus' centering pause practice is an ongoing practice, or the "custom," of Jesus. In one account, Luke tells us that "every day" Jesus was teaching in the temple, and "at night he would go out and spend the night on the Mount of Olives."[14] Since we know first-century Jews understood that the people of God are "formed" by contact with the *shekinah*[15] in thin places in the natural world, such as mountains and isolated places, it is likely Luke was implying that, despite no words of prayer being recorded, Jesus' "prayer" here is that of simply *being in God's formative presence.*[16]

The literal translation of the Greek in one Lukan account can be understood as even implying that Jesus is essentially praying "in" God, as it says Jesus "went forth to the mountain to pray, and was passing the night *in* the prayer of God."[17]

Luke uses even stronger action and intention connotations than Matthew and Mark to emphasize Jesus releasing the ongoing daily demands of his active life to take time with God. Luke uses the Greek verb *hupochereo*—to withdraw self—to make it clear that Jesus leaves the crowd to be with God *even as the crowd is gathering for Jesus to heal them.*[18]

"Obedience": To Listen Deeply

> When they had sung the hymn, they went out to the Mount of Olives. . . . They went to a place called Gethsemane; and he said to his disciples, "Sit here while I pray." He took with him Peter and James and John, and began to be distressed and agitated. And he said to them, "I am deeply grieved, even to death; remain here, and keep awake." And going a little farther, he threw himself on the ground and prayed that, if it were possible, the hour might pass from him. He said, "Abba, Father, for you all things are possible; remove this cup from me; *yet not what I want but what you want.*" (Mark 14:32–36)
>
> When they had sung the hymn, they went out to the Mount of Olives . . . then Jesus went with them to a place called Gethsemane; and he said to his disciples, "Sit here while I go over there and pray." He took with him Peter and the two sons of Zebedee and began to be grieved and agitated. Then he said to them, "I am deeply grieved, even to death; remain here, and stay awake with me." And going farther, he threw himself on the ground and prayed, "My Father, if it is possible, let this cup pass from me; *yet not what I want but what you want.*" (Matthew 26:36–39)
>
> He came out and went, *as was his custom*, to the Mount of Olives; and the disciples followed him. When he

> reached the place, he said to them, "Pray that you may not come into the time of trial." Then he withdrew from them about a stone's throw, knelt down, and prayed, "Father, if you are willing, remove this cup from me; *yet, not my will but yours be done*." (Luke 22:39, 31–42)

With each gospel writer's inclusion of Jesus' words "yet not my will but yours be done" in the Gethsemane passages, it is notable that the words "Let it be thy will, O Heavenly Father" are the opening and closing words of a common Jewish litany of petitionary prayers of this time period that were likely to have been very familiar to Jesus.[19] Certainly the *kenosis*, the release of Jesus' own egoic will, was integral to his way and being throughout his life and mission.

The acquiescence and *obedience* of Jesus here to the will of God may give us additional insight into the contemplative act of mindfully and intentionally turning to God in prayer in general. Even the very act of pausing to turn away from our innate drives and inner compulsions is *kenosis*, a release of one's egoic will, and is an opening to the awareness of the power and presence of God.

Remember the word *obedience* comes from the Latin *ob-audire*, which means "to listen deeply, or from the depths." We can discern Jesus' pattern of *deep listening* to God in the simple act of his repeatedly releasing his own will (or plans, or desires, or expectations) and returning to the will of God through prayer.

These prayers of Jesus in Gethsemane on the Mount of Olives are another revelatory example of Jesus' apparent dependency on the presence of the spirit of God for strength through prayer in relation to his ability to fulfill his call. Jesus often goes to the Mount of Olives, another place of *shekinah*, but in this encounter with God, he "is deeply grieved, even to death"[20] and in the Markan account lies prostrate in prayer to God.[21]

As is his pattern in his ministry, here on this night in Gethsemane, Jesus returns again to prayer, and then again, and then even a third time, "even more earnestly."[22] I believe we are expected to notice that Jesus is then later able to *face* rather than to fight or flee the horror and pain of his upcoming "time of trial" or "temptation."

In this passage, the gospels' first-century audience is especially able to understand the gospels' intention to demonstrate the strong relationship between Jesus' consistent and formative encounters with the *shekinah* of God in his prayer life and his ability to then carry the power and love and grace of God's love into his mission and ministry.

Noticing the Rhythm and the Pattern

From the perspective of a first-century Jew, we can now see that the gospel accounts of Jesus taking time to pray "in" God are passages that would immediately alert us to something unusual taking place. The accounts of Jesus at prayer are not accounts of prescribed daily times of prayer, though they are clearly incorporated into the daily activity of Jesus' ministry. These are accounts of Jesus intentionally taking time to be in silence and solitude with God, even when he is with his disciples and others. Jesus is going out of his way to pause and be completely available and open to God, without inner distraction.

At Baptism

> Now when all the people were baptized, and when Jesus also had been baptized *and was praying*, the heaven was opened, and the Holy Spirit descended upon him in bodily form like a dove. And a voice came

> from heaven, "You are my Son, the Beloved; with you I am well pleased." (Luke 3:21–22)

Alone, with Disciples Nearby

> *Once when Jesus was praying alone*, with only the disciples near him, he asked of them, "Who do the crowds say that I am?" They answered, "John the Baptist; but others, Elijah; and still others, that one of the ancient prophets has arisen." He said to them, "But who do you say that I am?" Peter answered, "The Messiah of God." (Luke 9:18–19)

Before Teaching What Is Traditionally Called the Lord's Prayer

> *He was praying in a certain place*, and after he had finished, one of his disciples said to him, "Lord, teach us to pray, as John taught his disciples." (Luke 11:1)

We can see the contemplative rhythm and pattern of Jesus' way of being throughout the arc of his ministry. Prior to his public ministry, Jesus retreated into sustaining silence and solitude with God at his baptism and in the wilderness, the *erémos*, known by all hearers of the gospel message to be full of the spirit of God. The practice of intentionally taking time to be alone and with God then was a practice that became "his custom."

First-century Jews would have noticed how frequently and intentionally Jesus departed from the crowds, and even (or especially) from his disciples, to be alone in quiet with the *shekinah*, the formative presence of God. Jesus took time on his own with God before he made important decisions, to cope with his own grief, to "rest awhile" in care for his own soul, to prepare for his teachings and healings and feeding of the masses, and to prepare for his own earthly death.

Even as Jesus was making time to be alone with God, he was, nonetheless, actively and fully engaged with his public ministry, so it would have been clear that the synoptic gospel writers were emphasizing Jesus' particularly contemplative and continual rhythm and pattern of prayer practice, with his inner practice being in service of his outer practice.

Through the model of his profoundly contemplative life, Jesus challenges us, as he did his disciples, to broaden our understanding of prayer, and really of any contemplative practice we are drawn to, as a way of staying continually engaged with that of God within us, with the indwelling spirit of God, in every aspect of our lives.

With this glimpse into how Jesus is drawn to pray alone with God, we begin to see how the gospel writers have presented a real sense of the contemplative rhythms of Jesus' life. In one account after another, throughout the synoptic gospels, Jesus is drawn to the *erémos* for an inner contemplative life in solitude "in" God and then drawn back out into his outer contemplative life with others (and "in" God).

Why Jesus' Prayer Time Seems Hidden

Now that we are able to see the prevalence of prayer throughout the gospels, we will see that not only does Jesus seek time to be in prayer with God alone, but throughout each of these gospels Jesus teaches prayer, Jesus prays with others, Jesus talks about prayer. Jesus prays and blesses and gives thanks and cries out to God in prayer. Jesus' contemplative life forms Jesus in such a way that he becomes prayer himself.

Realizing this practice as his custom, you may wonder why you've never really noticed these accounts or noticed how often the gospel writers point out that Jesus took time apart to be in silence and solitude with God. You may wonder why the prayers and prayer life of Jesus have seemed so hidden in the gospels until now.

It turns out, our own blind eye has something to do with the lens through which we were taught to understand the gospels.

Remember that Western Christianity is more *soteriological,* savior-oriented, and Eastern Christianity is more *sophiological,* or wisdom-oriented. So if you were brought up with a predominantly *Western* Christian orientation as I was, it is likely you were taught, consciously or unconsciously, to read the gospels primarily through the lens of *belief in* Jesus as an all-powerful, often even implicitly omniscient, Savior. With our more Western orientation, we were more interested in the miracles and dramatic healing scenes and other signs that would confirm our *belief in* Jesus.

With a more Eastern orientation, we would read the gospels primarily through a lens of *becoming like* Jesus, the Way-shower. We would be wanting to look for ways to *be like* Jesus, to take on his divine nature, to "put on the mind of Christ" by following Jesus' own practice of transformation.

We would have more easily noticed the many times Jesus went out to spend time alone with God as well as other ways of being that are integral to Jesus' character and way of being in the world.

So these events have been hidden in plain sight because we did not *know* to notice them.

But as soon as we begin to relearn Christianity as a wisdom pathway into a transformed consciousness, we begin to see the prevalence of Jesus' centering pause practice throughout the gospels, in both Jesus' inner contemplative life and in his outer active life. We realize Jesus' intentional times apart to be with God are a key and primary feature of the gospels that likely supported his ability to return to God in his outer, active life. We begin to understand Jesus' active and contemplative life and ministry not as something to *believe* in but as a contemplative-in-action *way of being* that can transform our own.

CHAPTER 11

Contemplation in Action: Jesus Practicing off the Mat

What if Christ is a name for the transcendent within of every "thing" in the universe? What if Christ is the name for the immense spaciousness of all true Love?

—Richard Rohr

In a particularly overly busy time in my life, when the meditation I had been practicing had gone all but completely neglected and I hadn't been to a yoga class in a long while, I signed up for a yoga class that incorporated a session of meditation. After the meditation, when I lay down on my mat to settle into the final *sávāsana* pose, I remember feeling unusually relaxed and open and spacious.

Flat on my back, arms and legs completely supported by the floor, I closed my eyes to settle further into this pose that some call the pose of complete surrender. It was then that I heard an inner voice say, as clearly as if it were spoken out loud, "Oh, *there* you are . . . welcome home."

And it actually did feel like a homecoming, like a kind of recognition moment when the inner me and the outer me were able to see each other after a long time of being apart.

As class ended that day, our instructor reminded us that yoga and meditation are called "practices" because the time we spend practicing on the yoga mat, continually pausing to return to our breath, to our center, to the Divine in us, even in the challenging poses of our sessions, is actually *practice* for our day-to-day lives. Our on-the-mat practice equips us for the challenging poses we are sure to encounter in our *off*-the-mat practice just as soon as we walk out the door of the yoga studio.

The Inward Sanctuary as Our Source of Strength and Meaning

When we become aware that Jesus makes his inner contemplative practice a priority, no matter the distraction, and that this time in God was integral to Jesus' character and ministry, the reality begins to dawn on us that the gospel writers were intent upon getting across a powerful and even revolutionary message that has been hidden in plain sight, waiting for us to see: Jesus' profound inner contemplative life in God was not only formative and transformative; it was always *in service to* his outer active life. Jesus' profound inner contemplative life of continual prayer in God informed and infused Jesus' outer active life of radically inclusive *metanoia*, his self-giving love toward others.

We know this message was quite clear, not hidden, for earliest Christians. Some even immediately saw this message as the transformative, contemplative way of *theosis*, "divinization," of realizing their own divine nature through the practice of Jesus. This was the revolutionary message that inspired early Christians and the desert mothers and fathers and, as we discussed earlier, remains the very purpose of life for many Eastern Christians today.

We even see the often-bumbling disciples finally get their act together around how essential the inner contemplative life is, but this does not apparently happen until *after* the ascension of Jesus, when it is said that they returned to the upper room where they were "constantly devoting themselves to prayer"[1] before the descent on them of the Holy Spirit on Pentecost ten days later. (This account is recorded in the Acts of the Apostles and does not appear in the gospels. In the gospel accounts, the disciples are never seen as being in prayer on their own initiative as Jesus is. Even after Jesus is crucified, the disciples are said to have gathered,[2] but it is not apparent that they are in prayer.)

Howard Thurman, contemplative theologian, pastor, and spiritual adviser to Martin Luther King, Jr., often spoke of the growing yearning in our modern world to live into Jesus' original example of a profound and intentional inner contemplative practice being the essential underpinning of *contemplative and compassionate social action*. Thurman says,

> I am determined to live the outer life in the inward sanctuary. The outer life must find its meaning, the source of its strength, in the inward sanctuary. As this is done, the gulf between outer and inner will narrow and my life will be increasingly whole and of one piece. What I do in the outer will be blessed by the holiness of the inward sanctuary; for indeed it shall all be one.[3]

Prayer in the Midst of Life—Prayer in Action

The gospel writers seem to be intent on showing us how Jesus' one-pointed focus on the Divine is a necessary means toward a profoundly contemplative way of being in prayer *as well as* a profoundly essential means toward being *in action* effectively. The accounts they chronicled of Jesus in his life and ministry *between* his retreats into stillness and solitude—when he was teaching through parables, feeding the four thousand (or five thousand in some accounts), offering himself at the Last Supper, and even as he was dying—are accounts where Jesus exemplifies what it is to be in intentional contemplative practice in *all* aspects of our inner lives and our lives in the world.

Jesus exemplified how our outer life can indeed be "blessed by the holiness of the inner sanctuary."

In these accounts, we see Jesus fully in prayer even in the midst of chaotic life, continually open to the Divine working in and through him. We see Jesus' entire life as an active, living, contemplative prayer.

The Radically Inclusive Open Table

> When it grew late, his disciples came to him and said, "This is a deserted place. . . ." Then he ordered them to get all the people to *sit down* in groups on the green grass. . . . Taking the five loaves and the two fish he *looked up to heaven, and blessed* and broke the loaves, and gave them to his disciples to set before the people; and he divided the two fish among them all. And all ate and were filled . . . (Mark 6:35, 39–42)
>
> His disciples replied, "How can one feed these people with bread here in the desert?". . . Then he ordered the crowd to sit down on the ground; and he took the seven loaves, and *after giving thanks* he broke them and gave them to his disciples to distribute. . . . They had also a few small fish; and after blessing them, he ordered that these too should be distributed. They ate and were filled . . . (Mark 8:4, 6–8)

> When it was evening, the disciples came to him and said, "This is a deserted place" ... And [Jesus] said, "Bring them here to me." Then he ordered the crowds to *sit down* on the grass. Taking the five loaves and the two fish he *looked up to heaven, and blessed* and broke the loaves, and gave them to the disciples, and the disciples gave them to the crowds. And all ate and were filled . . . (Matthew 14:15, 18–20)

> [Jesus] went up the mountain, where he sat down. . . . Then ordering the crowd to *sit down* on the ground, he took the seven loaves and the fish; and *after giving thanks* he broke them and gave them to the disciples, and the disciples gave them to the crowds. And all of them ate and were filled . . . (Matthew 15:29, 35–37)

> The twelve came to him and said, "Send the crowd away . . . for we are here in a deserted place . . ." And [Jesus] said to his disciples, "Make them *sit down* . . ." They did so and made them all *sit down*. And taking the five loaves and the two fish *he looked up to heaven, and blessed* and broke them, and gave them to the disciples to set before the crowd. And all ate and were filled . . . (Luke 9:12, 14–17)

Notice how, with our awareness of first-century Jewish spirituality, we can now see that each of the synoptic gospel writers set the stage for an encounter with God in their accounts of the feeding miracles. Each story is said to be located in a "deserted place" (or on "the mountain" in the second account in Matthew), using the same Greek word *erémos* to imply a privileged place for contact with the *shekinah* of God.[4]

In addition to the *shekinah* motif being highlighted in each of the feeding miracles in terms of physical location, the gospel accounts show Jesus moving beyond any sort of natural fight/flight response that one would naturally have in a situation like this.

Instead of giving in to the agitation and despair of the disciples and to the prospect of what was before them all, the gospel writers show us how Jesus turns to the Divine in every moment. In each of the feeding miracles, Jesus exhibits and models real intention, *kavanah*, in the ways he carefully directs everyone, through connecting to God in prayer, to come into a profound and deep awareness of the *shekinah*, the presence of God that is dwelling in the midst of and among them.

In all five gospel accounts of the feeding miracles, either Jesus himself urges the crowd to "sit down," or he urges his disciples to tell the crowd to do so. To convey this action, the gospel writers used Hebrew words that give a particular sense of taking one's place at a table, implying the spontaneous (often radical) open table fellowship that is characteristic of Jesus throughout his ministry. We are familiar with Jesus "eating with sinners and saints," but these feeding miracle scenes take Jesus' radically inclusive open table fellowship to an entirely new level.

Given Jesus' directive for the crowd to all sit down together, we can assume that some in the crowd had been standing, presumably in a similar state as that of the disciples—hungry, possibly worried about what to do about getting something to eat and about any number of other concerns, especially regarding with real apprehension the mixed classes of the crowd having differing purity laws regarding meal ritual.

In these stunning scenes, Jesus was inviting a restless crowd of four or five thousand people of all stations of life to disregard their purity laws and to all sit down and have a communal meal together. Then we watch as the profound *kavanah* of their teacher, Jesus, draws those four or five thousand people away from their own concerns and into an awareness of the powerful and all-inclusive *shekinah* of God.

In all five gospel accounts of the feeding miracles, Jesus orients the crowd toward an awareness of *and a remembrance of* the presence of God, either through his action of *looking to heaven* before praying or through his prayer of blessing giving recognition to God's power to bring forth bread from the earth or his prayer of giving thanks to God.

In those moments, hearing Jesus praying *in God's name*, Jesus is drawing the awareness of the crowd to the abiding presence of God, what the first-century crowd would have understood as the *shekinah* abiding within them. We can see that everyone—the crowd, the disciples, *and* Jesus—is united in the *kavanah* of the prayer and is able, together, to experience the power of the *shekinah* present in this *erémos*, this holy place, the privileged place of contact with God.

These scenes are reminiscent of Jesus later assuring his followers that they will experience his presence when they are gathered together in an awareness of him—"Where two or three are gathered *in my name*, I will be in the midst of you."[5]

The Power and Grace of Giving Thanks

It is important to note here that most standard, routinized prayer practices aren't generally recorded in the gospels.[6] So we know then that the synoptic gospel writers are particularly emphasizing both the act of Jesus blessing the food before the feeding miracles *and particularly of Jesus giving thanks.*

Remembering that in first-century Judaism the practice of offering a prayer of *thanksgiving* before a meal was not standard, it is notable that in Mark and Matthew, we see Jesus not only offer a standard prayer of *blessing* (likely the traditional blessing before meals recited over a whole loaf of bread—"Blessed art Thou, O Lord our God, King of the Universe, who has brought forth bread from the earth)";[7] Jesus also offers a prayer of *thanksgiving* as well. That this action was unusual and a memorable event is also implied later in the Gospel of John when the writer describes the site of the feeding of the five thousand as "the place where they had eaten the bread *after the Lord had given thanks*."[8]

The traditional *blessing* before a meal does indeed direct attention to God through an acknowledgment of God, but a prayer of *thanksgiving* is quite different. A prayer of thanksgiving solicits a personal and felt gratefulness resulting from a *remembered* experience of direct participation in God; thus, the very action of thanksgiving inclines those who are giving thanks to pause and actually *remember* their previous experience of receiving the grace of God—an action that then enables them *to be fully present* to God.

Through the *kavanah* of Jesus' prayers of blessing and thanksgiving, the disciples, the crowds of four and five thousand people, and Jesus himself were able to "re-member," to reconnect themselves with, the transcendent, loving power of God in the midst of them: *shekinah.*

The tenor of the scene then shifts from what we recognize as the disciples' and the crowd's instinctive fight/flight concern over scarcity and purity laws to an intentional, heartfelt offering of thanks and a shared collective experience of abundance in the presence of God. Jesus, the disciples, and the crowd were united in the spirit of God.

The gospel writers thus capture in this moment an overarching message of Jesus throughout his ministry: *By being present to God, we experience the presence of God.* By pausing to be present to God, we are equipped with the power of God in our daily lives.

Bread of Life, for You, Filled with God's Love

> While they were eating, Jesus took a loaf of bread, and after blessing it he broke it, gave it to the disciples, and said, "Take, eat; this is my body." Then he took a cup, and after *giving thanks* he gave it to them saying, "Drink from it, all of you; for this is my blood of the covenant, which is poured out for many for the forgiveness of sins." (Matthew 26:26–28)
>
> While they were eating, he took a loaf of bread, and after blessing it he broke it, gave it to them, and said, "Take; this is my body." Then he took a cup, and after *giving thanks* he gave it to them, and all of them drank from it. He said to them, "This is my blood of the covenant, which is poured out for many." (Mark 14:22–26)
>
> Then he took a cup, and after *giving thanks* he said, "Take this and divide it among yourselves; for I tell you that from now on I will not drink of the fruit of the vine until the kingdom of God comes." Then he took a loaf of bread, and when he had *given thanks*, he broke it and gave it to them, saying, "This is my body, which is given for you. Do this in remembrance of me." (Luke 22:17–19)

While several scenes of Jesus at table fellowship appear in the synoptic gospels, what is traditionally known as the Last Supper is the only *private* meal in the gospels that depicts Jesus saying grace, giving thanks, and eating with his disciples.

We can assume there were many meals shared between Jesus and the disciples, and because such everyday events are not recorded in the gospel accounts, we can be sure the descriptive passages leading up to the gathering of Jesus and his disciples seated at this Passover meal would once again be alerting first-century hearers of these gospels that an unusual event is about to take place.

The scene in the upper room becomes a mirror of the feeding miracles, with Jesus offering the grace of a blessing *and* of thanks, once again drawing the disciples into a deep awareness of the presence of God, despite the distraction of the foreboding events they have experienced in Jerusalem.

But the scene then moves into unfamiliar territory. With the prospect before them of the events of the next day, these next moments become a kind of transmission of his wisdom as Jesus opens the eyes of the disciples to the abiding nature of the indwelling spirit of God embodied in the basic elements of life so that they might know that the love of God is all and is in all.

Through this kind of profound *metanoia* awareness, Jesus discloses a present reality: Just as the spirit of God is embodied in the bread and in the wine, and in all living things, the spirit of God is *the love* that Jesus showed to be *his very nature*. And our very nature. The spirit of God is the love with which we love.[9]

It is as though Jesus is saying, with a profound sense of *kavanah* so that his disciples can have ears to hear and can understand the power and the mystery of what would be his eternal message to them,

> The love of God can be found in all that sustains you. The love of God *is*. I *am*. You *are*. When you have these eyes, the eyes that see, you will see that this bread also embodies the love of God that is me and is you. This wine also embodies the love of God that is me and is you. Now do you understand the feeding miracles? It can always be just as it was when we were there together. Do not think I will not be with you. Stay awake and pray, and you will know that I am with you. I am with you always, even

until the end of time. I *am*. You *are*. You will know this as often as you eat or drink.

In this passage, Jesus is inviting his disciples into a unitive experience of *metanoia*, of full and complete contemplative awareness. What does this mean? Jesus is giving his disciples a glimpse of how the inner contemplative life can flow into the outer lived life so completely that we can see the Christ, the Divine, in all things.

As Richard Rohr says, "What if Christ is a name for *the transcendent within* of every 'thing' in the universe? What if Christ is the name for the immense spaciousness of all true Love?"[10]

Jesus himself is immersed in the contemplative awareness of the love and grace of the spirit of God in all living things, and he invites his disciples to wake up into this reality so that they, too, might live in this profound contemplative *metanoia* awareness, and so that they, too, might experience the gifts that this knowing brings whenever they eat or drink and in every living moment of their lives.

Even the Moon

I experienced a glimpse of this concept of bread embodying the presence of God's love through my encounters with a wonderful man named Rich Fox, who was a member of the church I served fifteen years ago. Rich made bread for our Lenten simple suppers. Making that bread for us was Rich's joy. Each Tuesday evening during Lent, Rich would walk into the kitchen with a big smile on his face, flushed with excitement, and his arms laden with baskets filled to the brim with little individual rolls for each of us—a new and different kind of bread every time.

At supper one night, someone came in late and sat down at our table, and I let them know that Rich had made the bread. I held up one of the little rolls and said, "Rich Fox made these rolls!" When I said that, I noticed I felt a kind of holiness about that simple little roll, and then later when I really thought about what I was feeling, it occurred to me quite powerfully that this tiny, rather nondescript roll was indeed holy. I had just finished reading the chapter in *Living Buddha, Living Christ* in which Thich Nhat Hanh says,

> If we allow ourselves to touch our bread deeply, we become reborn, because our bread is life itself. Eating it deeply, we touch the sun, the clouds, the earth, and everything in the cosmos. We touch life, and we touch the Kingdom of God. . . . The body of Christ is the body of God, the body of ultimate reality, the ground of all existence. We do not have to look anywhere else for it. It resides deep in our own being.[11]

I decided to give a children's sermon about the holiness of Rich's rolls that next Sunday.

To describe this holiness to the children, I held up one of Rich's rolls left over from the supper, just holding it between the tips of my fingers, kind of twisting my wrist this way and that way to show all sides, and remarking that it looks like just an ordinary little roll.

But then I asked the children (and because they were present, also the adults, implicitly) what they thought this ordinary roll was made of. (God bless the child who immediately said "grain.") Then I invited the children to think about where the grain came from (the earth) and who made the earth (God). I then invited them to consider (to wonder!) what *else* is in the grain as it is growing out of the ground that God created. They named what else—the rain, the sun, the wind, the air—and when I asked what goes into the grain at nighttime when we're all sound asleep, a little girl who rarely speaks out loud looked up and said ever so quietly (I still remember her little mouth shaping the words), "The *moon.*"

Yes, the *moon*!

I reminded them that all these things that God has created, all these ways that God loves us in every day, all are *inside* this little roll. At this point, I was holding the roll up at my eye level, reverently, on the open palms of my hands, and I said, "See, then, how this little roll is *filled* with God's love for us? We open it up," I broke it at this point, "and we know that what is inside is God's love for us. It is *holy*." And then I shared this eucharistic image by inviting them to know that the bread we were about to receive in our outstretched hands at the communion rail is always God's love for us too.

~ ~ ~

No matter our theology or background, with a practiced contemplative awareness that is rooted in Jesus' centering pause practice, like the disciples, we, too, can be aware of our oneness with the Christ of Jesus in every moment and whenever we eat or drink.

It is notable that in some translations of 1 Corinthians 11:25, "Do this as often as you drink it," the definite article "it" is omitted, thus the direction actually becomes "do this as often as you *drink*."[12] Every time we drink, there can be this ongoing awareness of the love of the spirit of God with us.

This final time of prayer for Jesus and his disciples in the upper room is one of complete oneness with the presence of God and is a full manifestation of Jesus' contemplative life in the love of God.

Into Your Hands I Commend My Spirit

> At three o'clock Jesus cried out with a loud voice, "Eloi, Eloi, lema sabachthani?" which means, "My God, my God, why have you forsaken me?" (Mark 15:34)

> And about three o'clock Jesus cried with a loud voice, "Eli, Eli, lema sabachthani?" that is, "My God, my God, why have you forsaken me?" (Matthew 27:46)
>
> Then Jesus said, "Father, forgive them; for they do not know what they are doing" . . . . Then Jesus, crying with a loud voice, said, "Father, into your hands I commend my spirit." (Luke 23:34, 46)

Jesus' final prayers from the cross in the Gospel of Mark, and their parallel in Matthew, could be seen by some as Jesus apparently falling prey himself to the temptation to believe that God has forsaken him. But having just heard Jesus' teaching in Gethsemane to "stay awake and pray," to stay in the presence of God in order to resist temptation, we can continue to recognize Jesus' life pattern of consistently returning to the presence of God, even to death, even there on the cross.

Even in his last moments before death, Jesus does not abandon God as the disciples abandoned Jesus: despite fearing the possibility that God may have abandoned him, Jesus still calls God "my God"; Jesus still *prays* to God in his own darkness. In the Gospel of Luke, the Greek word *phoneo* is used, meaning to address or to cry *for*, and in Mark, the Greek word *boao* is used, meaning to shout for *help*.[13]

In this time of trial and temptation, the gospel writers continue to portray Jesus as still turning to God, calling on God for help, drawing from the Psalter in which he is immersed, praying what is the first verse of Psalm 22, "My God, my God, why hast thou forsaken me?"

But there is *a very important nuance here that many are unaware of*: Psalm 22 is a psalm that many first-century Jews would likely have known in its entirety. As such, first-century Jews would also be aware that Psalm 22 moves, as many psalms of the Psalter do, from fear of abandonment to assurance of rescue by God, as in the final verse of this Psalm 22—"for he did not despise or abhor the affliction of the afflicted; he did not hide his face from me, *but heard when I cried to him*."[14]

Jesus' last words on the cross in the Gospel of Luke are also drawn from the Psalter—"Into your hands I commend my spirit."[15] With powerful and unutterable poignancy, Jesus' final words mirror his contemplative pattern of ceaselessly, intentionally surrendering, giving himself over to, the power and presence of God that loved and sustained him throughout his life and ministry.

The Radical Call of Jesus Into Our Divine Potential

We can now see how the whole of Jesus' inner and outer life exemplifies his complete *Sh'ma* participation in the love of God—with all of his heart, mind, soul, and strength—which then infuses his abiding, "oneing" unconditional love of neighbor as himself: "Forgive them, for they do not know what they are doing."[16]

By his own example, Jesus calls us to connect with that of God within us and around us with all *our* heart, mind, soul, and strength so that we, too, might know the Divine within us more relationally, more intimately, more "oneing-ly," in ways that transform us and give us "the eyes to see and the ears to hear" so that we are able to carry the power and love and grace of our inner contemplative lives of God's love into every moment of our outer active lives, as Jesus did.

This is the radical call of Jesus into our divine potential. This is the transformative way of being truly awake and fully human like Jesus.

CHAPTER 12

Between Fight and Flight: The Revolutionary Third Way of Jesus

Between fight and flight is the blind man's sight, and the choice that's right.

—Jewel Kilcher, American singer-songwriter

I can't help but wonder what it must have been like for Jesus' disciples as they witnessed and experienced Jesus' way of being, both the way he was with them in private and the way he engaged with others in his public ministry. Did the disciples connect Jesus' steady practice of turning to God, in both his inner and outer life, with his apparent ability to respond to even the most challenging people and situations with courage, compassion, forgiveness, and even insightful provocation? Did they connect Jesus' steady practice of turning to God with his ability to resist reacting from a defensive, overattached, or fear-driven fight/flight posture?

No one could have known then that specific contemplative prayer practices can actually rewire the human brain, but many first-century Jews were quite aware of the very *formative* power of the presence of the *shekinah*, the spirit of God. So did the disciples see that Jesus' frequent and intentional time spent in interior prayer and awareness of God then naturally and powerfully carried into his way of being in his outer, active life?

I would say the answer is likely no, given that the disciples (who are so like us) appear to be pretty clueless much of the time. It is not apparent *in the gospels* that the disciples realized how transformative Jesus' own practices and way of being in God were. It is not apparent that they realized Jesus was living his own vision of transformation for them and for all of us to see.

But the gospel writers give us hints as to why this may be: In stark contrast to the numerous accounts of Jesus' contemplative prayer practice throughout the gospels, there is a noticeable absence of gospel accounts of the disciples being at prayer at all during the life of Jesus, even after they asked him how to pray.[1] We do not encounter an account of the disciples being at prayer until the Book of the Acts of the Apostles.

We can, of course, assume Jesus and his disciples would have engaged in ritualized, fixed prayer throughout the day in a way that was known to be customary for practicing first-century Jews. But as we read the gospels carefully, we can see its authors typically do not record otherwise normal occurrences of life, such as eating daily meals, sleeping at night, and normal washing rituals. With this in mind, the synoptic gospel writers' explicit and implicit references to the times Jesus takes to be in prayer in silence and solitude with God can each then be assumed to be highly significant and noteworthy events[2] that were purposefully highlighted by the gospel writers. And the contrasting complete *lack of* accounts of the disciples having a contemplative prayer practice like Jesus is also noteworthy.

As a natural consequence, the contrast is also stark between Jesus and the disciples in terms of their ability to respond from a higher, *metanoia* level of spiritual awareness or awakeness, as Jesus does. So, as can be expected, the disciples' track record in the gospels for getting past their egoic fight/flight instincts is—again, so like us—not that great.

The Disciples and Us

Throughout the gospels, we see the ordinary, nonreflective awareness and overreactive egoic impulses of the disciples in full view, set against the developed spiritual awareness and one-pointedness of Jesus toward the presence of God both in his inner and outer lives. As New Testament scholar Ched Myers notes, "Tragically, the disciples will sleep while Jesus sweats *in prayer* in Gethsemane, and they will flee when he turns to face the powers."[3]

The disciples are unable to live into Jesus' way of *staying*, rather than fighting or fleeing. They are unable to stay in connection with God, to stay awake, to stay *in* God. Continually relying on their own power alone, we see the disciples in fight/flight reactionary mode, caught up in their ego and fear for much of the gospel.

Often arguing among themselves regarding who is greatest among them, the disciples apparently completely miss Jesus' teaching that the greatest among them are the ones who are the most vulnerable in society. The disciples are preoccupied with concern at each of the feeding miracles; and they are simply unable to stay awake with Jesus in his time of greatest need.

Jesus points to the disciples' general malaise and lack of spiritual strength with his revealing question to Peter in Gethsemane—"Could you not stay awake with me one hour?"[4] The question is, more precisely, "Did you not *have the strength to* stay awake with me?" as the writer uses the Greek *ischuo*, which can be more accurately translated as "to be strong in body," or even, "to wield power."

The disciples' overreactive egos and overall weariness and lack of spiritual strength and awareness may be all too familiar to many of us. We are, as Jesus says, "worried and distracted by many things." We, too, may wish we could stay more awake to the big picture, stay awake to an awareness of God working in and through us, as Jesus did, in the face of the nonstop stressors of our everyday life and the general overwhelm of living in the twenty-first-century digital age.

Like Jesus' disciples, left on our own power, without an intentional and consistent centering pause practice, most of us easily fall prey to our ego's temptation to either fight our daily realities until we are exhausted or to flee and avoid those realities entirely.

Alternatively—the writers particularly highlight Jesus' deliberate efforts to pause and release his agendas and attachments to spend focused time in communion with God as a repeated, intentional, and purposeful returning to God's presence—perhaps even as a strenuous devotion to a prayer practice or regimen. This understanding opens the possibility that Jesus' practice was an intentional way for Jesus to "have the strength" to resist distraction, fatigue, resignation, and other reflexive fight/flight responses to "times of trial" or "temptations."

Jesus himself says to "Be on guard so that your hearts are not weighed down with dissipation and drunkenness and the worries of this life, and that day does not catch you unexpectedly. . . . Stay awake and pray for strength against temptation."[5]

Knowing what we know now about the power of practice to catalyze changes in the brain, we can see how these words and the ancient and familiar wisdom words of Jesus that come next in this passage echo the wisdom of new contemplative neuroscience and ancient spiritual traditions:

"The spirit wants to do what is right, but the body is weak."[6] Indeed—the body/brain builds strength against the temptation of fight/flight overreactions when we follow Jesus' directive to "stay awake and pray" as he does.

Practice gives us the strength to be transformed, body and soul.

The Disciples' Full Awakening

The disciples' apparent lack of spiritual strength throughout the gospels makes their transformation later in the Book of the Acts of the Apostles all the more vivid and astonishing. We see in Acts *a complete shift in the disciples' practice of prayer*, a shift that can inform our own call to live into the promise of being awakened contemplatives-in-action.

It is in Acts, the first book of the New Testament after the Gospels, that we learn that in Jesus' post-resurrection appearance to the disciples in the upper room, he tells them to stay in Jerusalem and "to wait there for the promise of the Father," which most scholars consider to be a reference to the coming of the Holy Spirit on Pentecost. The writer of Acts tells us that the disciples then, "together with certain women and his brothers . . . were *constantly devoting themselves to prayer*"[7] until the Pentecost event ten days later.

The disciples "were constantly devoting themselves to prayer"?

This is the first recording in the entire New Testament of the disciples actually being in prayer at all, either individually or together. (Acts is said to have been written by the writer of the Gospel of Luke, so this shift in perspective would not simply be a result of differing authors.)

Jesus' stay awake and pray message may have somehow finally landed. There were several post-resurrection appearances of Jesus. Although I wonder—might there be other explanations?

It can't go without saying here that there are several gospels missing from what were finally accepted by church councils as canonical gospels. One of those is the Gospel of Mary Magdalene, which includes a remarkable and extraordinary scene in that same upper room as the disciples were mourning the recent death of Jesus:

> [Jesus'] students grieved and mourned greatly saying: "How are we to go into the rest of the world proclaiming the Good News about the Son of Humanity's Realm? If they did not spare him, how will they ever leave us alone?" Mary arose then, embracing them all, and began to address them as her brothers and sisters, saying, "Do not weep and grieve nor let your hearts remain in doubt, for his grace will be with all of you, sustaining and protecting you. Rather, let us give praise to his greatness which *has prepared us so that we might become fully human.*" As Mary said these things, their hearts opened toward the good, and they began to discuss the meaning of the Savior's words.[8]

When Mary reminds the disciples that Jesus has prepared them so that they might become "fully human," the word being used is *anthropos*, meaning becoming a "completed" human being. Cynthia Bourgeault tells us:

> When this level is attained . . . either by sudden spiritual insight or by a long, tough slog through the mine fields of ego, a person becomes "a single one" (in Aramaic, *ihidaya*, one of the earliest titles applied to Jesus): an enlightened or "fully human" being. [It is a] union of the finite and infinite within oneself . . . so that there is one Heart, one Being, one Will, one God, all in all.[9]

Mary's words to the disciples imply what we have discerned here in our close observation of Jesus' contemplative way of being as recorded by the writers of the synoptic gospels: Jesus' way of being, in both his inner contemplative life and his outer active life, prepared his disciples to become fully human, as Jesus' way of being can prepare us today.

Mary confirms here that the heart of Jesus' preparation, his vision of transformation, is the capacity to become fully human, to raise awareness to a level of *metanoia*. Jesus has prepared all his followers to become fully human—his disciples, the earliest Christians, the desert mothers and fathers, the Christian contemplative tradition, and modern contemplatives today—by modeling a practical way of being that can enable us in mind and heart to move beyond the ego's fight/flight constructs inherent in our human nature and enhance our highest virtues, which are also inherent in our human nature.

In Jesus' vision of transformation, we can wake up to our divinity in the fullness of our humanity. We can find the way *between fight and flight* that makes radical, inclusive, self-giving love possible.

The Way *between* Fight and Flight

The concept of fight or flight was first described by physiologist and medical educator Walter Cannon in 1932 as the fundamental human response to stress, the instinctive reactions of the ego. The teachings of the wisdom tradition, which draw from the truths of all contemplative paths of ancient sacred traditions, have for centuries upheld the power of consistent, intentional contemplative centering practices to rein in our overreactive egoic impulses and instincts, including what we today call fight/flight. And now, as we have seen, new brain science is confirming this same phenomenon.

It is fascinating to examine Jesus' way of being in the context of fight/flight: Jesus shows us the way to consistently "have the strength" to stay attuned to the possibility of an alternative, loving, but nonetheless authoritative response to fight or flight, a "third way."

Through his prayer practice of pausing to release his egoic needs and open himself to God's love and power in a kind of ceaseless, interior prayer, he is equipped to thoughtfully *respond* with characteristic grace and understanding, and without apparent fear, to demanding and confrontational situations rather than fight his adversaries or flee from conflict or even danger.

Jesus is able to respond through his own "third way"[10] with courageous statements and actions of deep listening, compassion, and insight *in the midst* of conflict, remaining apparently grounded in the presence and grace of God within him.

We begin to clearly see how Jesus' on-the-mat practices of pausing for quiet within, in the *tameion*, in the solitude of his innermost self, and taking intentional time in silence and solitude with God *facilitate* his off-the-mat practice of being able to resist fight/flight and choose his third way.

Virtually all of the teachings of Jesus throughout his public ministry offer this third-way, "road less taken" alternative to the human inclination toward fight/flight in the face of threat or confrontation: "Love your enemy;[11] turn the other cheek;[12] forgive seventy times seven times;[13] you who have not sinned, cast the first stone;[14] consider the lilies of the field, they neither toil nor spin;[15] why do you see the speck in your neighbor's eye but do not notice the log in your own eye?"[16] as well as the many "fear not" passages in Luke's gospel.[17]

Cynthia Bourgeault says,

> While Jesus is typical of the wisdom tradition in his vision of what a whole and unified human being looks like, the route he lays out for getting there is very different from anything that had ever been seen on the planet up to that point. It is still radical in our own time and definitely the "road less taken" among the various schools of human transformation.[18]

Between Fight and Flight Is the Blind Man's Sight

We see Jesus' road-less-taken third way powerfully demonstrated by a follower of the Way in one of scripture's most stunning but perhaps least noticed scenes: After Jesus' death and resurrection, when Saul was blinded by his encounter with the risen Jesus on his way to round up and kill followers of the Way in Damascus, one of those followers, named Ananias, was told by God in a dream to go to Saul to heal him. Ananias at first protested, reminding God that Saul was the one who "had done great evil to [God's] saints."[19] But *rather than fight or flee*, Ananias not only goes to Saul; he *lays his hands on Saul and calls him "brother."*

It is said that *then* "immediately something like scales" fell from Saul's eyes, and he could see.[20]

Some say Saul's conversion was when he heard the voice of Jesus asking him, "Saul, why are you persecuting me?" I believe Saul was awakened to the love of Christ when he experienced Jesus' profound third way of being, the Way of Love, through the actions of his brother in Love, Ananias.

"Between fight and flight is the blind man's sight and the choice that's right," says singer-songwriter Jewel Kilcher.[21]

Between fight and flight is Jesus' *third way* and where our human potential for radical, inclusive, self-giving love resides.

Between fight and flight is our ability to authentically love our enemies in the way Ananias offers his love to Saul. We can have love even for our enemies and even for those who cause us harm, physical or emotional.

While the Ananias and Saul scene is described in the Book of Acts, the gospels are filled with many of Jesus' most well-known parables citing examples of his third way, the way of turning to and finding the love and power of God that is *between* fight and flight.

The prodigal son's father emulates the love of God for the son who deserted him, holding no grudge despite his wealth being squandered but picking up his robes and rushing to meet him and celebrate his return home. The good Samaritan (like Ananias) moves past his inclination to flee, and instead, he cares for an "enemy," whom he knew hated him and might otherwise harm him.

Jesus himself chooses not to fight or flee throughout his ministry and in his own passion and death. Even after being abandoned and betrayed by his disciples at his crucifixion, Jesus comes to them in the upper room after the resurrection and does not admonish them for their weakness but rather, as portrayed in the Lukan account, says, "Peace be with you"[22] and, as portrayed in the Matthean account, says, "Do not be afraid."[23]

The Heart of Jesus' Third Way

But lest we think of Jesus as being in any way passive or nonresistant, as Walter Wink, author of the groundbreaking social justice classic *Jesus and Nonviolence*, points out—Jesus' third way is emphatically *not* a stance of passivity or flight or even nonresistance to evil, "given the fact that on every occasion Jesus himself resisted evil with every fiber of his being."[24]

In his confrontations with the Pharisees, Jesus spoke truth to power, stood firm, and exposed their hypocrisy, sometimes with civil disobedience, sometimes even with humor. He challenged religious laws and angered religious leaders; he touched people no one would touch; he ate with people he wasn't supposed to eat with. His actions against systemic injustice were courageous, provocative, dangerous, and sometimes illegal. Jesus was never afraid to "make some noise and get into some good trouble, some necessary trouble."[25]

Jesus' revolutionary third way of being has been central to social justice movements through all these centuries later and into our modern time. Indeed, Jesus was honored as a model nonviolent revolutionary by Mahatma Gandhi, Martin Luther King, Jr., Dorothy Day, and countless current-day followers.

Jesus' active, unconditional hard skill of love is embodied in these words of Dr. Martin Luther King Jr., words that resonate fully with Jesus' third-way teachings throughout the gospels:

> To our most bitter opponents we say: . . . We shall meet your physical force with soul force. Do to us what you will, and we shall continue to love you. . . . Throw us in jail, and we shall still love you. Bomb our homes and threaten our children, and we shall still love you. Send your hooded perpetrators of violence into our communities at the midnight hour and beat us and leave us half dead, and we shall still love you.[26]

King's capacity to love his enemy seems beyond ordinary human capacity and is certainly "not the ego's default or preferred method."[27] Jesus himself calls this transformative third way of being the "narrow way": "Small is the gate and narrow the road that leads to life, and only a few find it."[28]

But loving our enemies is the *very heart* of Jesus' third way.

And "love of enemies is paramount," says Walter Wink. "Commitment to justice, liberation, or the overthrow of oppression is not enough, for all too often the means used have brought in their wake new injustices and oppressions."

Love of enemies is paramount, Wink says, because it "is the recognition that the enemy, too, is a child of God. . . . When we demonize our enemies, calling them names and identifying them with absolute evil, we deny that they have that of God within them that makes transformation possible."[29]

How Do We Choose the Third Way?

As we get more and more of a sense of just how narrow a path the third way is and why the road of the third way is so little traveled, the question then becomes: *How is it really possible to attain to this third way*? How can we possibly access this truth—that even our enemies have that of God within them? How can we possibly resist the fight and flight impulses that so often get in the way of us being able to make the more challenging choice of the third way?

And the hard-truth answer is: We take our cue from Jesus as the Way-shower.

If our desire is to truly live from our inner sanctuary and be able to choose the third way: We *must* practice.

And to reorient our mind, brain, and heart so that the third way comes through our innermost being, our Source, more naturally, we must practice the pause that Jesus has shown is what gets us there. And we must practice "ceaselessly,"[30] at least in terms of our awareness.

This sounds in some ways simple and in some ways beyond daunting. But, taking lessons from Jesus as the Way-shower, we can see that the alternative, creative response of the third way seems to *require* an intentional and consistent practice of pause-release-return in order to stay in awareness of the spirit of God working in and through us.

Otherwise our overreactive fight/flight nature takes over in those very stressful situations that need the choice of a third way. Our egos get overattached, our unconscious needs are triggered, and we lose the window to choose the third way. Our practice—this pause—and the awareness that it brings, is what can transform our entire way of being, including rewiring our brain.

It is in this kenotic pausing to return to the love of God that we remember and reconnect with who we are, and we remember who the other is, which sets us up as a first step toward *being able* to choose the often more difficult third way.

Throughout the gospels, step by step, we see how the example of Jesus' intentional practice of pausing and releasing egoic agendas and other impulses can empower *our own capacity to respond* to the stressors of our life in a way that is *between* fight and flight—not by fighting or fleeing but through a third way, a response that comes from our divine indwelling, from the infinite within.

We know now that what happens psychologically here is that the practice of *pausing* and returning to God, "re-membering" ourselves in God, eases our instincts for self-preservation and allows our inner, flawed motivations that present obstacles to deeper awareness to fall away. Without our usual egoic defenses getting in the way, we are able to become more aware of our own intrinsic goodness of self and the ever-present nature of the Divine in us and around us.

And neuroscience is now confirming that by continually releasing our egoic impulses and the returning to the present moment, to center, to a relational sense of Presence, we catalyze new neural pathways in the regions of our brain that can then equip us, day by day, to *more easily* pause and literally *make space for* the alternative third way between fight and flight. When we have a practice of pausing and turning to God our brain becomes wired to have more time—sometimes even just an invaluable fraction of a second—to make space for us to access the wisdom and power of the divine indwelling in us and avoid fight/flight.

So we can begin to understand that following Jesus' practice of pausing to stay awake and pray is not only for the sake of more effectively meeting the challenges of our day-to-day lives. Pausing to stay awake is revolutionary. Pausing in the way of Jesus ultimately rids us of our own overreactive fight/flight habits and ways of thinking that get in the way of us living into our *essential* nature, that of the divine indwelling within us, the image of God.

This takes practice.

I appreciate how Richard Rohr's Center for Action and Contemplation describes contemplation and its role in our own action in the world:

> Contemplation is a way of listening with the heart while not relying entirely on the head. Contemplation is a prayerful letting go of our sense of control and choosing to cooperate with God and God's work in the world. Prayer without action can promote our tendency to self-preoccupation, and without contemplation, even well-intended actions can cause more harm than good.[31]

Practice the Pause

I am reminded of author Lori Deschene's piece of wisdom: "Practice the pause. Pause before judging. Pause before assuming. Pause before accusing. Pause whenever you're about to react harshly and you'll avoid doing and saying things you'll later regret."[32]

A later anonymous meme has made its way through the internet that says: "When you're in doubt, pause. When you're angry, pause. When you're tired, pause. When you're stressed, pause. And when you pause, pray."

The "pray" part is key.

Phileena Heuertz is cofounder of Gravity Center, a center for contemplative activism. For Phileena, the unequivocal answer to the question of what gives us the *capacity* to choose the narrow way, the road less traveled, Jesus' third way: Pausing to spend time in silence, solitude, and stillness with God.

To Phileena, "silence, solitude, and stillness with God are the hallmarks of contemplative spirituality, which have never been more important for our society." With her deep personal experience of exhaustion and burnout in her own life and witnessing the same in the lives of her fellow workers on the front lines of poverty and homelessness, Phileena advocates the necessity of a sustained contemplative prayer practice—what she calls resting in God—in order not only to "do good" but to "do good better."

She says,

> [Resting in God in] contemplative prayer is for courageous, devoted seekers. It facilitates personal transformation for a world in need of healing love. Contemplative spirituality supports the way of following Jesus, which necessitates dying to self or emptying self to make room for the all-consuming presence of God (Philippians 2). But we are reluctant to choose this road less travelled. It's easier to walk through life asleep.

We can almost imagine Jesus saying, "Pause, and when you pause, pray: turn first to the *indwelling spirit of God in you* for strength. Turn to the love of God with all your heart, mind, and strength. You have that love and power indwelling in you." And Jesus does, in fact, tell us essentially this in the gospel of Matthew: "Seek first the kingdom of God."[33]

Here is the means to rewire our brain to resist fight or flight, to resist overreaction, *and to be able to see the third way.* By practicing ceaselessly, literally making space in our brain to reveal our innate nature, our spark of the Divine within, we make room *for the power of God to* facilitate a third, creative way.

Each of the synoptic gospels point to Jesus' invitation to his disciples (and to us) to join him in this ongoing pattern as a means to be able to give time for the movement of God's grace so that we are able to resist fight/flight and respond instead through the third way. Through Jesus' centering pause we are able to live from our grace-filled, grounded center of being, which is our essence and the spirit of God within us.

~ ~ ~

As the very essence of resisting fight/flight, choosing the narrow way, the road less traveled, Jesus' nonviolent third way of pausing is the way to wake up to our full human potential: By choosing not to fight, we do not destroy; by choosing not to flee, we do not abandon. When we are able to pause and resist fight/flight, we give time for the indwelling presence of God's grace to move us to a more loving and insightful response. Choosing this third way, we stay in relationship with God, with ourselves, and with others.

We stay in the heart of the *Sh'ma*, loving God with all our heart, mind, soul, and strength.

The Evolution of the True Self

Circling back to the exciting science of the power of practice, let's take a quick look at what modern psychology has to say about what happens to the psyche in this process of learning to resist our fight/flight stress overreactions. How is the "charade of the smaller self"[34] pierced through when we return again and again to the presence of God?

As we will see in more detail in the next chapter, from a psychological perspective, the container for our fight/flight instinct is our small self, the "false self." Neither false nor a self, we use this term to define what Thomas Keating describes as "the needy, driven, unrecognized motivations that govern most of our untransformed human behavior."[35] In other words, this false self contains our instinctual fight/flight need to overprotect ourselves; it is our self-reflexive capacity, our animal drives, or what some would even call our original sin nature.

Living through the lens of the twenty-first century, we have been given the gift of now knowing in spiritual *and* scientific terms that contemplative, mindful practice enables us to move beyond the needs of our false self and the learned, defensive, fight/flight behaviors in which we have engaged since childhood. These behaviors may have served us well as a species and helped us to survive thousands of years ago, but now they have become a threat to our survival. In addition, while these behaviors may have served us and even protected us when we ourselves were young, they now can get in the way of us leading the lives to which we aspire.

So in an intentional centering pause practice of sitting in the presence of God and of consistently pausing to release distracting thoughts and then returning to our essence, to God-in-us, then *the false self weakens over time, and the true self gradually emerges,* which for Thomas Keating is the real meaning of the term "transforming union" and "the gift of contemplative prayer."[36]

This action of releasing our own self-protective motivations and returning to God and to God's way of seeing has strong resonance with Jesus' exhortation to "stay awake" and with the ability to develop the capacity for seeing bigger and developing greater spiritual awareness.

Remember "repent" means *metanoia.* Staying consistent in Jesus' practice of pausing to "stay awake and pray," we turn away and go another direction, *toward God,* and are able to think differently, to go into the larger mind. *We are able to choose the third way.*

As the false self weakens and our basic instinctual fight/flight tendencies become less overpowering, we are then able to move into the challenges of our day-to-day lives in a more awake and aware state. We have the capacity to observe our life challenges in the way we do the distracting thoughts that arise during intentional and contemplative practice. In stressful moments, for a crucial fleeting moment, we are able to stop our usual reaction and turn in another direction. Turning to the awareness of God, we are less inclined to *react* automatically and defensively; we can instead *respond* from a more thoughtful and more potentially loving place.

According to Bourgeault,

> Every time you are willing to release a thought, to perform the gesture of self-emptying, this gesture is patterned and strengthened within you. In time, with patience and persistence, it begins to take shape as a magnetic center within you, a deeper pull or gravitation that is clearly perceptible, like a tug to center. In the process there is a kind of "dying to self" as the false self begins to "dismantle" and the true self emerges from beneath the defensive passions of the false self.[37]

In his essay *Changing Your Mind: Contemplative Prayer and Personal Transformation,* Brian C. Taylor says, "In dying to self, the divine life that has always been within us can arise and become known."[38]

In dying to self, we allow room for the divine indwelling to be more at work in our everyday lives so that, ultimately, we are able to live into the radical call of the gospels for personal and social transformation. We are able to love as Jesus loves and choose the third way of Jesus.

~ ~ ~

With twenty-first-century scientific and psychological studies confirming the power of contemplative practice to enhance our capacity for wisdom and compassion, the character of Jesus himself exemplifies the transformative potential of contemplative awareness to transcend the ego limits of the human psyche and to live in wisdom and compassion.

Jesus' words "stay awake and pray" can be heard in a wholly new way: each pause, release, and return to God re-forms us, transforms us, and reveals the likeness of the Divine within us.

When we pause and return to the love of God, we can live *between* fight and flight and respond through the love and power of God in the third way of Jesus.

When we pause and return to the love of God, we can be more fully human, like Jesus.

CHAPTER 13

Ancient/New Teachers: The Desert Mothers and Fathers

You were taught, with regard to your former way of life, to put off your old self . . . to be made new in the attitude of your minds; and to put on the new self, created to be like God in true righteousness and holiness.

—Paul of Tarsus (NIV)

The early *abbas* (fathers) and *ammas* (mothers) of the desert spirituality tradition, as they are affectionately called, appeared on my spiritual landscape during a midsummer afternoon seminary class on Eastern Christian spirituality, and I have been drawn to them ever since.

It was there that I learned the entirely new (to me) wisdom-oriented Eastern way of understanding the gospels. It was there that I first heard of the call to not only follow Jesus but to practice ways to *be like and become like* him from the inside out, so that we, too, might put on the mind of Christ and see through the eyes of our own loving, divine nature.

It was there that I learned of the desert call to be touched and transformed by Love.

Looking back now, I remember how immediately at home I felt with the *way* of Eastern Christian spirituality and with the people of the Eastern deserts and their school of radical love.

Here were ardent followers of Jesus, born just a few generations after Jesus himself lived on this earth, who, like the disciples Peter and Andrew, "dropped their nets," completely upended their lives, left everything they knew before to follow the way of this wisdom master from Nazareth, who showed them how to become fully human, to be able to live a life fully awakened and transformed, and to "love as God loves."[1]

Here were followers whose hearts were warmed and minds were awakened by Jesus' holy charism. When hearing the story of Jesus, these followers had the eyes to see how essential Jesus' own centering pause practice was to his way of being, so they ventured in, eyes wide open, to practice that same revolutionary way of being for themselves.

Now, here in the twenty-first century, with new science shining its spotlight on the benefits and even the *necessity* of contemplative practice and inner transformation as a means toward spiritual and psychological wholeness, Christians and non-Christians alike are rediscovering the practical wisdom of the desert mothers and fathers of the fourth and fifth centuries and the contemplative practices of desert spirituality.

Thomas Merton, Henri Nouwen, Richard Rohr, and other writers who explore the dynamics of contemplation in action can be credited for reawakening the West to the simple, straightforward, but transformative sayings and practices of these ancient followers of Jesus who fled to the desert by the thousands to freely practice the way of Jesus apart from the dictates of either Roman or church authority.

The simple but profound and rigorously honest way of life of the desert mothers and fathers so closely followed the practices of Jesus himself that the desert experience is still today considered to be a school of radical love, a way of being that, when practiced, can awaken us to a profound awareness of that of God within ourselves and within all things, an awareness that can attune us to live and love in the radically inclusive and self-giving way of Jesus.

Original Blessing, Not Original Sin

The desert mothers and fathers are perhaps most known for their genuine and basic love of humanity. It is not surprising, then, that the practical experience of these mothers and fathers of the desert had as its cornerstone an understanding of humanity as being created in the image of a God of profound love.

Theirs was not a Western theology of the original sin of humanity. Theirs was an Eastern understanding and experience of original blessing, of the original goodness of humanity. All attitudes and actions of the desert mothers and fathers either moved toward or grew out of their understanding of the biblical commandment to *love*.[2]

This compelling and foundational understanding of humanity, along with the central and fundamental spiritual disciplines the desert mothers and fathers practiced to empty themselves of the constraints of their ego, directly mirrors the overarching pattern of the Jesus practice we highlighted in the first chapters—Jesus taking time apart to "just be" in the presence of God, his continual and *kenotic* "not my will but thine" letting go of ego, and his full and constant immersion in the awareness of God.

By so closely following Jesus' teachings and way of being, the desert mothers and fathers are our closest-to-Jesus wisdom mentors—and certainly our most practical. Their simple but transformative way of living life in the desert close to two thousand years ago can serve as a surprisingly appropriate icon of the "desert" journey of inner transformation in our modern time.

Through the centuries, their desert way has transformed the lives of Christians and non-Christians alike by showing us all how to be awake like Jesus and anchored in the love of God. Now we can look to their way of being as we explore our own practices of centering pause to rewire our brains, reorient our hearts, and live into the full potential of our own humanity made in the image of profound Love.

A Proper Introduction

Allow me to properly introduce these enigmatic people of the desert to you in hopes that you, too, might be drawn into their school of radical love and to their simple but profound way of being.

Keep in mind that one of the most powerful aspects of the life and prayer of desert spirituality is its archetypal nature. The desert mothers and fathers' call to the desert, and the journey in and out of the desert, is full of profound symbolism for our own inner spiritual journey.

We are all invited into this life-changing journey of *just being* in God.

~ ~ ~

In a quick aside, be sure not to confuse the desert mothers and fathers with the church fathers, the Christian theologians who hammered out the creedal phrases, what they felt was "right belief," and other doctrinal foundations of the newly established church, notably the Apostles' Creed, the Nicene Creed, and the Chalcedonian Creed. In contrast, while the *desert* fathers and mothers to whom I am referring flourished in roughly the same time period as those church fathers, their emphasis was not the same. The emphasis of the desert fathers and mothers was not on what constitutes right belief about who Jesus is. Theirs was an emphasis on *how to be like* Jesus and on a spiritual *praxis* that would get them there.

So the way of the desert tradition, then and now, is one of direct experience rather than an adherence to a specific set of laws and belief systems. The desert mothers and fathers were Christians who weren't formed through systematic theology and creedal doctrine. Their simple, profound wisdom was rooted in experience, and much like Jesus, they shared their wisdom not through formal theology but through short, compelling stories similar to Zen koans about ego, humility, God's inclusive love, the power of Spirit, surrender, and inner freedom.

The desert mothers and fathers speak the language of *practice.*

Getting a Sense of Time and Place

The desert mothers and fathers lived in Egypt, Syria, and present-day Turkey primarily in the fourth and fifth centuries. Around the time of Constantine's rule as emperor of Rome in the early fourth century, these men and women chose to leave the corruption of society to go out and live in the deserts outside the cities, either alone or in small groups, where they could establish their own alternative Christian societies of small, essentially monastic communities.

Constantine had converted to Christianity. The last persecution of Christians had ended. In 313 CE, Constantine made Christianity legal with the Edit of Milan, which first declared "tolerance" of Christianity in all of the Roman empire. Ten years later, Christianity was the official religion of the Roman empire.

At first, it would seem reasonable to assume that if the persecutions of Christians had ended and Christianity was legal, wouldn't this be an ideal time for Christians, whose desire was to be free to follow the teachings of Jesus?

But almost the opposite was true.

With Christianity as the official religion of the Roman empire, Christians were not free to follow the teachings of Jesus in the way they chose. The (Western, patriarchal) Roman empire now had full jurisdiction over the doctrine and even the protocol of Christian gatherings and practices. As just one example of how this played out, this meant that Christian communities could no longer be open to women sharing full leadership with men.

Prior to Christianity being sanctioned by the state, both men *and women* led Christian worship, prayer, and Eucharist gatherings, all of which were open to and inclusive of all people. But under Roman rule, women could no longer serve in leadership positions. (We are all too familiar with this discriminatory restriction in our own modern time, as some Christian churches to this day still exclude women from leadership, nearly two thousand years later.)

As Laura Swan observes in her book *The Forgotten Desert Mothers*,

> While many women found in Christianity a freedom that enabled them to break with their culture and exercise leadership that they could not in Roman society . . . as leadership opportunities within mainstream Christianity decreased, the desert and the monastery offered women a greater sense of physical and spiritual autonomy.[3]

As well, when Christianity became the official religion of the Roman empire, being "Christian" became simply an easy label for Roman citizenry. Anyone and everyone was considered Christian just by virtue of being a Roman citizen. Every member of every sect in Roman society—finance, agriculture, trade, the military—was deemed to be Christian. Christianity became mainstreamed, diluted of its initial fervor, and suddenly had little to no connection to the essential message and promise of a revolutionary and transformative way of being in the world. Christianity became an identifier rather than an invitation into a transformed consciousness.

The irony was as stark seventeen hundred years ago as it is today: the way of Love was being co-opted, institutionalized, and used as a means of exerting power by the reigning empire.

The collective response of thousands of early Christian men and women of that time to this co-opting of their chosen way of faith was a kind of radical deconstruction of their very lives: Experiencing a fervent call and desire to follow the open, inclusive, life-changing way of Jesus, but constrained by the hypocrisy and dictates of the established social, political, and religious authorities, they each made the momentous decision to leave their lives as they knew them. Jettisoning the rules and constructs of an oppressive outside authority, they freed themselves to pursue and embrace an alternative, though enormously challenging and rigorous, way of living in the world so they could follow that fervent call.

They left the city and headed to the wilderness of the desert, to the *erémos*, to follow an irresistible impulse to embark on their own arduous (inner and outer) desert journey to follow the vision of Jesus.

~ ~ ~

This collective city-to-desert exodus of the fourth and fifth centuries was one of great magnitude and was well known in this time, with records confirming tens of thousands of communities and close to *seven hundred* monasteries across the entire region between the ancient cities of Cairo and Alexandria alone. Every community established its own practices of solitude (time apart with God), silence (resting in God), and prayer (ceaseless awareness of God) as disciplines of inner transformation. Each community was immersed in continuous study of the gospels, with each member of every community being expected to spend time alone reading aloud both Hebrew and Christian scripture daily.

Over time, several *abbas* and *ammas* of the desert actually became household names, as many Christians who remained in the cities would periodically travel long distances to the desert specifically to meet with and receive spiritual guidance from these desert teachers and then would return home with stories and wisdom sayings that would equip them in their own spiritual journeys.

The Original Call of Love

The Jesus story of the gospels must have been riveting and mind-blowing to these early Christians of the desert.

They would have been able to hear and follow the extraordinary Jesus story without the distracting overlay of later Western church doctrine telling them who the church thought Jesus was and wasn't. These were an Eastern Christian people whose first glimpse of Jesus of Nazareth was unencumbered by formalized doctrine or by societal overfamiliarity.

I am imagining what such a clear and fresh look at the life of Jesus might have been like.

Here was an obscure first-century Galilean who had been born into poverty, whose parents had to seek refuge from their country's ruling authority, who as a young man had answered the call of the Spirit to the *erémos* and then began living and teaching a radical, inclusive, self-giving Love that he ultimately died for.

Here was a young man who touched those who no one would touch, who ate with those who no one would eat with, who healed and comforted those who were suffering, who made whole what was broken, who said things like "give your shirt to someone who steals your cloak" and "the last shall be first and the first shall be last."[4]

Here was someone who saw beyond his own finite ego-self, spoke truth to power, confronted structural racism and economic inequity,[5] who said go into your "inner room" to pray, who forgave those who betrayed him, who forgave even those who killed him.

Here was someone whose magnetic charism inclined many who came near enough to hear his words to then drop everything, leave their former lives, and follow him into his way of *metanoia* and non-judgmental tenderness. Here was someone who again and again took time apart from the relentless demands of his own life to pause and spend time with God and told us *this* is the way to ultimately realize that we each, and all, embody the Source of this radical, inclusive, self-giving Love.

Here was someone who reminded us that "the Kingdom of God is within you."[6]

~ ~ ~

Reading the gospels through their own fresh lens of perception, the early Christians of the desert knew Jesus wasn't a demigod. They could see, and some had personally experienced in their own communities, that the inclusive, self-giving Love in which Jesus "lived and moved and had his being" was an innate and *attainable* state of being, not an unattainable superpower.

Through the story of the life of Jesus, they could see the possibility that they, too, could become "a human being the way God intends human beings to be—loving God, and every bit as important, loving God's image, the other people who share the world with us."[7]

Through the story of the life of Jesus, the desert *ammas* and *abbas* could see that they could be like Jesus, not only in the sense of following him—trying to carry out Jesus' ministry of caring for the poor and welcoming the stranger and advocating for the outcast—but in the sense of being *themselves* transformed by *their* time spent alone in silence and solitude. They understood that they could attain to *the mind* of Jesus and the spiritual awareness of Jesus (what they called the "kingdom of heaven") that would equip them to see as Jesus sees, understand as Jesus understands, and realize that they, too, live and move and have their being in Love.

What Gets in the Way

One of the most compelling aspects of the desert way, and the reason both modern science and religion are drawn to study the way of the desert even now in our modern time, is the desert mothers and fathers' clear-eyed understanding of the inevitable psychological obstacles that they knew got in the way of their call to inner transformation and their clear-eyed understanding of how to overcome those obstacles.

These people of the desert who were so fervently called to be like Jesus also understood the ever-present and challenging obstacles to getting there: these obstacles were what they called their "demons" and their "passions," what we would call our fears and anxieties, our ruminating thoughts, our obsessions and addictions, and the egoic compulsions and hidden agendas that become the distractions and static noise of everyday living. These demons and passions are the "shadows" within us, which we desperately don't want others to see. We work hard, after all, on developing a strong persona, a personal identity to show the world who we want the world to see.

So it is apparent that these early Christians knew all too well that their own ego's manipulative control of their lives posed as much of a threat to their call to become like Jesus as the constraints of any oppressive outside authority. They knew it was ultimately their own passions that posed the greatest threat to their ability to rid themselves of their overreactive impulses and compulsions and then *be able* to live into Jesus' call to, as Mary Magdalene said, "become fully human."

These people of the desert tradition were a dependably pragmatic people who knew that if they were to be able to participate fully in the active, loving flow of Divine Love, they especially needed to find ways, as Jesus did, to free themselves from the ever-present egoic reactions and compulsions that so totally possessed them.

And they were up to the challenge.

Their answer: The centering pause of Jesus.

Just being. With God. Alone.

And this practice took on many forms in the desert tradition.

Primary among these was their act of leaving for the desert itself. As Jesus did, these early Christians had fled to the desert, the physical desert, an outer *erémos*, to be in the *formative* presence of God. Once there in the desert, like Jesus, "as was his custom," their practice was centered on retreating to their own *inner* desert, the inner *erémos*, to be in the formative presence of God. Here in their heart of hearts, day after day after day, the desert mothers and fathers intentionally and consistently practiced and taught powerful and ongoing daily spiritual disciplines of solitude, silence, and prayer.

These everyday practices were the desert mothers and fathers' essential psychological *means* to free themselves from the hold of the manipulative control of their egos, their false selves, or, in their own words, their "old self within."[8]

These disciplines are practiced today in much the same way they were seventeen hundred years ago. They were the foundation of Christian monasticism and now are the foundational practices of countless contemplatives-in-action around the world.

Solitude: Being with God

But whenever you pray, go into your room and shut the door and pray to your Father who is in secret; and your Father who sees in secret will reward you.

—Matthew 6:6

The desert discipline of solitude is rooted in Jesus' teaching to pray to God in the *tameion*, in what I like to call the inner room of you. The call to the desert itself is a call into the *tameion* to be in relationship with God in your innermost self. Being alone with God while studying scripture was integral to daily life in the desert. As an answer to any request for knowledge, "Go and sit in your cell and your cell will teach you everything"[9] is one of the most common phrases of the desert sayings, alluding directly to the transforming power of finding an inner sanctuary away from distractions, releasing one's own will, and allowing the illusions of the "small self" to fall away through silence, solitude, and prayer with God.

Silence: Resting in God

> *He said to them, "Come away to a deserted place all by yourselves and rest a while." For many were coming and going, and they had no leisure even to eat.*
>
> —Mark 6:31

The wordless prayer of the desert, a kind of meditation practice called *hesachasm* (from the Greek for "stillness, rest, quiet, silence"), was traditionally practiced in silence and with eyes closed, "empty of mental pictures" and visual concepts, but with the intense consciousness of God's presence.[10] The practice of *hesachasm* is central to the desert tradition and is similar to today's practice of the contemplative prayer that develops out of Centering Prayer. The practice is said to have originated with the desert mothers and fathers, though we can now see how the people of the desert clearly developed this practice in response to their witness of Jesus' *tameion* teaching and of his own practice of praying "in God" on his own for long periods of time.

Prayer: One-Pointedness in God

Rejoice always, pray without ceasing, give thanks in all circumstances; for this is the will of God in Christ Jesus for you.

—1 Thessalonians 5:16–18

As a means to their commitment to Jesus' own "one-pointedness in God," life in the desert was characterized by a constant "clinging utterly to God"[11] through continuous prayer, studying scripture, reading the psalms, celebrating liturgy, and cultivating the prayer of the heart, also called the Jesus Prayer. The people of the desert strove to practice prayer in all its forms and engage with prayer continuously, taking seriously Paul's directive to pray ceaselessly.

Notice that each of these desert spiritual disciplines has as its mainstay what the desert mothers and fathers knew to be the revolutionary release-and-return movement of the centering pause of Jesus that again and again reorients the psyche away from the distractions of ego and toward being fully aware of, and even within, Divine Presence. This full orientation to the spirit of God within all is what the desert mothers and fathers called having "purity of heart."

To these *abbas* and *ammas*, having purity of heart meant being single-minded, or single-eyed, "not attached to anything or anyone except God,"[12] and it was the objective of each and every one of the desert disciplines. Having purity of the heart was what Thomas Merton called "the proximate end of all their strivings."[13]

Release. Return. Release. Return. Release. Return.

In this context, we can see how this purity of heart desert practice of complete and total focus on, and immersion in, God's love is manifested in the action of the *Sh'ma*, to "love God with *all* your heart, with *all* your soul, with *all* your strength."

Laying Aside the Old Self

The ongoing task of striving toward purity of the heart through solitude, silence, and prayer had as its primary intent the laying aside of the "old self" and was in answer to Paul's directive:

> You must live no longer as the Gentiles do, in the futility *of their mind* . . . [that] is not the way of life you learned when you heard about Christ and were taught in him in accordance with the truth that is in Jesus. You were taught, with regard to your former way of life, to put off your old self, which is being corrupted by its deceitful desires; to be made new in the attitude of your minds; and to put on the new self, created to be like God in true righteousness and holiness.[14]

Allowing the old self within themselves to die so that the new self may come alive is a prevalent theme in the desert sayings, with obvious symbolic imagery of our own ordinary, reflexive awareness and automatic egoic impulses contrasted with the developed spiritual awareness and one-pointedness toward God that are embodied in Jesus.

The writings of Evagrius Ponticus (345–399 CE), who is believed to be the first desert father to organize the teachings of the desert fathers and mothers on prayer,[15] point to how the laying aside of passions, or the old self, and the putting on of the new self frees us from our subtle compulsions and hidden agendas so that we are free to love others.[16]

Evagrius describes the striving for "purity of heart, the full orientation toward God" in the desert practices as the key to laying aside the old self and to bringing "concord and harmony between the parts of the soul."[17] His description seems to echo today's ground-breaking contemplative neuroscience studies explaining how modern-day contemplative practices *integrate* regions of the brain. Indeed, Evagrius believed that through purity of heart, "the psyche's faculties begin to come together, to *reintegrate*, to work the way God originally had made them to work."[18]

Seventeen hundred years later, Cynthia Bourgeault explains these shifts in psyche this way: "A life of continuous and deepening surrender brings about a profound transformation in the psyche: a deepening and gentling of the human being . . . [as] the ego begins to relativize of its own accord."[19]

Evagrius knew these shifts in psyche, he experienced these shifts in psyche, and he taught his own followers in the desert about these shifts in psyche. Scholars in the fields of both religion and psychology have noted how ahead of their time the desert mothers and fathers were in terms of their understanding of human psychology and psychological wholeness.

Indeed, knowing what brain science now says about how certain ancient practices can dramatically change the usual flow of our brain's neural pathways, we can see how closely aligned the teachings and insights of the desert mothers and fathers' school of radical love are with those of esteemed psychologists, neuroscientists, and religious writers today.

Clearly these ancient people of the desert were on to something.

The Desert as a Bridge to Our Own Practice

As we follow the sayings and the lives of the desert fathers and mothers, their particular and unique spirituality can indeed be for us a school of radical love and nonjudgmental tenderness, teaching us how *to be* like Jesus and how to see as if seeing through the lens of God. The desert fathers and mothers boldly declare that the goal is Love, and then they lift the veils that might obscure what can assist us in reaching the goal. They encourage us to follow a way of singleness of heart through humility and freedom from attachments and a one-pointed focus on the loving movement and flow of life, what some call *God*.

To study, and learn about, and live into the lives of these people—the so-called desert people of the first few centuries after Jesus—is to be given a kind of map guiding us on our journey toward realizing God *in us*, a spiritual pathway that is still relevant to Christians and non-Christians today, and is a surprising and hopeful vision of how our world could be.

Through the witness of their lives, this guide, a standard, as they say, can accompany us as we learn to be more fully human, like Jesus, and to walk this way of Love. Like Jesus before them, the desert mothers and fathers can be our Way-showers on this journey of the heart and mind that begins and ends with just being with God and embracing with full *metanoia* awareness the ever-present Divine in every moment of our lives.

IV

AWAKENING OUR INNERMOST SELF

CHAPTER 14

Just Being with God

But how does one make this shift in consciousness? It's one thing to admire it from a distance, but quite another to create it within oneself. This is where spiritual praxis comes into play. "Praxis" means the path, the actual practice you follow to bring about the result that you're yearning for.

—Cynthia Bourgeault

I am aware that if you were brought up in the Western Christian tradition, then taking on a steady and intentional *contemplative* practice of silence and solitude in God may be uncharted terrain for you, and you may not know where to turn first or how to begin your journey. And some of us feel as though we are charting new territory these days anyway as we continue managing our lives through a pandemic and through the nonstop challenges and demands of the twenty-first century swirling around us 24/7 as they are these days.

But I am aware, too, that you may feel called in some way to the life-changing contemplative-in-action rhythm of Jesus' centering pause practice. And while the way of a new contemplative practice may be an unexplored path in an unfamiliar land for you, your intuition may be telling you at this point that if you can just practice quieting your mind in some way every day, you will not get lost in this new land; you will find your way.

And in my experience, this is so.

~ ~ ~

I remember a time not long ago when I actually was literally lost in the woods. I had taken a long walk down to a nearby river during a light snowfall on the first day of a monastic retreat. As I began walking back up the hill, I realized the dusting of snow had covered any sort of indication of the already traveled path.

I began feeling a bit of panic. I didn't know which way to turn. I was lost. And I was a long way away from the monastery.

But then I paused for moment. And was very, very still.

And at that moment, something caught my eye. I realized that standing there, from my angle, I could see through the snow to where the very next step of the path was. The snow had slightly melted in the place I had walked before.

I took that step and then looked up, relieved and fully expecting then to see the entire path ahead of me and which directions the path would turn along the way. But I could not see any sort of path at all.

I looked down again at what was just right in front of me, and I realized I could see then just the very next step, this time turning slightly right.

Step. Pause. Step. Pause.

For the entire way back through the woods to the monastery, I never could see past my very next step. But pausing and taking that next one step led me to see the next one.

And that is how I made it back home to the monastery, one pause at a time, one step at a time.

~ ~ ~

For thousands of Western contemplatives, Eastern Christians, and non-Christians around the world and throughout the ages, the first uncertain pauses and steps they took toward beginning their own centering pause practice of just being, in quiet, with God ultimately became the joyfully freeing dance steps of coming home to themselves and to the power of God within them.

The always heart-warming Persian (Eastern!) lyrical poet Hafiz reminds us that this sacred dance of life is our call and our natural birthright. He says,

> I sometimes forget
> that I was created for Joy.
> My mind is too busy.
> My Heart is too heavy
> for me to remember
> that I have been
> called to dance
> the Sacred dance of life.
> I was created to smile
> To Love
> To be lifted up
> And to lift others up.
> O' Sacred One
> Untangle my feet
> from all that ensnares.
> Free my soul.
> That we might
> Dance
> and that our dancing
> might be contagious.

This beloved Persian poet, along with two-thousand-year-old gospels *and* recent revolutionary twenty-first-century neuroscience discoveries, are all sharing the same good news:

We can feel fully alive, we can be "free from all that ensnares," we can find enlivening rest and attunement with the divine that is deep within ourselves, "through all, and in all."[1]

We can dance the Dance.

And the gospels' full-on spotlight on the practice of Jesus is an invitation into that dance.

It is an invitation to experience *in ourselves* the transformative power of Jesus' centering pause.

It is an invitation to be *able* to equip ourselves to release the hold of our egoic fight/flight reactions and live into the freedom and full human potential of bringing good to the world, "lifting others up" through the power of our true, innermost selves in God.

So—This Word Practice

The life-changing power of having an intentional and steady spiritual *practice* of resting *in God* is not a concept that many of us in the fast pace of the twenty-first century grew up learning about. That Jesus himself had a profound and transformative *practice* of regularly spending time in silence and solitude in God is easy to miss for those of us who have been more savior-oriented than wisdom-oriented in our understanding of the person of Jesus. And unless we were brought up in a Quaker family, most of us were never taught in Sunday school that a quiet practice of being in complete silence, just us and God, was actually an option.

But this was not always so.

As impossible as it is for us to imagine today, during the first centuries of Christianity, the spiritual practice of taking a few minutes to be alone in quiet, wordless "rest in God" was the completely natural and expected outcome of daily prayer and scripture reading. This silent, apophatic time of prayer was integral to Christian practice, as modeled and taught first by Jesus and then by the desert mothers and fathers.

We know now that it is this apophatic aspect of early Christians' prayer—being beyond words, thoughts, and feelings—that brings a deep and fully *experiential* kind of knowledge by engaging our whole being—body, heart, soul, and spirit—and not just the mind.

And it is this apophatic practice that is being revitalized today.

In a perceptible shift, a growing number of Western Christians today are coming to know that we can't experience the full power of Jesus' transformative practice by simply observing Jesus, or by reading about him, or by talking about him (or even to him) week after week after week. It is not enough for us to read the gospels and simply watch as Jesus models for us his life-changing, relationship-changing, even world-changing practice that could equip us to attune us to the movement of the Divine within us.

If we want to change at a fundamental level, if we want to rid ourselves of the unconscious psychological baggage that often triggers our fight/flight impulses and gets in our way of living from our essential, true self, our Source, the divine in us, we have to actually engage in a practice of being in silence and solitude with God.

It is this *practice* that shifts our spiritual attentiveness in ways we can otherwise come to know about only conceptually. The contemplative pause-release-return rhythm of intentional practice in silence and solitude with God incorporates a new awareness, a new and expanded way of being, into our intuition, into our psyche, and into our bodies. We are changed from the inside out, so to speak.

So if we are to truly know and understand the power of the transformative contemplative practice of Jesus to change us in ways that we can fully embody, we ourselves must decide to begin an intentional steady practice *of our own.*

~ ~ ~

The reason the gospel writers made a point to include their many accounts of Jesus returning to the presence of God was not so that those hearing their message could marvel at the power of Jesus' full and centering practice or marvel at how centered in God Jesus was. The gospel writers were offering those who would hear their message, then and now, an invitation to *experience that power ourselves* in ways that are real and relevant to our day-to-day lives and relationships.

Active, engaged, world-changing contemplatives since the desert mother and fathers of the third century have realized how life-transforming, even world-transforming, that gospel invitation is.

And we can too.

So where to begin?

First Steps—A Pause

The spiritual journey begins with a pause, a centering-in-God pause, and over time becomes a constant and ceaseless prayer, an honoring of and a connection with the Divine in you that awakens your essential self.

Depending on where you are in your contemplative journey, the idea of practicing a steady spiritual practice might at first feel far removed from your usual day-to-day life, like a way of being that is meant only for monks living in monasteries.

So I believe the first vital step to intentionally beginning a contemplative journey is to become more aware of the spiritual practices you already practice in your daily life. You can begin to be aware of the rhythm of the everyday practices you are naturally called to and how sustaining they are in your life.

Many of our favorite pastimes are spiritual practices, whether we call them that or not—listening to our favorite exquisite or joyful music; taking a long, hot bath; reading a book to a child at night; making a special dinner with someone you love; going on your regular need-a-break walk or run. These meaningful practices can all be thin places where our essential self and the spirit of God meet.

Jane Woods, a teacher of mine who leads an online community called Waking House, leads wisdom circles for contemplative women and describes herself as a "inter-spiritual Jesus follower." Jane encourages her community to try to "bust myths about spiritual practices," just as we will try to bust myths about what prayer is in chapter 17. Jane's primary spiritual practices currently are "motherhood, Centering Prayer, and Pilates," and they will shift with the natural seasons. (Jane's inner joy reminds me of Hafiz.) She reminds us all, "On the spiritual journey, there is nowhere to go, only perpetual arriving where you already are."[2]

I find this to be so.

I find spiritual practice to be about noticing where we are and becoming more and more aware of the Divine in us that is already an essential part of us. This returning to our center again and again is a kind of in-and-out, in-and-out movement, like breathing: breathing in, we gather strength and calm, maybe an insight, maybe a sense of an injustice needing to be righted, and then breathing out, we go back out in to the world to live into what we've been given and what we've received.

You may be concerned that you don't have extra time to devote to new practices or especially to a separate Centering Prayer twenty-minute sitting meditation once or twice a day. We are living in a digital age with an impossible amount of information demanding our attention.

But the surprising good news about incorporating a transformative few minutes of intentional contemplative practice into your day is that while such practices will require intention and some discipline, the essence of even the most powerful ancient and universal practices is to "just be," as even our most beloved teachers tell us.

Take Time Just to Be

I recall Father Keating speaking at St. Benedict's Monastery in Snowmass, Colorado, particularly about the practice of just being with God, and he described this particular contemplative stance as *the essential* life practice. He said our ultimate goal is to connect and integrate our inner contemplative practices with our outer active life, as Jesus did, and that being able to do this is what some mystics call ever-present awareness, enlightenment, or waking up.

Then Keating surprised many of the listeners when he described how effortless this waking up can be. He said,

> To handle the details of living a human life without being distracted from this primary vision is not attained through thinking, but through what might be called the practice of *just being.* To take time just to be, which is to do nothing but be in God's presence for a regular period of time every day, seems to be the shortest access to the mystery that is beyond any conceptual consideration.[3]

~ ~ ~

I can't help but notice the pattern. The world's greatest masters of wisdom, from Jesus himself to our beloved teachers of today, are broadcasting the same message: To be awake and truly human like Jesus, you don't need to *do* anything. You need to just *be.*

But notice what is essential and holy here in what Keating said: You need to just be. *In quiet. Alone. In God's presence. A few minutes every day.*

And as simple as it sounds, the practice of just being, in quiet, in God's presence, a few minutes a day is the foundation of a profound inward spiritual journey. This is a journey where you can come to be reacquainted with your innermost self, the part of you that is easily forgotten in all the busyness of each day. This is a journey where you can be reacquainted with that of God within you, with the divine indwelling in you that has been there all the time.

This is a journey that can indeed change you "from the inside out."[4]

Yes, we know the neuroscience now—that by returning to inner silence, solitude, and stillness in these few minutes every day, your amygdala will be smaller. We know now you will be much less reactive and forgetful. We know you will have a larger insula, more gray matter, and overall much smoother connections to your very human prefrontal cortex. You will have greater awareness and insight and focus and even compassion.

But when you engage in any one of several centering practices that are available to us today, practices in which you can just be, alone, in quiet, in awareness of your innermost self *with God,* then over time, something holy and extraordinary happens in ways that, as Keating said, we can't imagine or foresee. The closeness of your inner, *relational* life will be changed, to yourself, to others, to God, and to the world around you. Your relationship to your own life will shift subtly but profoundly.

It is not an exaggeration for me to say that every person I have encountered who has begun a steady centering pause practice has spoken of this relational dynamic in one way or another. Some speak of how their practice "fills a kind of reservoir of peace inside," enabling them to be have a wider and more loving perspective of the events that happen throughout the rest of the day. Others speak of a "gentling" that happens with such a practice as they begin to feel a deeper sense of connection to themselves and others and aren't as quick to judge and overreact.

You may not notice this at first. I know I didn't. Usually it is your closest loved ones—particularly the loved ones who live with you—who will notice subtle but real changes in the way you relate to them and to others around you.

The Emergence of the Real Self

We talk about how *transformative* a contemplative spiritual practice is, but what I believe really is happening here is that such a practice is *revelatory*. A contemplative spiritual practice gradually lifts the veil that obscures our spiritual awareness of the basic core of our own goodness, our essential, true self and that of God within us. A contemplative spiritual practice *reveals to us what has always been there.* It gently vacates the often unconscious obstacles that prevent us from seeing the essence of ourselves, our bigger, real self, the basic inner core of goodness that resides in each one of us and that is full of God, that *is* God.

As the thirteenth-century Persian poet Rumi reminds us, "You are the drop, and the ocean."[5]

~ ~ ~

As I developed a steady and intentional daily contemplative practice, over time I began to feel as though I was occasionally seeing through a different lens, perhaps the lens of *metanoia* that I spoke of in earlier chapters. It was as though my camera lens occasionally shifted from standard photo to panoramic. It was as though I was occasionally seeing through a lens that sees beyond the surface of things. It was a more expansive and connected way of seeing.

And as the way I was seeing was changed, I noticed the place *from which* I was seeing was gradually changing. I began to have a sense of that of God in me and in everyone and in all things. It was as though I began to be able to differentiate between two versions or realities of me, one of whom I think I had largely overlooked for much of my life.

The version of me with whom I am most familiar is the fight/flight, overattached-egoic me, the one who still has much work to do to realize why certain emotional encounters still trigger my hurt and sensitivity and anger that swing me out of a place of being able to see more clearly.

The other version of me is one whom I feel I have been reintroduced to after a long time of being away. I have come to know this version of me again ever so gradually in these years that I have been practicing a steady centering practice. It has been a lovely reintroduction. This version of me, the one I often sit with in Centering Prayer in the morning, the one who tries to practice returning to God again and again, is one that on a good day, in a good moment, has come to be able to see more expansively, to (sometimes) go meta, and to respond from the center of my being—toward myself, toward others, and even toward what can sometimes feel like the world's despair.

I am thinking this me version may be close to what some call the essential, true self and what I like to call the bigger self, the real self, or the "I AM" of me.

Poet, playwright, and 1992 Nobel Prize winner Derek Walcott captures this gift of recognizing our real self in his luminous poem entitled "Love After Love":

> The time will come
> when, with elation
> you will greet yourself arriving
> at your own door, in your own mirror
> and each will smile at the other's welcome,
>
> and say, sit here. Eat.
> You will love again the stranger who was your self.
> Give wine. Give bread. Give back your heart
> to itself, to the stranger who has loved you
>
> all your life, whom you ignored
> for another, who knows you by heart.
> Take down the love letters from the bookshelf,

the photographs, the desperate notes,
peel your own image from the mirror.
Sit. Feast on your life.

The Real Self in Action

Retreat leader and teacher Jill Benet gave an illuminating presentation on this real self in a recent *Closer Than Breath* online conference on Centering Prayer.

Benet suggested that in times when we experience strong emotions such as real anguish or anger, having a steady centering practice will help equip the real, true self in us to be able to understand that *only a part of* ourselves is actually feeling that hurt or anger. When we can understand that our anguish or anger is not the whole of us, then we aren't as likely to be completely overtaken by it. We can say to ourselves, "A part of me is feeling angry" and know that there is another part of us, a bigger self, if you will, that is holding steady.

This bigger self is able to pause, to notice that a part of us is hurting or angry, and then can care for that part of us and can even listen to that part of us, perhaps in ways that that part of us has never before been cared for. The process is not unlike good therapy or spiritual direction, where a loving and more objective person can sit with your pain or anguish or happiness or joy.

This way of understanding ourselves does not in any way delegitimize any anxiety or anger or fear or trauma we experience. Quite the contrary. This way of understanding ourselves is a grace-filled extension of our particularly human capacity to observe ourselves with *metanoia* eyes.

When our real self is moved to pause, pull back, and respond from a loving place to another part of us that is hurting, we are able to actually honor that hurt part of us and allow it to be seen and to maybe even take steps forward, perhaps the first steps forward it has ever taken toward healing.[6]

When we are engaged in a steady practice, we are more able to pause for these revelations of our different selves because, through our practice, we have trained our minds, our brains, our psyches, and our bodies to *pause* and to release the hold of our own egoic needs, our reflexive defenses and agenda, and to return to God. Again and again and again.

Repetition is key.

And after learning even just the basic neuroscience of contemplative practice, we know now of Hebb's law, how neurons fire and wire new circuitry together when we pause. We come to know the space, the pause that is then created by our own intentional pause practice. We come to know that there in the space Victor Frankl speaks of, "the space between stimulus and response," is indeed our freedom.

Practicing the Pause

And remember, no matter how much we want to calm our habitual fight/flight nature and live a more connected and meaningful spiritual life, no one can simply wake up in the morning and just decide they are going to stop reacting/be less angry/be less anxious, whatever we are trying oh-so-hard to manage in our lives. As much as we'd like to, we can't simply *will* ourselves to be rid of our fears and anxieties, our defensive psychological triggers, our ruminating thoughts, addictions, and obsessive looping.

And that is the magic, the grace, of a steady centering pause practice.

When we practice the pause in steady, everyday practices, we train ourselves to move into that pause naturally and unconsciously. This happens not only physically, in the rewiring of our neural pathways, but it happens in our consciousness, in our psyche, and in our heart center.

And in a spiritual practice in which coming back to center means coming back to that of God within us, not only are we more able to pause in important moments and in important ways, we are also connecting with the "I am" of ourselves, with our steady, bigger, real self. We find we begin to pause in these crucial moments without having to think about it. The movement becomes more automatic because we have the wiring set in our brain, and we have an awakened, abiding sense of Divine Presence residing in our heart center.

~ ~ ~

Our centering pause practice reveals our essence, the basic goodness at the core of our being.

We become in our outer life what we already are in our essence, in our true, real self. As you are able to connect your inner contemplative life of God-within yourself with your outer life of God-within others and in all things, you will notice you are attuned to and living through a new frequency.

A frequency that is Love.

Feeling More Awake, More Aware, More "Prayed"

It was during several retreats at Holy Cross Monastery that I learned firsthand how transformative contemplative practice can be when it is intentionally and consistently woven into the inner and outer fabric of our lives.

Immediately upon arriving at Holy Cross Monastery for a weekend retreat, I could see that the Episcopal monks of this community are very busy twenty-first-century monks. Their primary call is to offer their grace-filled overnight hospitality to as many as five thousand guests a year—an active ministry in itself. These monks are not cloistered. Each monk of the order is active in his own personal ministry—as priests, teachers, psychotherapists, social activists, or managers of the monastery's fully stocked bookstore.

And yet, in the midst of their busy lives, the beautiful bells of the monastery ring out five times a day, much like in the well-known Muslim tradition, to call the monks and monastery guests to gather together in communal prayer, chant, and quiet meditation. At first, I wondered how the monks could get anything done. I found I was even a bit resentful of the constant interruptions of these calls to prayer!

But on my next visit to the monastery, I began falling into the rhythm of the monks' daily prayer, their transcendent plainsong chanting of the psalms, and their long moments of resting in God. I even considered the possibility that there might be some monks who actually prefer the restful and contemplative prayer times to the busyness of their daily responsibilities.

Finally, on my third or fourth visit to the monastery over several years, a shift happened in me. In living the monks' movement from prayer, back to work, to prayer, then back to work, I could see that this constant return to being with God in prayer was affecting, even shaping, the rest of even *my* own day. In my time outside of communal prayer, I felt more aware, more open, more "prayed."

The daily prayer-work "rule" of these Episcopal monks showed me how the day lived and the day prayed could be the same thing. The inner and outer life could be one.

Might we also be called to join in?

CHAPTER 15

Reading with God: When Scripture Shimmers

Listen . . . and incline the ear of your heart.
—St. Benedict

Amid the vast array of powerful and life-changing spiritual practices available to us today, two contemplative practices have become foundational in my life—the ancient practice of *Lectio divina*, or "holy reading," and the practice of Centering Prayer, which is a kind of modern-day "gateway"[1] to the contemplative beyond-words prayer of simply resting with God.

I now realize that the few minutes I spend in these practices in the morning have overflowed into the way I experience and move through my daily life. So I would like to take a short walk with you here through both of these practices and share with you some of the treasures I have discovered in them along my own journey.

~ ~ ~

I don't think I'd given the idea of having a steady, daily contemplative practice a single thought in all my life until I was introduced to the power of the contemplative life through a life-changing chance encounter I had with an Episcopal monk.

I was thirty-three years old. I didn't even know monks could *be* Episcopalian.

So I was surprised when the rector of the small Episcopal Church I was attending with my young family invited an Episcopal monk to give the sermon one Sunday. The monk's name is John-Julian.

That's all. Just John-Julian.

He had been an Episcopal priest of a church in Norwich, Connecticut, and took a pilgrimage to Norwich, England, to learn more about the founding families of his church's town. While he was visiting Norwich, he learned about Lady Julian of Norwich, the fourteenth-century author of *Revelations of Divine Love*, a compilation of mystical visions Julian had in her time as an "anchoress" cloistered in Norwich Cathedral. John-Julian then experienced a life-changing call to found an order of monks and nuns devoted to Julian of Norwich and her teachings.

He became a monk himself, and he changed his name to John-Julian.

I will never forget John-Julian or that day. He seemed otherworldly standing there in the pulpit, wearing his simple monk's habit in the midst of young and old New York City suburbanites donned in their Sunday best. His sermon was on the spiritual life and inner transformation, and he included a story about an eaglet who had grown up in a chicken coop and didn't know she could fly and about how God is always calling us to become who we already are.

His words touched something in me that had been stirring. Church for me had felt like a not-quite fit for a few years by then, and yet there seemed to be something mysterious there that I felt I hadn't yet quite touched.

I have three daughters, and at that time my eldest was three years old and my twin daughters were eleven months old, so our lives were jampacked most days, but I knew I needed to come back that afternoon to attend the Sunday forum that John-Julian was leading. I walked in late and saw that he had written "R U L E" in big bold letters up on the whiteboard. My heart immediately sank as I imagined this meant this afternoon session was going to be all about the rules and doctrine and structure of the church. But when I sat down, I found myself riveted again by John-Julian's way of being, and his groundedness in something I couldn't name.

He wasn't talking about church doctrine at all. John-Julian was talking about the ancient monastic way of life and prayer called the "Rule" of life. He talked about this balance of work and prayer, *ora et labora*, prayer and work, contemplation and action, as an essential, life-giving rhythm of life, a way of coming to know ourselves and God in ways that transform our inner and outer lives.

I remember raising my hand and asking this mysterious monk who had just appeared in my life, "What do we have to do if we want a deeper spiritual life?" When he responded, it felt as though time stood still for a moment. I imagine everyone in the room felt the same way. John-Julian paused—I remember it was completely quiet—and then he said, "If you want a deeper spiritual life, you have to find time to just be alone, in quiet, with God."

Just be alone.

In quiet.

With God.

It was as though his message was emblazoned on me: Just Be Alone. In Quiet. With God.

He spoke to us with a kind of palpable spiritual authority and assuredness about how being with God in quiet is something our innermost selves long for, and how time alone in quiet with God shapes us, changes us, wakes us up, and ultimately draws us to others.

The tricky part for me was that in this season of my life, I was a young mother with three little ones and was preparing for a big family move to Virginia, so I had no time. Or I thought I had no time. But John-Julian said the best way to start finding this time alone with God was to get up early and sit for a few minutes in the morning with scripture. Any scripture. Read slowly for a short while and then rest, alone, in quiet, with God.

Discovering the Monk Within

I was so drawn to the mystery and call of a deeper inner spiritual life, and into an inward journey to what might be true and meaningful, I actually did exactly as John-Julian told us.

The next day, I woke up half an hour before my husband and three little girls did, walked down the stairs to the living room as the light of dawn was just peeking through the windows, and sat cross-legged in a chair (that I had probably never really sat in before) with a big hardcover Bible open in my lap and a pencil in my hand. (Something in me had inclined me to take the plunge and, rules be damned, I was going to actually *write* in this Bible. *Why not?* I thought. Holy studying, right? Reading with God.)

But I knew I was not going to start with Genesis. I had tried that several times in my younger years and always got caught up or confused or bored with all the *begots* and *begats* somewhere in Exodus. No, it was clear to me that I would begin with the gospels. And I did. I read slowly and sometimes would underline phrases or passages that stood out to me.

I quickly came to look forward to those few minutes in the morning.

I realized that in my memory, I hadn't really ever set aside specific time to be truly and intentionally *alone* with my thoughts and certainly not alone with God, reading in this slow and relaxed way. And I think that part was key. I noticed I wasn't reading in my usual analytical way. Being alone, in a holy sort of way, with God, reading scripture, made me read differently. It made me experience my reading differently.

Sometimes tears would come, and that was perplexing to me. I would go back through the passage I had just read, wondering what had made tears come. I remember once it was Matthew 6:33 when Jesus said, "Seek first the kingdom of God and all these things would be added to you." This was very unfamiliar language to me. I hadn't ever studied the Bible or the gospels. I didn't know why tears had come from the reading. Nonetheless, something brought tears, though they weren't sad tears at all. They felt like a kind of quiet overflowing. They felt like tears from a deep, loving place. I didn't feel saddened by them. I think I actually felt bathed by them.

There was, in those early-morning moments in time, a felt sense of not being alone but being somehow accompanied on a deep soul level. When we are "alone" with something holy, we don't actually feel alone at all.

And just as John-Julian had said, small shifts began happening in my life, almost right away, first in my thoughts, then in my outlook, then in my priorities. I began having powerful dreams and becoming aware of meaningful synchronicities in my daily life.

Synchronicity and Serendipity

I remember one morning, a remarkable set of coincidences happened to me that became immediately meaningful to my new journey. I had decided to read over the passages that had been read during the memorial service of Louise, an older woman in our parish. I had for some time been drawn to her sparkle-eyed intelligence and wit and grace. So I pulled out the memorial service bulletin and saw that what was listed as the designated Hebrew scripture passage for the service was Isaiah 61:1–3:

> The spirit of the Lord GOD is upon me,
> because the LORD has anointed me;
> he has sent me to bring good news to the oppressed,
> to bind up the brokenhearted,
> to proclaim liberty to the captives,
> and release to the prisoners;
> to proclaim the year of the LORD's favor.

This seemed a fitting passage for Louise to choose as it seemed her quiet life's mission had been to notice and care for the souls of those in need. I then turned to the place I had marked in the gospels where I had left off the day before and continued on with my own scripture reading for the day. My bookmark was in Luke, chapter 4. The reading that morning began at Luke 4:16, which read

> The Spirit of the Lord is upon me,
> because he has anointed me
> to bring good news to the poor.
> He has sent me to proclaim release to the captives
> and recovery of sight to the blind,
> to let the oppressed go free,
> to proclaim the year of the Lord's favor.

Well, I thought I was seeing things. I could have sworn I had *just* read those very words in Isaiah. I looked back, and indeed they were the same. Now those of you who know the Bible well may be thinking, *Well, of course*, but this was very confusing to me. Remember, I was not at all familiar with the Bible. I wasn't aware until that morning when I finally read the bottom-of-the-page notes that the words recorded in the gospels as the first words of Jesus' ministry were indeed the words of the prophet Isaiah.

Later that day at a meeting for prospective Sunday service scripture readers, one of the other lay readers handed me a training book that was being given to new readers. When I opened it up, the very first quote at the top of the first page above the first paragraph of the first chapter was:

> The Spirit of the Lord is upon me,
> because he has anointed me
> to bring good news to the poor.
> He has sent me to proclaim release to the captives
> and recovery of sight to the blind,
> to let the oppressed go free,
> to proclaim the year of the Lord's favor.

Whether it was a coincidence or an intuition that my innermost self in God was pointing to, it felt like a spiritual two-by-four, saying, "Hey, wake *up*! Stuff is happening here, and you need to pay attention." My awareness was up, and I was open, and these and other coincidences by day and more powerful dreams by night started doing their work on my unconscious. I began pondering existential questions I hadn't had (or made) time for, like "What is actually important to me?" and "What is actually *most* important to me?"

Words began jumping off the page of whatever reading material drew me. Like God's spiritual guard rails, I call them, it seemed all things in those days kept pointing me more and more toward my own true center.

The Two Holy Questions

When our one-year-old daughters were going to be baptized and we were preparing for the service with our priest, he went over the questions asked of parents and godparents during the baptism ceremony. One question was "Will you seek and serve Christ in all persons, loving your neighbor as yourself"? Another was "Will you strive for justice and peace and respect the dignity of every human being?" These two questions made me stop cold. Did I seek and serve Christ in *all* persons? Did I respect the dignity of *every* human being? I suddenly was face to face with the fact that, actually, I didn't really focus all that much on this really fundamental aspect of life very much. It wasn't something I thought about in my day-to-day life. I was thirty-three years old, and respecting the dignity of every human being wasn't a *priority* for me? I began wondering, *How could that possibly be?*

I thought about this the rest of the day and for months after. As I continued my new morning practice, I began to notice my life beginning to reorder itself. A subtle but real shift was happening, moving me from "What do I need to do to be successful?" to "How can I *serve*, how can I be a part of something bigger than I am? How can I somehow bring good (God)?"

This moment now reminds me of what a dear friend of mine said in one of her sermons: "And this is why you were born—to make God close and near."[2] At the time I thought this meant that our call was to make God close and near to others, but as I have grown older, I realize my friend also means that our call is to realize God's very closeness and nearness to *ourselves*. As Julian of Norwich tells us, "Between God and the soul, there is no between."[3]

As we recover that closeness, we are recovering the potential of who we are meant to be.

I share all of this here because since then, I have realized that in John-Julian's class on living a R-U-L-E of life, he had been quietly and unobtrusively teaching us a rich and profound and transformative contemplative *practice*—a very basic way to be with God *and* a powerful and radical and life-changing ancient prayer and meditation practice. He was imparting ancient spiritual knowledge rooted originally in Jesus' own practice and later in the teachings of the desert mothers and fathers and other monastic communities who were foundational to the Christian contemplative tradition.

I had no idea then that over the next ten years I would discover the contemplative "monk" within my own self, apply to go to seminary, and someday be riding a train along the Hudson River, listening to Oksana tell me about the monastery in her heart and feel a quickening of recognition in my own.

An Introduction to the Divine Listening of *Lectio Divina*

It wasn't until my first year of seminary, in a course I was taking on the desert mothers and fathers, that I realized the practice I had learned through my awakening encounter with John-Julian is *Lectio divina* (pronounced LEX-ē-oh de-vē-nah). *Lectio divina* is Latin for "holy reading," though the practice actually is a way of attentive and holy *listening.*

Some people actually describe *Lectio* as a listening practice, and historically it has been so as monks as early as the desert mothers and fathers would actually recite scripture aloud as part of their daily prayer practice and would be listening for the messages they could then live into during the rest of their day.

I realized that, under John-Julian's quiet and life-changing tutelage that Sunday afternoon so many years before, I had learned an ancient, time-honored wisdom practice of moving my focus from my head to my heart, of listening to short passages of scripture, just a couple of lines or so, and then noticing which words and phrases stir my heart. I had learned the mysterious power of the words of scripture to open our hearts and enable us to come to know ourselves.

I think it was John-Julian's particular instruction to me to read scripture *with God* that made all the difference: By opening myself, even the tiniest bit, to a more spiritual experience, I wasn't as inclined to analyze or examine the text as I would have been otherwise. I didn't know it at the time, but by reading scripture in this way, I was reading in more of a heart-centered way. I was reading through the perspective of divine indwelling (i.e., with God). I was actually praying scripture and incorporating the aliveness of its words into my body, mind, and spirit.

That is *Lectio*.

The practice of *Lectio* is enjoying a resurgence of interest today as more and more people, young and old, Christians and others of many belief backgrounds, are being drawn to practicing the contemplative dimension of ancient Christian practices in new and life-giving ways that easily fit into their day-to-day lives.

The Practice Itself

The reason *Lectio divina* is often called a "methodless method" of prayer is because its four movements are so natural to us. Many of us tend to read poetry or spiritual texts in this same way.

Here is how it goes:

You choose a very short passage of scripture or of a spiritual reading, and as you read, you "listen" to the words in a different frame of mind from what we're used to. You don't analyze the text as you would a newspaper story, or a book, or even as you might a Bible passage in a Bible study. You listen, waiting for and *expecting* a word or phrase to emerge or "shimmer" from within the text. Upon reflection, this word or phrase often brings insights that pertain to your particular life situation and choices.

Many of us have had an unprompted "shimmering" *Lectio*-like moment in our lives at some point: It is that moment when, as you are listening to someone read a poem or some verses of scripture or a spiritual reading of some kind, and you feel as though what was read was exactly what you needed in that particular moment. It gave you an insight, an epiphany, or a feeling of connection you'd not had before.

Lectio is also similar to times when you are reading a book and you come upon a thought or an idea or an image, and you can't help but stop and look up from the page for a moment to take it in more fully.

Writer Maria Popova beautifully recalls such moments in our lives, saying, "A single poetic image can lift us from the plane of our storied worldview toward the gasp of a whole new vista, where in the spacious silence of the unimagined we imagine ourselves afresh."[4] In the gift of that "spacious silence," we are given the gifts of insight and imagining. We pause to savor the moment, letting it settle in before getting back to our book.

This flowing natural movement from one moment to another is very natural and is much like the four movements of *Lectio divina* that have been practiced for centuries:

Lectio—Reading

Meditatio—Reflecting

Oratio—Responding

Contemplatio—Resting

(I learned *Lectio* with the Latin terms, and I know some people love Latin, but some find it a bit off-putting. If you're in the latter camp, you just add a letter N at the end of each Latin word, and a corresponding English term emerges!)

For those readers who may be connected to a church liturgical tradition on Sundays, notice how *Lectio* is the very template for traditional worship services and has been for thousands of years: We listen to the scripture readings (*Lectio*), the celebrant gives the sermon (their version of *meditatio*), we pray the prayers of the people (*oratio*), and we have communion followed by our own quiet prayer (*contemplatio*).

In a very real way, the practice of *Lectio* can be like our own morning service, and our own thoughts about the *Lectio* word or phrase that shimmered on any given day can become today's sermon for each of us, all on its own.

Marjorie Thompson, author of *SoulFeast: An Invitation to the Christian Spiritual Life*, describes the *Lectio* process well;

> In lectio divina we begin by reading and savoring a short passage of scripture. Our inner posture is one of a listening heart filled with an expectation that God has a message to convey especially suited to our condition and circumstance. We read and ruminate with the ears of our heart open, alert to connections the Spirit may reveal between the passage and our life situation. We ask "what am I to hear in this passage, story, parable, prophecy?" Listening in this way requires an attitude of patient receptivity in which we let go of our own agendas and open ourselves to God's shaping purpose.[5]

I will briefly describe in more detail the texture of each of *Lectio*'s four stages:

But first, you will want to settle yourself in any way that is natural to you, and choose just a few lines of scripture or another spiritual reading that you would like to "listen" to: The gospels are a good source. The noncanonical Gospel of Thomas is particularly good as Jesus' sayings themselves there are quite short. The Episcopal, Catholic, and Lutheran Church share a lectionary of designated readings for each day that you can reference online. Thelma Hall's book *Too Deep for Words: Rediscovering Lectio Divina* offers a treasure trove of five hundred scriptural passages for *Lectio*.

You might want to take a few long breaths to settle and calm yourself. Perhaps you could invite the Spirit to give you inspiration and guidance.

Reading (*Lectio*)

In *Lectio*, we are invited to listen with what monastics call "the ear of the heart," as if we are in conversation with the innermost part of ourselves and with the divine indwelling in us—because we are! So begin by reading the short passage you chose, slowly and prayerfully, out loud if possible, listening with your body, soul, memory, and imagination for a word or phrase that emerges or shimmers[6] from the text. You may want to reread the same text several times to help quiet yourself interiorly. Feel yourself receive the word or phrase.

Reflecting (*Meditatio*)

When a word or phrase captures or even just gently draws your attention, stop and rest with it. Gently repeat the word or phrase to yourself. Read the passage again, reflecting on the word or phrase. Something inside of us shifts in a powerful and lovely way when we ourselves shift our attitude from our usual stance of analyzing a text to receiving the text and then savoring it. This shift of stance is a profoundly contemplative one. So allow the word or phrase to speak to you in a personal way by pondering the word in your heart, reflecting on what it means to you, allowing it to interact with your thoughts, hopes, memories, and desires. In what ways does the word or phrase connect to your day-to-day life situation? Be attentive to what speaks to your heart.

Responding (*Oratio*)

Allow noticings and wonder to appear. Feel the invitation to have a back-and-forth conversation with your innermost self; feel the invitation to have a back-and-forth conversation with that of God within you, voicing questions or thanksgiving or petitions or prayer. What do you want to say to your inner self and to God in response to your noticings and wonderings? Enter into a loving conversation that comes from your heart.

Resting (*Contemplatio*)

Now for a few quiet moments, you can just let go of all these thoughts about your word or phrase and even about your conversation itself. Settle in for a few minutes of just simply being in this moment—being rather than doing—and as thoughts come to mind, simply return to an openness to that of God within you. Soak in that moment of rest and peace with your innermost self and God.

Mission (*Missio*)

You may find the word or phrase that came to you in *Lectio* will bubble up in your consciousness throughout the day in a way that seems to incorporate the insights you may have received earlier in the day into your soul and psyche. While I was attending seminary, a professor of mine, Rev. Jonathan Linman, wrote a book on the practice of *Lectio* and added this fifth and critically important *Lectio* movement that points to the importance of intentionally carrying our Spirit-led *Lectio* insights into our lives, our relationships, and our world. Just as with all our centering pause practices in our lives, through our growing relationship with ourselves and with the Divine within us, our inner contemplative life can inform, inspire, and equip us in what naturally becomes our more and more socially active contemplative life.[7]

This is contemplation in action.

The *Lectio* Resurgence

One aspect of the spiritual revolution is that a growing number of Christians are turning away from church theology that is based only on the church's interpretation of scripture. Some are turning away, too, from church theology that is based only on traditional church doctrine. People are yearning for their spiritual lives to be more directly connected to the presence and action of the spirit of God in their daily lives. They are yearning for their spiritual lives to be relevant to the comings and goings of the rest of their daily lives, and they are less inclined to lean on church authority to tell them what to think *about* God. They want to directly experience God in their lives.

This is where *Lectio* comes in and why there is a surge in popularity in *Lectio* and other centering practices, particularly those practices involving silence and solitude with God. Many Christians who are in the midst of reconstructing their faith today are adding in the third leg of Richard Hooker's three-legged stool concept[8] into their spiritual lives: they are wanting to ground their spiritual lives in the three-pronged foundation of scripture, tradition, *and reason,*[9] and *Lectio* is an ideal way to incorporate the ongoing activity of the Holy Spirit into their lives through their mind and heart and imagination.

By inviting us to slow down and reflect on a word or phrase of scripture, Lectio allows us to receive quiet but powerful insights, guidance, comfort, or timely challenges along the way of our journey into a deeper spiritual life. In *Lectio,* we are given the chance to collaborate with the spirit of God within us, using insight from scripture to form us, to give us ears to hear, and to help us listen for insights, truth, and guidance that can impact every part of our lives.

Lectio is finally once again a practice for the masses.

Lectio is indeed revolutionary.

CHAPTER 16

The New *Lectio*: Noticing and the Seven-Second Pause

The spiritual journey is a journey of self-discovery, since the encounter with God is also an encounter with one's deepest self.
—Thomas Keating

What I perhaps find most remarkable and life-giving about the pause of *Lectio* is that it is profoundly a "noticing" practice. *Lectio* nudges us to notice and pause.

Our minds and hearts become more and more trained to have "eyes to see" what has been right in front of us.

I have heard that in Celtic Christianity, the Bible is called the Little Book, as it is book-size, and that life and nature itself are considered to be the Big Book.

This makes sense to me.

I am reminded of spiritual director and photographer Christine Valters Paintner, who offers an alternative, contemplative approach to the act of taking photographs as a way to pause and pay attention and as a way to receive the "grace and generosity of life."[1]

She points out that our common language for photography is that we "take" photos and that this is actually how we, as a culture, approach much of life. "But instead of 'taking' photos when you go out into the world," says Paintner, "try becoming aware of how you are 'receiving' them as a gift, and this will shift your awareness and how you move through life."[2]

With this same orientation Paintner has toward the wonder of the everyday, she has created a delightful revision of the four traditional *Lectio* movements, renaming them *shimmering, savoring, summoning*, and *stilling*. She encourages us to notice invitations not only in scriptural texts but also in "the texts of everyday life." You can see how these movements parallel traditional *Lectio* but can be easily applied to our outer contemplative life.

Shimmering

Just as Paintner listens for a word that shimmers or catches her attention when she sits to pray each morning with her scripture reading, she finds that as she moves through her day, there are *moments* that "shimmer forth," and she honors them, as well, as being "important and sacred."[3]

Savoring

In those moments in daily life that stand out to her, Paintner carries them along in her imagination, allowing them to evoke feelings and memories that arise. She says, "Our lives are so rushed that savoring can become a counter-cultural practice."[4]

Summoning

Both in her prayer time and in her daily life, Paintner attends to hints of how God may be calling her into a back-and-forth conversation in those shimmering moments, either to something new or ways to handle certain situations.

Stilling

Stilling is Paintner's lovely word for the space of rest and stillness we are called to in which we can bask for a moment in the experience of being rather than doing. Paintner says her *Lectio* practice helps her to notice moments of stillness that appear in the midst of life's busyness.[5]

The Seven-Second Pause Practice

Moments of stillness like these are not only nice to have in the sense of being a welcome chance to slow down and take a breath in the midst of the rush of the day. They are this, of course. But scientists have determined that even a centering pause of between just six and ten seconds throughout the day is also very effective at resetting and calming our body and mind. As with intentional contemplative practices of long duration, even seconds-long pauses in our daily life have a significant and beneficial effect on developing our ability to pause before overreacting during stressful situations that come up later in the day.

There are both neuroscientific and psychological reasons for this. The slow and easy breath we take during even a few-seconds-long intentional centering pause activates the parasympathetic nervous system, which then reduces your heart rate and blood pressure and calms you down. By pausing to bring your awareness completely into the present moment, in those few seconds you are free from past regrets or future worry, which gives your body and mind a signal and a chance to rest and recover.[6] These pauses can be worked into your everyday life so they become habitual and refreshing.

I work remotely most of the time, and I live near a church that chimes the hour throughout the day. I find this a natural time to look up from what I am doing and stop for what I call a seven-second pause. So for those few seconds, I pause and become present to myself and to where I am. (Sometimes if I am concentrating especially hard on something, I feel almost surprised to find myself there!)

I notice my breath. As Thich Nhat Hanh reminds us, "I take an in-breath, and know I am taking an in-breath." I intentionally relax the muscles around my eyes and mouth, I move the thinking of my mind down to my heart center, and I "find my feet."[7]

After even this very short time, I find I do feel somehow refreshed and more aware. Seven-second pauses are another way to just be alone, in quiet, with God.

They can be what Carmen Acevedo Butcher calls "micro-moments to rest in God." As Butcher tells us in her luminous book *Practice the Presence*, "The practice of the presence is a form of micro-prayer done on the fly. A mini-conversation with God. A brief 'lifting up of the heart.' Done anywhere, anytime, the practice is perfect for anyone."[8]

I invite you to find a way that works well for you to take time in your day for a centering pause of a few seconds. A friend of mine, even when eating alone, pauses to really "see" the food on her plate, and "see" the people who made it possible. Another older friend of mine uses his phone as a reminder. Even before cell phones were ubiquitous, when he gets a phone call, he has always paused and waited for the second ring and prays for whomever is on the other end of the line.

Much like the foundational on-the-mat practices like *Lectio* and Centering Prayer can prepare our brain, psyche, and body to be able to pause in high-stress and/or emotional encounters rather than automatically reacting through our unconscious defensive reflexes, having an off-the-mat practice of set centering pause times throughout the day can set us right as well.

But just a reminder here: Even establishing a long-time centering pause practice does not mean you will no longer be inclined to overreact in emotional situations. It does mean you will have gone a long way to creating an automatic pause in your brain and your body so that you will be *more aware* of what's going on in those emotional situations. You will indeed see a bigger picture, and you will be able to respond more thoughtfully and from your heart. You will come to know yourself, and you will come to more closely know the call of that of God within you.

Lectio in the Christian Tradition

Over time, practicing *Lectio* pauses in both our morning practice and our daily routine informs our lives and helps us to come closer to who we are called to be.

I love to "listen" to Thomas Keating's words about *Lectio* as the practice is understood in the ancient Christian contemplative tradition. (Keating first became interested in the practice, he says, at the age of seventeen while he was attending Yale University, which means Keating practiced *Lectio* for seventy-eight years before his physical death in 2021.)

I invite you to listen to Father Keating's words here, perhaps even to savor them, and "attend to them with the ear of your heart":[9]

> As you continue practicing the Lectio movements and the deep rest in the Spirit that is integral to Lectio, you will find over time that the Spirit will then naturally anoint your daily life—your conduct, your speech, your relationships, your imagination. Then you, without even trying, will be able to express this Mystery. You will become a channel of God's presence in the world.

> And even in ordinary ways: Whether you're a grandmother, or a lawyer, or a homemaker, or a professional person, there is a divine way of being that person. And that's what you will be. The overflow or result of having rested deeply in God is that that anointing of the Spirit anoints you at every level of your being.

Keating continues speaking here, I believe, of the Universal Christ and the role *Lectio* plays in the sustainability of contemplation in action and social justice:

> The triumph of grace is to lead ordinary life with extraordinary love. This is the thrust of the Lectio movement, of moving from knowing Christ casually, to learning about him in the scripture, interacting through conversation and communion, until that presence of Christ *becomes* our resting place, both in prayer and action. And that makes action more *active*. Because then your action can sustain the stress and major difficulties and the opposition of persecution and other things, without you getting upset. So there is more and more energy from the divine source and the Spirit is gradually succeeding in transforming us body, soul, and spirit into the image of Christ. That's the project of the Gospel, isn't it?! And Lectio is a marvelous invention precisely to do this.[10]

~ ~ ~

I like to call *Lectio* the "pearl of great price" practice. There truly is buried treasure in this practice of *Lectio*. And, inevitably, the treasure we discover is ourselves and the love of God within us.

CHAPTER 17

The Centering Pause: Nourishing the Roots of Our Essence

Even from a purely human perspective, everybody needs some solitude and silence in daily life, just to be human and creative about the way one lives. This sort of spiritual discipline is a therapy for the tyranny of the false self . . .

—Thomas Keating

On many Sunday mornings, when I was a young mother, my husband and I would make breakfast with our three preschool-age daughters, get everyone fed and dressed, and then all pile into the car and head to church. After dropping the girls off at Sunday school, we would settle into our pews for a few minutes before the service began. The organist was playing his prelude, people were perusing their bulletins, and the choir and clergy were gathering in the back of the church getting ready for the procession.

And then something I looked forward to every Sunday would happen: When the prelude ended, instead of the organist immediately beginning to play the first notes of the first hymn of the service, the sanctuary became quiet, and everyone waited for the priest to say this prayer out loud, slowly, for all to hear from the back of the church:

> O God of peace . . . who hast taught us that in returning and rest we shall be saved . . . in quiet and in confidence shall be our strength . . . by the might of thy Spirit lift us we pray thee, to thy Presence . . . where we may be still . . . and know that thou art God.[1]

And then, before he said "Amen," the priest would pause.

It was just this unusual—and in a way gloriously—weighty pause.

I'd never experienced this in any other church. After he had just spoken the words "where we may be *still*, and know that thou art God," the priest would do exactly that: be still.

He would be completely still.

And every single one of us in the sanctuary was, collectively, also completely still. It was a moment when I felt full of something wonderful and mysterious and full, something I will call God.

And *then*, after the glorious pause, the priest would say, "Amen." And the organist would launch into the hymn, and everyone would stand up and start singing, and the choir would process, and on and on.

But I will always remember that pause. Strange as it sounds, I lived for that pause. At the end of busy nonstop weeks that seemed to somehow always spill over even into Sunday mornings, the full stillness of that sanctuary pause at that moment every Sunday morning filled my heart and soul.

And then I was ready for the next week.[2]

Awakening Into the "Is-ness" of God

How can silence be so full and centering?

I wonder if Jesus ever wondered the same thing. I imagine Jesus planned for these full and centering pauses in the silence and solitude that he sought on so many occasions that the gospel writers let everyone know it was "his custom" to do so.

Thomas Keating speaks to how the quiet and the fullness of silence can somehow break through the busyness and uncertainty of our lives and make us aware of the spirit of God within us and all around us:

> We rarely think of the air we breathe, yet it is in us and around all the time. In similar fashion, the presence of God penetrates us, is all around us, is always embracing us. Our awareness, unfortunately, is not awake to that dimension of reality. The purpose of contemplative prayer, the sacraments, spiritual disciplines, is to awaken us.[3]

This image of the movement and love of the presence of God being completely a part of us and around us all the time is one of my favorite ways of understanding all the ways God "is." As the psalmist said, we "live and move and have our being" in the spirit of God.[4] Which means—have you heard this?—humans asking the question "What is God?" is like a fish asking another fish, "What is water?"

The flow and movement and power and love of God *is*—and is always present as the holy and sustaining conversation between all the elements of creation: between the stars and the planets, between the trees and the air and us, even between the elements of our own body, mind, and spirit.[5] When Moses asked for a name, God simply responded, "I . . . *AM*." You can almost imagine the shrug.

So God *is*, all the while we are generally caught up in the doing of the moment rather than being in the moment, so we aren't always aware and awake to the ongoing movement and flow and Presence that simply *is*.

But as Episcopal priest and author Barbara Crafton tells us,

> God is transmitting all the time. And we are wired to receive that transmission. We are wired to have a deep and profound spiritual life. Think about that when you step into the shower in the morning, and feel that spray washing over you. If you're "awake" and tuned in, you will know there is God's grace in every drop.[6]

These moments are, to me, a kind of prayer, and as Keating said, sometimes it is the pause of prayer itself that wakes us up.

Prayer That Is Bigger

In that full and centering pause I experienced while sitting in the pew on those many Sunday mornings, I felt awakened to Mystery, to a sense of something other but also of something within.

In that full and centering pause, I felt an invitation to reconsider what I named as prayer.

Prayer is one of those words that often has preconceived notions, or misunderstandings, even baggage, that for some people may put up real obstacles to pursuing a meaningful daily spiritual practice. In a series I lead on contemplative practices, we spend some time in the first class working together to demystify the idea of prayer for all those who were brought up with the Western Christian experience of prayer mostly being about talking *to* God.

So let's begin here by busting the myth of what prayer can be.

When we pray, we may talk to God, praise God, ask God to do things for us, ask God for help, and these are all important and good practices. But prayer is not only discursive and one-way. As the desert mothers and fathers taught us, prayer is also apophatic, without words.

You've heard that St. Francis of Assisi said, "Preach the Gospel; when necessary use words." I think of prayer in the same way: If necessary, we can use words, but a lot of time it is not necessary to use words at all. In fact, using no words when we want to open to that of God within our hearts can sometimes be more prayerful.

I think we can say that we actually are in prayer whenever we find ourselves drawn out of our ordinary awareness and toward a felt sense of awe of the Holy, of what we somehow know to be what is real.

I think prayer is being aware of the power of this Great Mystery, this great Love, right in the midst of our "ordinary" lives—catching sight of the full moon, watching a baby being born, being captivated by a glorious sunset or by the eyes of someone you adore gazing into your own while you are talking about something that is important to you.

Even a person can *be* prayer.

I imagine Jesus of Nazareth was prayer.

What Is Contemplation?

In one of Krista Tippett's *On Being Project* conversations, poet Naomi Shihab Nye offers a captivating and I think spot-on definition of what can be an oh-so difficult word to capture or define—contemplation.

Nye describes contemplation as "a long, loving look."

She says "when you take a long, loving look anywhere, you feel more bonded with whatever you've looked at."[7] It took my breath away when I first heard this. And I replayed the moment over again several times. "Contemplation is taking a long, loving look."

And I so appreciate Krista Tippett's compelling invitation for us to experience a long, loving look *at our own lives*, inner and outer:

She says, "Summon your best long, loving look at what's happening around you and inside you."[8]

I invite you to try it out for even just a moment now and see what happens. See what happens when you take a long, loving look at what's happening around you. And at what is happening inside you.

Contemplation is that accessible and is that essential to our well-being.

So I don't think contemplative *prayer*, then, was ever meant to sound or seem as lofty and unreachable as Western Christians have been taught it is for many generations, centuries, even. I believe contemplative prayer can be simply this quiet, wordless long, loving look we are talking about, a beyond-thoughts-and-feelings state of being that each of us has experienced naturally in one way or another—like the dappling-light-in-the-tree moment when we pause and sense that the movement and spirit of God are fully in that moment. And in us.

It is in this "long, loving look" of contemplation that we experience the "oneing" of a full and centering pause. In the full centeredness of such moments, we feel the fullness of Mystery and Spirit and the Divine in and through and around us.

So, then, the *practice* of contemplative prayer is when we spend *intentional* moments in time connected to the Holy in this way that is beyond our thoughts and beyond our feelings and "opens us to experiencing God."[9]

Keating draws an analogy with how naturally a conversation with a loved one over dinner might move from the kitchen table to the fireplace to just sit and be together. In the same way, we can simply be with God, rest in God, in the way we would be with someone we love.

I am reminded of when one of my daughters was about four years old, she told me she had a dream that she was sitting on Jesus' lap. I told her I thought that sounded like a lovely dream. And then I couldn't resist asking her if Jesus had said anything to her in this dream. She paused for a couple of seconds, then shrugged matter-of-factly and said, "We were just quiet together. It was really nice."

Nourishing the Roots of Our Essence

We can make contemplative prayer our daily practice both within the few intentional moments we devote to sitting and just being, alone, with God and then by attempting to carry the Spirit of that encounter into the rest of the moments of our daily life.

This intentional practice of resting in stillness, silence, and solitude with God in a way that is beyond thoughts and feelings is one way to describe the inner action of contemplative prayer, but it doesn't do contemplative prayer full justice, I admit.

Keith Kristich, founder of the online contemplative community *Closer Than Breath*, and one of my primary Centering Prayer teachers, opened my eyes to understand contemplative prayer as a practice that "nourishes the roots of our innermost self, our own *essence*, our divine indwelling."[10] I had never thought of this before. I have found myself captivated by this truth, that our divine indwelling, our innermost selves, is our essence, and that resting in quiet Presence nourishes that essence in us.

In his recent essay on silence, poet and philosopher David Whyte beautifully captures the power and beauty of our own essence and the essence of the Divine:

> In silence, essence speaks to us of essence itself and asks
> for a kind of unilateral disarmament,
> our own essential nature slowly emerging
> as the defended periphery atomizes and falls apart.
> As the busy edge dissolves we begin to join the conversation
> through the portal of a present unknowing, robust vulnerability,

> revealing in the way we listen, a different ear, a more perceptive eye,
> an imagination refusing to come too early to a conclusion,
> and belonging to a different person
> than the one who first entered the quiet.[11]

In the way a retreat is a rest from the emotional turmoil of our lives, twenty minutes of contemplative prayer can be a mini-retreat from the swirl of daily living, a mini-retreat from the spin of our own daily preoccupations. But, importantly, as Kristich reminds us, quiet prayer is not a "spiritual by-pass" or a "feel good" escape from our lives. Taking time to be with God in silence and solitude is about "waking to our groundedness, to our rootedness, to our 'beingness' in God. It's about finding that goodness within ourselves and giving that to the world."[12]

I am reminded of when I began having monthly sessions with a spiritual director, and at the beginning of each session, she would invite me to sit in silence for a few minutes, as long as I wanted. I began noticing that in those moments of silence, even if I was sitting there still in the swirl of everything that was on my mind, I found I would settle into a clearer way of seeing things. My spiritual director told me that sitting in intentional silence "in God" in this way often invites our entire being to relax and "shed our roles." In moments like these, we let go of each of our outer, more egoic selves—our job titles, the parts we play in our daily lives, even "wife," "mother," "sister," "friend," "minister." We find our goodness within ourselves. We come close to the essence of who we are, the "I am" of who we are in God.[13]

Henri Nouwen spoke to how contemplative prayer awakens us to this core goodness of ourselves and enables us to live *through* that true self in our daily life:

> The practice of contemplative prayer is the discipline by which we begin to "see" the living God dwelling in our own hearts. . . .

> The divine Spirit alive in us makes our world transparent for us and opens our eyes to the presence of the divine Spirit in all that surrounds us. It is with our heart of hearts that we see the heart of the world.[14]

We may wonder, But is this really possible? How can we attain to these eyes that see the heart of the world of which Nouwen and so many masters speak? And how, especially, do we respond when we face the challenges that present themselves when we *do* see into the heart of the world?

I believe the answer is: We practice the practice that we've been shown can get us there.

We practice the centering pause practice of Jesus.

A natural next question might be: But how can we practice as Jesus himself did two thousand years ago?

I believe that in our modern day and time, the closest we can come to practicing the way Jesus himself practiced, and to the way Jesus actually *instructed* us to pray, is by practicing the new but ancient practice of *Centering Prayer*, a practice that is enjoying a surge of interest today in both spiritual and neuroscientific circles.

A Thumbnail Sketch

There is much that is fascinating and even thrilling about the transformative practice of Centering Prayer and its connection to scripture, psychology, and science. Before we move into the life-changing benefits this practice can bring to our day-to-day lives, here is a thumbnail sketch to give you a sense of the practice itself.

Centering Prayer is a very simple but profound method of Christian meditation that leads us into the quiet "stilling" of contemplative prayer. In the usually twenty minutes of designated time for the practice, we allow ourselves to rest in a silent place beyond thinking, "a kind of oasis in a day of emotional turmoil."[15] When thoughts arise as they always do, we let them pass through our awareness and, ever so gently, we return to a sacred word we have chosen that reminds us to consent and open ourselves again to an awareness of God's presence and action within.

This returning to center, over time, incorporates in our mind, body, and spirit a natural means of staying centered in God's love in times of challenge and stress in our daily lives. By training ourselves to let go of and not get drawn into compulsive thoughts and emotions, we gradually develop freedom from our attachments and compulsions.

Centering Prayer is not meant to replace any spoken prayer practices we may have; it is considered another way to be aware of God and to experience the presence of God.

Through this simple practice of our own, we can peel away the overlay of our egocentric fight/flight, I-am-too-busy reactions that are rooted in the depths of our unconscious and that get in the way of us waking up to the inner power and intrinsic goodness of our true self, our essence, the soul of us, the divine that is within us and within all of us.

- <u>Centering Prayer is scriptural</u>: Current-day religious scholars and theologians have written extensively on how closely Centering Prayer connects with scriptural accounts of Jesus' own *tameion* teaching in Matthew 6:6 on how to pray in our "inner room," the indwelling presence of God in us.
- <u>Centering Prayer is psychological</u>: Centering Prayer is a practice that grows our capacity for an awareness of the Divine, as well as plumbs the depths of the false self in our unconscious, and releases their hold on us, so that, indeed, as Mary Magdalene said, "we might be prepared to become fully human."

- Centering Prayer has neuroscientific benefits: Recent neuroscience studies on the basic movement of practices like the basic method of Centering Prayer have been proven to catalyze positive changes in the neural pathways of brain regions connected with focus, empathy, and compassion.

I would like to introduce you more fully to this "treasure for the soul,"[16] the practice of Centering Prayer, which is now being experienced by thousands of people worldwide as the very cornerstone of their spiritual life, nearly fifty years after it was developed by three Trappist monks from St. Joseph's Abbey in Spencer, Massachusetts.

Centering Prayer: A Worldwide Phenomenon

When Thomas Keating, Fr. William Meninger, and Fr. Basil Pennington first introduced Centering Prayer as a new form of an ancient contemplative prayer method to a group of non-contemplatives in the mid-1970s, I don't think anyone could have predicted that over the course of nearly fifty years, it would become a worldwide phenomenon,[17] that thousands of people in dozens of countries would be committed to its daily practice, and that a far-ranging international network of volunteers would be teaching the practice throughout the United States and around the world.

But through their own experience, these three Trappist monks did know that the daily practice of this prayer could lead to a healing and transformative experience of the movement of the Divine in the lives of new practitioners. As well, a number of people were leaving the Christian church at that time, yearning for a practice that would bring meaning and transformation to their lives, having no awareness that their own Christian tradition offered meditation practices that could cultivate the connection with the loving spirit of God that they were looking for.

The fervent hope of Meninger, Pennington, and Keating was to distill the profound, centuries-old tradition of contemplative prayer into a simple practice that laypeople as well as clergy and monastics could understand and practice. That the popularity of their new but ancient practice would grow so dramatically was beyond their hopes and dreams. At a talk in 2003, Keating said, "I feel like somebody who, even though I don't look like it, is a surfer on the tide that is coming in and riding this wave of interest in a deeper meaning in life."[18]

The simple, easily learned practice that they developed, which they named "Centering Prayer," is deeply rooted in the early Christian contemplative prayer tradition. Meninger, Pennington, and Keating drew from the practice and teachings of Jesus himself, from Jesus' own Matthew 6:6 instructions on how to pray in our "inner room," from the anonymously written fourteenth-century guide to contemplative meditation *The Cloud of Unknowing*, and from the writings of, among others, the desert mothers and fathers, John of the Cross, and Teresa of Avila, as well as from the writings of their friend and colleague Thomas Merton.

Thomas Merton and the Center of Our Being

Not everyone is aware that Thomas Merton had been a profound influence on the lives of Meninger, Pennington, and Keating. Even now, more than fifty years after his death, Merton is a captivating mentor and inspiration to countless Christian and non-Christian laypersons, scholars, and theologians who are new and emerging leaders in the contemplative movement worldwide. Merton died just a few years prior to the development of the new practice of Centering Prayer, and his writings were integral to their process.

Merton's *The Seven Storey Mountain* (published in 1946, when he was thirty-one years old) introduced the psychologically healing power of quiet, wordless prayer to a wide secular audience. Prior to

Merton's writings, the experience of prayer without words or images, and the concept of being a contemplative-in-action, were "simply not on the radar screen of most contemporary thought."[19]

That each of us has an essential, true self—who we are in the fullness of our humanity—was also a common theme in Merton's writings, as was his understanding that to discover our truest vocational identity requires "seeking and discovering God in prayer."[20]

In Merton's last years of his short life, he opened the eyes and hearts of many to an understanding of the ways that Eastern spirituality and practice parallel and illuminate the Christian tradition. Notably, Merton developed a close correspondence with the Vietnamese Buddhist monk Thich Nhat Hanh, who wrote the introduction to the Merton classic *Contemplative Prayer.* By Thich Nhat Hanh's own account, his concept of the Holy Spirit of God that he writes about later in his bestselling book *Living Buddha, Living Christ* was profoundly influenced by his relationship with Thomas Merton.

Merton's orientation toward the importance of engaging in interreligious dialogue was yet another influence on the Centering Prayer process. As Fathers Keating, Meninger, and Pennington were developing the Centering Prayer method, they engaged in deep conversation with Eastern practitioners and leaders of nonmonastic backgrounds in order to develop a form of prayer that could be easily practiced by an audience of varied backgrounds.

A Peek behind the Scenes

In what may be an apocryphal story, it was Fr. Meninger who found a "dusty copy" of *The Cloud of Unknowing* and proposed the method taught by its anonymous fourteenth-century writer (who is imagined by many to have also been an older monastic teaching a younger monastic the power and practice of resting in the divine indwelling through contemplative prayer). It was apparently Meninger who suggested the repetition of a *single sacred word*, a concept articulated in *The Cloud*, that would symbolize the Centering Prayer practitioner's consent and intention to release egoic thoughts and to open to the movement and presence of God. This sacred word concept became a key element of the practice, the monks found, as the return to the sacred word assisted in the releasing of the thoughts and feelings that invariably come into one's awareness during the silence of prayer.[21]

Meninger, Pennington, and Keating then got to work drawing from their other sources and engaging in sustained dialogue with others, and over time they began teaching this simple form of meditation to prospective practitioners, instructing them to, once or twice a day for twenty minutes, find a place to sit with eyes closed and surrender their minds, thoughts, and feelings to the presence and action of God within them.

Centering Prayer teachings have been able to reach a wide and still-growing audience through dozens of publications by Keating, Meninger, and Pennington and then later by followers and colleagues of theirs, including Cynthia Bourgeault, James Finley, Carl Arico, and David Frenette, as well as through online Centering Prayer groups like Keith Kristich's *Closer Than Breath* community, Cynthia Bougeault's *Wisdom Waypoints* wisdom practice circles, along with retreats, conferences, and audio and video recordings created and offered by hundreds of Contemplative Outreach volunteers.

Teaching the practice of Centering Prayer is a call and endeavor that Keating described in a 2003 talk as "inviting people throughout the world across all boundaries—geographical, religious, racial, ethnic—to a deeper meaning in life, a deeper experience with the Ultimate Reality, or God, as we call that reality in the Judeo-Christian tradition."[22]

What Should We Call This Practice?

Because much of the actual method of Centering Prayer is taken from *The Cloud of Unknowing*, the practice was originally called "The Prayer of the Cloud." But it is said the method was renamed *Centering Prayer* in reference to Thomas Merton's description of his own experience of contemplative prayer.

In a letter written to Abdul Aziz, a Sufi scholar, Merton described his own contemplative prayer as "*centered* entirely on the presence of God and [God's] will and love, and as rising up out of the *center* of nothingness and silence."[23] (Remember also Merton's teaching on the divine indwelling that he described as the "point or spark which belongs entirely to God [that is] at the *center* of our being.")

Keating, Pennington, and Menninger found that the name "Centering Prayer" was easier to teach than The Cloud.[24] As well, the concept of being entirely centered on God is generally thought to be an excellent summary of the theological and spiritual root of Centering Prayer.

The Way It Works

In his book *Open Mind, Open Heart*, Keating explains that the practice of Centering Prayer, as practiced in the Christian contemplative tradition, is based on the core principle that the "fundamental goodness of human nature . . . this basic core of goodness, our true Self, is capable of unlimited development, indeed, of becoming transformed into Christ and deified."[25] There is an understanding that at the center of our being is divine love, the divine indwelling, the spirit of God, what some call the Universal Christ. This divine love is present and actively at work in the depths of our being and in the wholeness of our lives at all times and in all places.

The full and centering silence and stillness of Centering Prayer invite our awareness of this power and presence of divine love within us. Here is a four-step process of Centering Prayer that is drawn from the writings of Thomas Keating and Contemplative Outreach:

(1) Choose a sacred word as the symbol of your intention to consent to God's presence and action within you.
(2) Sitting comfortably with eyes closed, settle briefly, and silently introduce the sacred word as the symbol of your intention to consent and open to God's presence and action within you and all around.
(3) When engaged with your thoughts, return ever so gently to the sacred word.
(4) At the end of the prayer period, remain in silence with eyes closed for a couple of minutes.

The guideline for the practice is twenty minutes, once or twice a day.

~ ~ ~

I would like to add a few notes here from my personal experience in the hope that they may be helpful in your practice.

About Your Sacred Word

Try not to be concerned about having the perfect-for-you sacred word. The word is not as important as its intention to be open and receptive. The word is considered to be sacred because of its intent, not because of its meaning. You can always change your word. Examples of a sacred word are *peace, rest, still, Jesus, Mary, love.* You may also use your breath to symbolize your intention.

Some people use a non-English word to minimize meaning-making of their sacred word during their practice. One friend of mine uses *amma* as his sacred word. My sacred word at this time is *kairos*, as the exquisite silence and spaciousness of Centering Prayer are to me much like the full and centering pause of *kairos* time that we experience in thin places, where heaven and earth come closer and we catch a glimpse, a sense, of the Divine in us and around us.

I am reminded of Thomas Merton's words about his own silent prayer "rising up out of the center of nothingness and silence."[26] Or, as a wise and dear older friend of mine has said, "In the mysterious silence of Centering Prayer we move from nothingness into . . . Everything."

About Your Physical Posture

I used to either sit on a zafu cushion or on the edge of a hard chair for the duration of my practice. I situate myself now in a way that may be a little unorthodox, but it has helped me make time for, and to very much look forward to, my times in Centering Prayer, even on very crowded days: I make sure I am very comfortable! I add in a short ritual of being fully aware as I make myself a mug of hot tea or coffee. I sit cross-legged, my back upright but up against a comfortable couch or upholstered chair, with my mug of tea in my lap. I drink some of my tea and gather my thoughts for a just few short minutes before I move into the silence. Sometimes trying to be absolutely, *completely* still at the very beginning of your prayer time is a way to bring a kind of stilling that is helpful. Another personal note here: Notice and release any tension in your face, particularly around your eyes and around your mouth. And then after you do that, do it again—you may be surprised how much tension we habitually hold around our eyes and mouth.

About How You Settle In

I find it helpful to read or say a short line of a spiritual reading to attune myself to the *kairos* time of my practice. My two favorites are "in you we live and move and having our being" (from Acts:17:28) and the Book of Common Prayer's prayer for quiet confidence, which I love to say in its ancient language: "O God of peace, who hast taught us that in returning and rest we shall be saved, in quiet and confidence shall be our strength, by the might of thy Spirit lift us, we pray thee, to thy Presence, where we may be still, and know that thou art God."

And I love using "we" rather than "I" in these introductory prayers as a way to remind myself that I am spending these moments of silence and solitude with God *with many others around the world.* We are sharing in a kind of collective holy silence, together. (Notice how the Lord's Prayer begins with the word "*our*," not "*my*.")

About Your Daily Timing

I also practice first thing in the morning. I remember I initially avoided that time, thinking I would fall right back to sleep, but I have come to love the time before everyone else has awakened, and the tea and cozy chair ritual has become a welcome way to invite the day in. Adding the second time in the day is trickier, but either three o'clock tea time (again) or just before making supper can work well (if you don't have little ones in your midst). This, of course, is on ideal days.

But remember—sitting for twenty minutes of Centering Prayer during the day can happen in any space, not only in quiet spaces. I know people who have seen Thomas Keating himself often practicing Centering Prayer in the airport!

~ ~ ~

You will find that in a very short time, the constant ever-so-gently returning to your word or breath centers you in God and, over time, trains your body, mind, and spirit to also return to center in God in your daily life when thoughts and challenges, and even emotional triggers and times of crisis, pull at your attention.

An experienced practitioner told me recently that they found practicing Centering Prayer once a day to be "maintenance" and twice a day to be "transformative." I said, "Then we all have much to look forward to."

Fruits of the Practice

In her book *Mindful Silence: The Heart of Christian Contemplation*, Phileena Heuertz chronicles the deconstruction of her "identity, worldview, and faith" she experienced after many years of leading an international grassroots humanitarian organization in Sierra Leone. The practice of Centering Prayer was what she calls the "crucial remedy for her fragmented condition." She said,

> When I had hit a wall and come to the end of myself . . . contemplative prayer, in the form of a Christian meditation method called centering prayer, became the only way in which I could attempt to encounter God. There, in solitude, silence, and stillness, I could just show up—as I am with all my doubts, questions, and pain. And over time, the gentle, secret, grace-filled presence of God began to reveal a love so enormous that it has the power to transform all of the pain of the world—beginning with my own.[27]

Phileena and her husband Chris then founded Gravity Center, a center for contemplative activism to nurture what she calls the integral connection between contemplation and action.

I have attended several retreats hosted by Contemplative Outreach, a network of individuals and small faith communities committed to living the contemplative dimension of the gospels. The teachings of these retreat leaders mirror Phileena's descriptions of the ways she has found a daily practice of Centering Prayer develops our human capacity for love and insight and a profound connection with others and the world.

This human capacity for love and insight becomes more evident in many ways—"freedom from self-centered motivation, action in service to others, a sense of interconnectedness with all creation, disidentification with our self-image, healing of fear, conviction of our basic goodness, and capacity for union with God."[28] Not a bad list!

Many people notice a significant difference in their way of being in even just a few short weeks of a steady practice. But don't look for experiences or signs in the actual experience of sitting in prayer. You will notice results of your practice as you emerge *into your daily life.*

I would say that one of the first fruits (usually noticed by others in our lives) after we spend some time in a Centering Prayer practice is that when presented with a conflict or challenge, we tend to respond more thoughtfully and not react as instinctively by either lashing out impulsively in defense or by withdrawing or repressing our emotion.

Knowing some of the science now, we are aware of several basic mechanisms making this so. And once again, we can recall the space we covered in the neuroscience chapters that Victor Frankl points out to us: "Between stimulus and response is a space, and in that space is our freedom." By conditioning ourselves, through our practice, to return to ourselves in God—no matter the thought or distraction—our minds and hearts and brain create a space, sometimes just a nanosecond of time, so we are less apt to "react" in challenging situations. We are more inclined to "respond" through a more (literally) thoughtful perspective and from a place of love and understanding.

But for all the exciting science of this practice, we cannot overlook the profound *grace* of its rhythm of continual return to the Spirit, to that of God in us and in all things. The profound grace of Centering Prayer underlies all of its other fruits. Cynthia Bourgeault notes this blessing here:

> Perhaps the subtlest fruit of the practice of Centering Prayer (and the most delicious!) is a gradually deepening capacity to abide in the state of "attention of the heart," as it's known in the Christianity of the East. . . . Once you get the hang of it, attention of the heart allows you to be fully present to God, and at the same time fully present to the situation at hand, giving and taking from the spontaneity of your own authentic, surrendered presence.[29]

Monkey Mind

A primer on Centering Prayer would be incomplete without talking about the universal and inevitable experience of "monkey-mind," thoughts darting around here and there, like a monkey swinging from tree limb to tree limb.

Those first experiencing Centering Prayer as a "simple" method of prayer are immediately confronted with the intensity and the non-stop constancy of their thoughts. When you become quiet in prayer, the first thing you are likely to notice is how busy your mind is! Ideas, observations, little injustices, shopping lists, time schedules, memories, and worries will likely appear again and again at first. The overattached egoic mind *loves* attention.

All of us have monkey mind. You are not alone.

So when you sit in a time of Centering Prayer, you may find the interior noise overwhelming at first. This is normal too. Understand that these intruding thoughts are expected. It may seem as though you have more thoughts coming into your mind when you're quiet, but actually, when you're quiet, you're able to notice how many thoughts you're being constantly bombarded with all the time.

So what to do about all these thoughts floating in and out of our consciousness? I've noticed that even some long-time practitioners of Centering Prayer call these thoughts "distractions," but remember the new neuroscience and Hebb's law about this that we know and are aware of now: what actually catalyzes the neural firing of new pathways in your brain is the pause-release-return movement—that moment you pause and gently release the thoughts and open back into your intention.

In this way, your monkey mind will actually be integral to the transformative power of your practice.

So intruding thoughts are a not a bad thing! Every time you notice a thought and ever-so-gently turn back to your sacred word, you are creating new neural circuitry in your brain and creating new ways to be less reactive and more compassionate. I've encountered many teachers who say that the more monkey mind you have, the more opportunities you have to come back to being, as Thomas Merton says, "centered entirely on the presence of God."[30] And indeed, when we explore Keating's psychological model of Centering Prayer in the next chapter, we will begin to understand that intruding thoughts are not only inevitable; they are an integral part of how the Centering Prayer process brings profound psychological healing and growth.

Remember, the quality of your prayer time is not measured by the quality or intensity of your thoughts or by how often your attention is captured by them. When your mind wanders, as it will, simply ever so gently return to the sacred word. As Thomas Keating says, return to the sacred word "gently, incredibly gently, as if you were laying a feather on a piece of absorbent cotton."[31]

You Are the Sky

My first Centering Prayer teacher, who was of the Quaker tradition,[32] taught me an effective way to manage and actually *use* all the monkey-mind thoughts in a positive way, and I practice this almost always. In the quiet of your Centering Prayer sit, he told a group of us, the thoughts and sensations coming into your consciousness are actually just like clouds passing by. "You are the sky. Constant. Eternal. Part of the Holy. So we just let the clouds pass by. They always do. You are the sky."

I have found Chris' wisdom to be an eye-opening lesson in day-to-day life in general.

This sky and clouds imagining is similar to the process Fr. Keating suggests in *Open Mind, Open Heart*. In the quiet of your Centering Prayer sit, the thoughts and sensations coming into your consciousness are like boats floating by on a river. You just let them float by. When you find you're "checking out the boat to see what's in it" or you start "climbing all over that boat," you know then that you've been drawn away from the quiet, so then you just gently return to the sacred word.

One of my favorite analogies that gets across this same idea is to think of keeping the front and back doors of your house wide open. You can let the thoughts walk in, but just don't invite them to have tea!

What I love about each of these ways to manage monkey mind is that they can be so easily carried over into our daily lives. We—the essence of us, who we are in God—are the river, we are the sky, we are even the house with the open front and back doors. Emotional situations and events and even people in our lives to which our ego wants to over attach itself are like the boats on the river, the clouds in the sky, and the people walking into our house. Just as in our sitting practice, we do not need to allow ourselves to be hooked by them and then flood them with our attention.

Flooding our egoic thoughts with overattachment, i.e. with our attention, just serves to nourish our ego when it is overreacting, and these intrusions will just keep coming back again and again and again. We can instead simply notice the annoyances or disruptions they cause, and be even curious or amused by them. Then allow them to *pass us by*, and return ever so gently to nourishing our essence by connecting to that of God within us.

Opening to God

I heard someone say that when Westerners are asked where God is, they point to the sky, and when Easterners are asked where God is, they point to their hearts.

So in Centering Prayer, when we return to our sacred word, our intention is to open into that love of God, wherever and however we might envision its Source, and to consent to the presence and action of that love within us. This movement of release and opening into the presence of the Holy that is already within us can profoundly deepen our connection with the ground of our being, our divine indwelling, and our basic core of goodness.

I find the movement is one of opening into the love of God that is present in my heart, and at the same time, it is opening to what is all around us; it is as though I am stepping into the flow and movement of a kind of river that courses through all the workings of the universe. It is a flow that we are all a part of.

There is saying by Rumi that points to what I am trying to describe: "When you do things from your soul, you feel a river moving through you, a joy."

The continual surrender of one's soul, of one's whole being, into the loving flow and movement of God over time develops a natural orientation to the Holy and to the Divine in all things and all people. There is a sense of God with us and in us that is always working through us.

So in the practice of Centering Prayer, while you may choose your breath to be your sacred symbol for your intention to open to the indwelling presence of God in you, this is not the same as meditations in which you clear your mind of all thoughts and then focus moment after moment on your breathing to quiet your mind in meditation. The fundamental dynamic of Centering Prayer is not to resist, retain, or repress[33] thoughts as they arise but rather to allow them to *pass through our awareness*. We can then gently return with our whole being to being "in" God.

I should note here, too, that Centering Prayer is also not like some other spiritually oriented meditations that involve an expectation of having a spiritual experience of some kind by concentrating on a particular posture, mantra, or mandala. Also the practice Centering Prayer is not a relaxation exercise, although it may bring relaxation as we engage with, and surrender ourselves to, the presence and action of God in all and through all.

Then There's That Surrender Resistance

I remember I had a hard time at first with the term *surrender* that we hear a lot about when we talk about Centering Prayer and contemplative prayer. It can feel against our very nature to relinquish control in the way some of us think about when we think of surrendering ourselves to something or someone.

But every Centering Prayer teacher I have known has emphasized the point that the intention in Centering Prayer is to *open to, to give ourselves over to,* the love of God in our heart, which is the ground of our being. The practice itself is a kenotic practice of releasing the hold of our egoic thinking, which is itself a "self-surrender." Or a "self" surrender, a *false self*-surrender.

If the word *surrender* jars you in some way, as it did me for a while, it may be helpful to know that when I say the movement of

Centering Prayer is a kind of self-surrender, I don't mean this in a sense of giving something or someone autocratic and oppressive rule over you. A closer, truer understanding of what I believe the intended meaning of *surrender* is came to me in the way a dear and wise friend of mine described her own time of what she calls Quiet Prayer:

> To me Quiet Prayer is really about curling up on the lap of the Great Mother—like a child would—quite literally lying on my bed as if the pillows are indeed Her lap. It is a place of comfort; and it is there that I do surrender, I suppose, as there's no place else to go, no place else to rest my weary head and heart, except in that space of Love, "resting in God's love." The words "give myself over" . . . that takes effort, and I find it's more like finding comfort in those ever-waiting arms, leaning into them . . . and turning my full attention—body, mind, and spirit—to being held in the lap of the Divine.[34]

We can see how in this practice we are sharing in the practice of Jesus. This kind of giving oneself over to the love of God is that same release of will, the same *kenosis*, that we witness again and again in the centering pause of Jesus throughout the gospels. In this self-surrender, we experience a gradual weakening of the false self and its obstacles that prevent us from knowing in full awareness our true self, the image of God in us.

I believe Keating captures the power of Centering Prayer when he says, "When we offer ourselves in total self-surrender, God then transforms each level of our being into the divine way of being human, something Jesus gave us an example of."[35]

So when we practice in this way, we too can grow our capacity to attune, align, and connect with that of God and our deepest, innermost *true* self in God.

When we open into and receive the Divine in this way, again and again and again, we reveal to ourselves our own basic core of goodness, and we join into the flow and movement of the Divine that is in and all around us.

I do believe we transform into the likeness of what we hold in our heart, as Jesus of Nazareth showed us two thousand years ago.

In that transformation and revelation, is our potential to live into our full capacity to know the Divine in the midst of our full humanity.

In that transformation, we sense we are a part of Something. We sense we are a part of Love.

And so we are.

~ ~ ~

A primer on profound, transformative spiritual practices would not be complete without including online resources I use quite frequently and often daily: The Insight Timer app offers guided meditations and has temple bells you can time for the beginning and end of your Centering Prayer sit. The Jesuits of Britain organization's Pray-As-You-Go app reads daily scripture aloud, and offers thoughtful prompts using a helpful Lectio-like method. *On Being*'s Wisdom app and Keith Kristich's weekly Zoom Centering Prayer sessions and six-week Centering Prayer courses are invaluable.

CHAPTER 18

Centering Prayer: Divine Therapy for the Human Condition

If you do not make the unconscious conscious,
it will direct your life, and you will call it fate.
—Carl Gustav Jung

I have a favorite folklore legend that illustrates the promise of the journey of revealing and rediscovering our essential, true self within. The legend is based on the events surrounding the 1955 discovery of the Golden Buddha:

A long time ago, there stood a Golden Buddha, nearly ten feet tall, in front of a village monastery. When the village received the news that an army from a neighboring country was about to invade their village, the monks covered the Golden Buddha with stone and plaster. For many, many years, the Golden Buddha remained covered, until after several generations, no one remembered the secret of the Golden Buddha.

One day, a young monk was meditating, sitting on the knee of the stone Buddha. When he stood up, a small piece of the stone fell off of the Buddha, and the monk saw a glint of gold. He pushed away small pieces and then larger pieces of the stone, realizing, finally, that the entire stone Buddha was actually golden.

~ ~ ~

I love the wonderful metaphor of this story. Over time, most of us come to believe we are the stone Buddha, not the golden one, allowing the layers of our insecurities to get in the way of our relationships, our dreams, and of who we really are.

Then something, or someone, comes along and shakes us free of a bit of our stone casing. We see a glint of gold; we catch a glimpse of our soul and its completeness, just as we are.

We realize our "hidden wholeness"[1] is golden. And if we allow it, this foundational reality of who we are then has the power to guide us through our lives in transformative ways. As author Parker Palmer tells us, "When we catch sight of the soul, we can become healers in a wounded world—in the family, in the neighborhood, in the workplace and in political life."[2]

Dissolving the Not-Real Self

So how do we remove the rest of the stone covering of our own inner golden self?

Every major world spiritual tradition (and now neuroscience) offers us the same answer: *it is the gift and the nature of contemplative practice to dissolve that part of us that perceives a need to project an outer false image of ourselves to others in order to be seen as competent or successful—what some call our "false self."*

As Thomas Keating says in his book *Intimacy of God*, "We can bring the false self to liturgy and [even] to the reception of the sacraments, but we cannot bring the false self forever to contemplative prayer, because it is the nature of contemplative prayer to dissolve it."[3]

We understand that the way this works in our psyche is that the contemplative rhythm of continually releasing egoic thoughts and returning to the presence of God in our essence gradually weakens the constructs of the false, reactive self. Remember, this "self" is not really even an entity, a self, so much as it is an incorrect perception of ourselves. It is any overattached needs we may have developed since childhood. When we continually release the hold of these needs through our contemplative practice, then our true, responsive (golden, hidden) self can begin to emerge more completely.

Keating and the Psychology of "Who Am I?"

Thomas Keating has a recognized gift of weaving together the insights and language of modern psychology with Christian theology and spirituality in ways that make not only the practice of Centering Prayer readily accessible but the mysterious workings of this "attention of the heart" practice easy to understand. I think you will find it remarkable here how the insight of Keating's work, particularly on the psychology of Centering Prayer in his "false self in action" model, parallels and illuminates the new contemplative neuroscience we have covered in previous chapters.

~ ~ ~

Keating says the great question of the second half of the spiritual journey is "*Who* are you?"

I invite you to take a moment to observe what happens when you ask the question yourself: Who am I? Am I who others want me to be? Am I who I think I *should* be? Am I who my career path says I am? Am I who my friends think I am? Which friends? Who am I in my essence? *Who* am I? As we answer the "Who Am I" question for ourselves, Keating provides the basis for who we have unconsciously grown to be in our outer lives: "All of us come into this world as little bundles of emotional needs," he says, "of which we can identify three in particular: security and survival, affection and esteem, and power and control."[4]

By the time we are three years old, each of us has experienced unmet needs in each of these three primary human instincts. This is not a matter of good parenting or bad parenting. Simply by virtue of our limited rational abilities as an infant or small child, we are not equipped to understand why we may be experiencing one thing or another, and we are not equipped to adequately process our experiences, particularly not with any actionable sense of the Divine within us.

Keating calls these unmet needs our "emotional programs for happiness."

These instincts and motivations are a conglomeration of needs that on an unconscious level our ego believes we must have and fears that we don't. They are the basis of what I call our "not-real self," the false self that is clamoring to attain each and every one of these needs and motivations. They are the basis of what Keating calls our "false-self system." And they are the basis from which most of our words, attitudes, and behaviors flow.

In the assumed absence, or "not-enough-ness," of this group of emotional needs in our life—of affection and esteem, power and control, and security and survival—our unconscious inclines us to overcompensate for our vulnerability. We try to create an environment around us in which those needs are more likely to be met: we exert our power in situations to avoid feeling out of control, we find ways to earn approval and affection from those we want to impress, we have our own secret agendas that make us feel more safe and secure in the unpredictability of the world around us.

We then inevitably get triggered by something that conflicts with our behavior, at which point we start the complaining and the inner storytelling about how "no one understands, this always happens, how could they say such a thing," which then reinforces our unconscious programs and the vicious looping cycle of the false self in action.

Of course, all of these basic needs are natural vulnerabilities and are valid. To be healthy human beings, we need a good dose of each: we all need adequate amounts of affection and a sense of security and control in our lives. It is only when our ego overattaches to any or all of them that they become obstacles to our health and well-being and to our spiritual life in God. (Which is, sorry to say, a lot of the time.)

This is not some of us; this is all of us. None of us gets a pass!

And most all of this is unconscious. (Carl Jung apparently thought 90 percent of our "energy" expended in any given day is unconscious!)[5] I recall the quote attributed to Jung that applies well here: "If you do not make the unconscious conscious, it will direct your life, and you will call it fate."

What Gets in Our Way: Our Hidden Unconscious in Action

Keating's fascination with the psychology and science of the spiritual journey led him to masterful insights into the human condition and into the power of contemplative practice to relativize the power of our emotional programs for happiness to overtake our day-to-day behavior and our relationship dynamics. I had the honor of participating in a 2006 Contemplative Ministry Project conference of theological school staff members and students, led by Father Keating and the Rev.

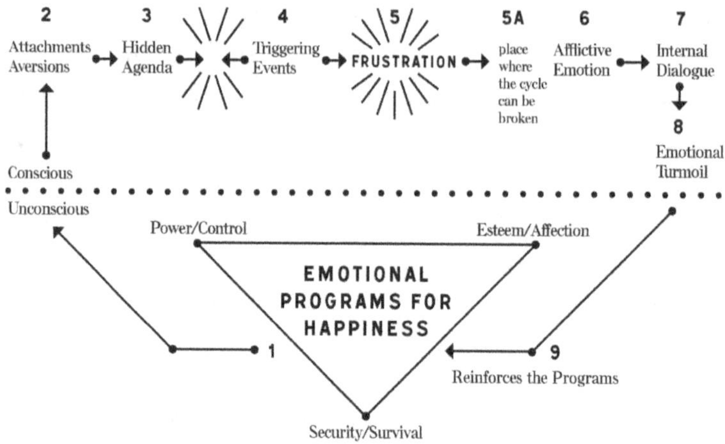

David Keller, where Father Keating shared with us his model of how a steady Centering Prayer practice can assist us in "dismantling the strait jacket of the false self."[6]

Notice in Thomas Keating's model above that all of our vulnerabilities, our "wounds of a lifetime," are, indeed, hidden deep in our unconscious (#1). We are not aware of them most of the time. We may not even have any memory of what caused these hurts or oversights or traumas. Most of us have little real awareness of why we act the way we do and why certain particular behaviors or events seem to inevitably trigger us into hurt, humiliation, anger, even rage, while they may not trigger other people at all. (Though other people have their own to manage.)

Keating's model shows us how relentless the cycling of our false-self system can be when unexamined. We act out of our ego's overattachment to our unmet needs (#2). We try to compensate for what we think we lack (#3). And this is where our unconscious behavior shows in any number of ways through our unique personalities.

Some of us may overreact with anger or hurt when someone is critical of us in order to convince ourselves that we are lovable; some of us will withdraw or be deceptive or aloof. Some will work harder; some will play harder. Some of us may be overcritical of either others or ourselves. We may be manipulative and have a hidden agenda to maintain a sense of control or safety. We may try to fix everything to keep things safe. We may become obsessed with how we look. We may overachieve and overwork at appearing to be successful.

At some point or at many points in our day, our way of expressing ourselves inevitably bumps up against someone else's, and there is conflict (#4). Because our false motivations have been either frustrated or completely undone by this triggering event, we move emotionally into hurt, anxiety, full-fury anger, or any number of other intense emotions (#5), and our bodies move into full fight/flight mode. We often react at this point in ways that were described well in Siegel's "flip your lid" explanation in chapter 5. (And, indeed, this is the place where we do flip our lid.)

Without any sort of awareness or centering practice, in our unconscious drive to right the wrongs of the triggering event (#4), and being in the throes of fight/flight, we completely bypass the crucially important point #5A without a thought, moving right into resentment and other emotions (#6) and all the storytelling and rumination and internal dialogue (#7) about how wronged we are and how bad things are because of what just happened.

These emotional binges can happen for hours, even days, and can bring us into real emotional turmoil (#8), all of this just reinforcing whichever emotional program for happiness has been triggered (#9) and ensuring we will continue to act out our unconscious needs in this way over and over and over again.[7]

This all sounds rather bleak, but hold on . . . there is good news coming.

Calming Down the Static

Keating explains that because of the noise of the emotional binges of our false-self system (our ongoing internal emotional chatter about our frustrations with every which thing), we aren't able to hear what he calls the "delicate inspirations of the Spirit"[8] that could actually begin to be heard through the process of letting go of our false-self system, if we could only do so.

This point in Keating's brilliant analysis of our emotional programs for happiness dovetails in remarkable ways with the new neuroscience we discussed in previous chapters. With our unconscious constantly pushing us to compensate for what it thinks it is lacking, we end up in the same ruminating thoughts and obsessions and inner storytelling about all the ways our needs aren't being met. Our fight/flight sympathetic nervous system can't calm down and remains in a state of continual false-self static noise and often chronic stress. Until the "static" calms down, the Spirit cannot compete with this noise. Keating offers an old-fashioned, easy-to-understand analogy here:

> It's like static in the receptive apparatus of a radio set. Until the static calms down and is quieted, you can't hear the news of what the announcer is going to say, or if you do, you just catch a word here and there. As the static or the noise, (the false-self system with its turmoil and emotional distress), calms down and diminishes through Contemplative Prayer and the active practice of virtue, then, little by little, the message of the Gospel, or more exactly, the higher transmissions of the universe, begin to be heard with greater and increasing clarity.[9]

Dismantling the False-Self System

Keating talks about how Centering Prayer and the contemplative prayer it leads to can quiet down the static of our false-self system. He describes Centering Prayer as "contemplative divine therapy," in the sense that the deep rest and peace that come from a regular practice of contemplative prayer inclines our usually vigilant inner defenses to relax, inclining our body, "with its great capacity for health, to say, 'Let's get rid of these emotional blocks once and for all.'"[10] This trust and rest of the Centering Prayer practice allows the defensive and fearful aspects of ourselves that are hidden in our unconscious to begin to come forward. Through our practice, "little by little, [they] fall away, and finally lose their lasting effect on us."[11]

This means that during our Centering Prayer time, thoughts from our unconscious can come bubbling up out of our unconscious, sometimes into our conscious awareness as thoughts or sensations, other times remaining unconscious, so we may not even become aware of the specific hurt or trauma that caused us distress when we were younger. We may find that a feeling of deep sadness or possibly some agitation suddenly comes over us, but when we return to our sacred word and open to the Divine Presence, the feeling is gone.

Grace in action.

Point 5A: The Power of the Centering Pause

Now I invite you to look at Thomas Keating's model through a different lens—not as a day in your life but as a session in your Centering Prayer practice.

Following the model, the thoughts or sensations come out of our unconscious and may become known either as a feeling that comes over us or as a conscious event that comes to mind. There is that #5 experience of frustration as we begin to react, but then, as part of our practice, we don't engage with the emotions. We ever so gently return to our sacred word and open to the power and movement of the divine within us. And in doing so, we do not pass point #5A! We hang out there for a while. We don't reinforce our unconscious insecurities with stories and grievances and emotional binge chatter. We turn to the Divine in us.

Despite the numbers and letters contrivance, this point #5A juncture is a *profound and life-changing one:* The *power of our practice* is at this point #5A. Our few minutes of daily practice sitting in Centering Prayer, on the mat, so to speak, continually releasing thoughts and opening to the Divine, makes it easier to break the cycle of our unconscious attachments at point #5A.

Point #5A is the centering pause that breaks that cycle, both in our practice and in our daily life. It is the letting-go point, the release, the *kenosis* that frees us from the shackles of what holds us back from living into our human/divine nature. Here we are now seeing the science of Centering Prayer from a psychological perspective and how point #5A holds the possibility of a shift that creates the Victor Frankl "space" that is our freedom.

This is the way a steady Centering Prayer practice "relativizes the insecurities of the ego." Rather than get caught up in the emotion that our egoic thoughts or needs can bring, when we instead release those thoughts and needs and open ourselves to the presence of God in and around us, we relativize all the shoulds and must-haves of our unconscious needs. At the same time, we reinforce our awareness of our basic core of goodness, that of the Divine within.

So it is our intentional and steady practice that assists us in relinquishing our overattachment to these unconscious programs or vulnerabilities.

If we don't practice such a profound contemplative prayer practice, a practice that reveals what is hidden in our unconscious, we will change very little over our lifetime, says Richard Rohr: "*If we do not transform our pain, we will most assuredly transmit it*—usually to those closest to us: our family, our neighbors, our co-workers, and, invariably, the most vulnerable, our children."[12] He goes on to say,

> But if your prayer goes deep, "invading" your unconscious, as it were, your whole view of the world will change from fear to connection, because you don't live inside your fragile and encapsulated [not-real, false] self anymore. . . . You move from ego consciousness to soul awareness, *from being fear-driven to being love-drawn.*[13]

~ ~ ~

An important note here: Keating notes the "gentleness" of Centering Prayer in the way the Spirit allows the bubbling up of the unconscious to happen slowly and in such a way that thoughts or emotions can come and go, sometimes unconsciously, sometimes by returning to our sacred word that is our intention to open to God's presence. The process can for some people sometimes unloose uncomfortable earlier emotions, even early traumas. If this should happen, the emotion will usually lose its power when you return to your sacred word and open to the presence of God. If you find the emotions are more intense than you feel comfortable with, it is helpful and important that you seek companionship and guidance along the way through a spiritual director or a therapist who is attuned to the spiritual journey.

A Paradigm Shift

In this compelling explanation of the cycling of our unconscious needs, what Keating calls our false-self system, Keating is answering one of the questions that plague most of us in our emotional encounters with others:

Why are some of us completely overtaken by emotion when someone is being rude and uncaring to us? When either our spouse or other loved one says something hurtful or rude to us, or even when we get cut off in traffic, or a coworker doesn't include us in a group decision, why do we get so upset?

We see now that many of our overreactions are rooted in our unconscious. Our egoic false-self system of emotional programs for happiness is all set up deep in our unconscious to be triggered and to remind us of all that it thinks we don't have enough of. With just one thoughtless comment or one annoying incident, our programs are triggered, and at an unconscious level we're afraid the esteem that we thought we had is gone, that we don't have control, and that we certainly don't have security.

Because all of this is unconscious, we have no idea or memory of why certain events go right to the heart of our emotional sensitivities. We could have been excluded from a birthday party. We could have been blamed and even punished for something we didn't do. We don't know why. But what we do know is that when whatever happened, we weren't old enough to make sense of the pain of it, so it got buried, and fed other unmet needs until we could make sense of it all.

Which is now.

Now we are able to realize at some level that we don't need to be overtaken by our emotions in these encounters. Through our practice, we become more identified with our basic core of goodness, the Divine within. And through our practice, we are able to more easily notice when we are about to be overtaken by our emotions.

As Keating says in his inimitable and animated way, "It doesn't even make sense when we think about it! Why should we get upset? There is no commandment that says 'Thou shalt get angry when someone is rude to me.' But we do because our false-self system thinks we desperately need to defend ourselves in order to get the esteem and control and security it thinks we don't have."[14]

Contemplative Divine Therapy

I have found that this new understanding of the *psychology* of contemplative practice can enliven our understanding of the *neuroscience* of contemplative practice in a particular way: yes, pausing to release thoughts and open into a sense of Presence in our practice eventually develops more efficient neural pathways so we don't get so overtaken by emotions and react so dramatically in day-to-day life. And yes, coming back to center in daily encounters builds certain pathways that make us calmer and more resilient.

But now that we know the psychology of Centering Prayer, we have some real personality around our personal thoughts and the encounters that trigger a dramatic stress response particularly in us. We can recognize our triggering emotions and better understand their source. They become ours in a way, even though they are universal. We realize that when our sympathetic nervous system goes into full tilt and we flip our lid in certain particular-to-us emotional situations, it is because our unconscious is terrified that we don't have what we need to survive.

And as we begin to relinquish our overattachment to the unconscious vulnerabilities that get in the way of us experiencing the loving realness of our lives, we begin to recognize our innate esteem, control, and security is actually more intact than we knew, and is even grounded—and grounded in a deeply spiritual sense. We can rest in and connect with a deep and spiritual awareness of feeling "I really am okay" at our core, at our very center. We begin to finally have some space to slow down the frames of the movie of our life that we are living in and actually *choose* the way we want to respond. We can choose in any given situation to respond in a way that is informed by our own real truths and not just driven by the perceived needs of our unconscious.

This is good news.

Keating offers us a hopeful imagining here:

> Through a spiritual practice like Centering Prayer, we begin to experience spiritual awareness. . . . We live more and more out of *self-actuating* motivation rather than the domination of our habitual drives to be esteemed, to be in control, and to feel secure.[15]

So you can see how in Thomas Keating's psychological model of the practice of Centering Prayer as "contemplative divine therapy," we gradually become aware on an *experiential* level of the basic core of our own goodness. At the same time, our Centering Prayer practice *reinforces our capacity of letting go*:

> So if you learn to let go of all thoughts in contemplative prayer, returning to the sacred word when you notice you're thinking some particular thought, or have some particular impression or feeling, then in daily life it is *going to become easier* when you have some distressing thought or feeling that is emerging out of one of the energy centers to let it go and not react.[16]

It is going to become easier because, with practice, there will be a pause there now. The more we practice, the more of a pause there seems to be. And because we aren't engaging as much in the stories we tell ourselves or in an explosive reaction, we aren't reinforcing those hurt places in our unconscious.

The Highway Works Project of the Soul

Keating says,

> Just like *weeds in the desert,* if you can keep them dried out by not reinforcing them or watering them with your imagination

> or by giving into them, very quickly they wither up and die. There's no substance to them. They're just childhood habits that we never got around to changing when we became an adult. A habit can be changed by another habit. And so this is the invitation then to respond to the Gospel.[17]

By this "invitation to the Gospel," Keating may be referring to Jesus' Matthew 6:6 invitation "when you pray, go into your inner room, and close the door," which is the very basis of the Church's centuries-old tradition of contemplative prayer. Your inner room, your monastery of the heart, your divine indwelling is where God will meet you. It is our essential self.

So we understand that when Keating tells us that a habit can be changed by another habit, he is saying our habit of "watering the weeds," the unconscious needs of our false self, can be changed by taking on a centering pause habit such as the habit of our Matthew 6:6 inner-room, on-the-mat Centering Prayer practice or the habit of our seven-second-pause, off-the-mat practice.

Does this "watering the weeds" analogy sound familiar?

Here is another highway works project in the making. Remember in Chapter 7—the insula highway between the amygdala and the prefrontal cortex? This is the same highway, just in a different country. Perhaps it is the same project. The spectacular news here is that when we practice, the pathways of our unconscious are cleared of the overgrowth of our unconscious grievances and frustrations and despair.

In our practice, our constant opening to God rather than getting hooked onto thoughts *makes it easier* in our daily life to open toward God in our encounters with others.

And in our daily life, every time we pause at the point we would normally engage in all the ruminating thoughts, the chatter and the stories of how wronged we have been by whatever has triggered us, when we instead turn to our body or to our heart or to the remembering of God with us, we are also then clearing the path for, and building the muscle of, surrender. We are giving over to the power and love of God within.

Do you see what is happening here?

In the Centering Prayer pause practice of contemplative divine therapy, *we are nourishing the roots of our true self's essence rather than nourishing the roots of our false self's emotional triggers!*

As we nourish the roots of our *essence*, then the roots of our unconscious, unmeetable needs gradually wither and fall away, and our true, completed, divine self is gradually revealed.

So while yes, it *is* our human condition to overcompensate for our unconscious, unmet needs for affection, security, and control, the good news is that, *at the same time*, we as humans are equipped in our mind and in our spirit and even in our brain to relinquish our overattachment to these unconscious drives and motivations and to live into our basic core of goodness, the Divine within us.

"Inside everyone is a great shout of joy waiting to be born," says poet David Whyte.

Human/Divine Evolution

Metaphysics, psychology, the religions of the world, and now new neuroscience are all explaining this remarkable capacity that we as humans have to be healed of our unconscious emotional wounds. Even the "wounds of a lifetime"[18] that can sometimes take over our entire lives and our closest relationships can be released and healed. And through this healing we are able to live into our potential full humanity, to become fully human.

But what does this mean—to become fully human?

Certainly new science has given us a clue: In the previous science chapters here in *Practice the Pause,* we have seen that there is evidence now that engaging in our own steady, transformative contemplative practice may improve our capacity for our innate human virtues of compassion, empathy, kindness, and awareness. And remember, some scientists believe, as science writer Sharon Begley has said, the power of these contemplative practices *may even bring about* the "exceptional states" of each of these virtues in ourselves.

But I think this is only one aspect of what it could mean to become fully human.

We also have a new awareness of the potential for us as human beings to evolve into higher levels of spiritual consciousness. Keating believes we are experiencing a spiritual evolution, "a prelude to a divine-human way of functioning in all the virtues of which humans are capable, but which we have not yet learned to put into practice."[19]

Notice that Keating calls this evolution a *spiritual* evolution. As we realize the transformative potential of Centering Prayer's *kenotic* pause and the contemplative prayer to which it leads, we can see that the spiritual aspect of living into the potential of our full humanity may be finely woven into the exciting science.

What this is all leading up to is quite profound.

Through the contemplative pause practice of Centering Prayer, we are not only unloading our unconscious and freeing ourselves from the shackles of our emotional wounds. The contemplative divine therapy of Centering Prayer is *not only* a practice of healing.

Through the contemplative divine therapy of Centering Prayer, we are *also* ceaselessly opening to an awareness of the love of the Divine within us. This means contemplative divine therapy is *also* a practice of grace. Indeed, the purpose of divine therapy is nothing less than to "heal the roots of all our problems" *and* to "*transform the whole of our nature into the mind and heart of Christ.*"[20]

As a spiritual practice, by virtue of continually practicing this centered-in-God pause of Jesus, our Centering Prayer practice, with grace, transforms us into the likeness of our essence, of what is in our hearts, of Love itself.

Keating says,

> The purpose of our spiritual journey is not just to become a better person, as important as this is. The purpose of this journey is to change us into the *divine way of being human*. This is a much bigger and more comprehensive project and opens us to the full extent of human possibilities and capacities.[21]

In a very exciting way, we have come back around, full circle, to chapter 1. This "changing us into the divine way of being human" of which Keating speaks is what he and the Church call *theosis*. Remember that, for Christians in the East, that path of *theosis* is not only modeled for us by Jesus; it is understood to be the very purpose of life itself—to transform into the likeness of the love of God, *to be fully human like Jesus*.

~ ~ ~

I encourage you to notice what happens in you as you read these more wisdom-oriented words of Eastern Christianity, words pointing to the possibilities of a path toward living into the likeness of the love of God. The very words *theosis* and its companions *divinization* or *deification* tend to trigger (there's that word again) our Western Christian ego resistance to the notion that we might presume to aspire to such a lofty prospect. So then it becomes all too easy for us to revert to the old and comfortable, more Western, lens of thinking, "Well, I know *Jesus* could, but, oh no, *I* can't do *that*."

I've come to believe that this way out isn't an option anymore.

In fact, Thomas Keating believes that "to submit to the divine therapy is something *we owe to ourselves and the rest of humanity*." He says,

> If we don't allow the Spirit of God to address the deep levels of our attachments to ourselves and to our programs for happiness, we will pour into the world the negative elements of our self-centeredness, adding to the conflicts and social disasters that come from overidentifying with the biases and prejudices of our particular culture and upbringing.[22]

Keating is reflecting here the vision of our wisdom masters, ancient and new, who are making sure we know that taking time to be alone with God through a transformative centering pause practice is now nothing short of paramount—not just for each one of us but for our collective future.

~ ~ ~

Think back to scripture for a moment and notice how the synoptic gospel writers start off right away with Jesus *being led by the Spirit* into the *erémos*, a place full of God, where he stays and is "in prayer" for forty days, all the while resisting the temptations of . . . what? Jesus resists the very temptations that are the unconscious vulnerabilities of the human condition: Jesus resists the temptations of esteem, security, and control.

And then remember what Jesus does "immediately" thereafter: Jesus leaves the desert to begin his mission, and the very first message of his mission is for all of us to return to an awareness of God within and all around, to change our (unconscious) ways of thinking, and to see in new ways—*metanoia*.

Jesus says, "The Kingdom of God is within you," which sounds to me a whole lot like,

> You have a basic core of goodness in you that is your very essence, that is your divine indwelling, so reclaim who you are, reclaim that true self, and see the big picture: See how connected

> everything is in the Love and power of God, the Christ that is in all things. Live into my radically inclusive, self-giving love. Live into what it means to be fully human. You can do this too.

And then Jesus shows us how.

"As was his custom," Jesus practiced the full and centering pause that centered him in the power and love of God. And he practiced again and again and again, perhaps with every breath he took.

Jesus himself showed us how to put on the mind of Christ and to live through the heart of Christ.

Jesus himself showed us how to be fully human.

~ ~ ~

And so spirituality and science are, indeed, dancing together.[23]

We are now able to understand the compelling *psychology* of the breakthrough new contemplative *neuroscience* studies on what ancient *religion* has taught for thousands of years about the power of contemplative practice to equip us to live into our highest human virtues.

Psychology. Brain science. Religion.

The new good news of each field, as our human race journeys together into this twenty-first century, is a harbinger of real hope and promise for the future exploration of what it means to be human and the role contemplative practice must play for us as we begin to live into the radically inclusive, self-giving divine love that is, for us, humanly possible, as shown to us by one Jesus of Nazareth.

We can be a part of what wants to happen naturally. We can be attuned to the "transmissions of the universe,"[24] to the flow and movement and power of the transformative love of God within us and all around us, from the smallest cell within us to the far reaches of the galaxies.

This is possible. We can do this.

I keep in mind always the words spoken in a sermon delivered by a dear friend of mine one Sunday morning in the glorious height of springtime:

"Just take a look around—the entire *world* is rigged for transformation!"[25]

EPILOGUE

Even as I complete these pages of *Practice the Pause*, I know there will be days for all of us when the stresses and strains and demands of life take over, and we may ask ourselves: Who can attain to such a thing, truly—to be truly awake *and fully human*? Did even Jesus himself . . . every day?

What we do know is that when we practice, as Jesus himself practiced, *we can come close*. We can wake from sleep, and on some days, we can come pretty darn close to understanding ourselves and understanding our lives through the bigger, clearer, inclusive lens of *metanoia*. We know others since Jesus' time who have done so, who have in their own quiet and dramatic ways changed either the world or their corner of the world. I know some who are doing so now.

We share the same DNA as Jesus. We share the same divine indwelling as Jesus.

I am reminded of my daughters' baptisms when I and others were asked the two Book of Common Prayer questions that are asked at every baptism, those two questions that get right to the heart of things: "Will you seek and serve Christ in all persons, loving your neighbor as yourself?" and "Will you strive for justice and peace among all people, and respect the dignity of every human being?"

And the Book of Common Prayer answer to these questions is not "Yes, sure, I can do this." Neither is the answer to these questions "Wait, who could do this all the time, really?"

The Book of Common Prayer's answer to these questions is "I will, with God's help."[1]

With God's help.

We are not going it alone. And that's what the centering pause practice of Jesus is all about: every time we practice, every time we intentionally pause to "nourish the roots of our essence,"[2] to rest in that of God within us, we are quieting the static noise of our unconscious and opening to, attuning to, aligning with, and being in full collaboration with the divine Spirit working in and through us. Always.

Every time we practice, we are being transformed into the likeness of what we hold in our hearts.

And we become more aware of this reality . . . *with practice.*

So as we practice, we and the spirit of God are setting us right so that the love of God can do its work in us, weaving together the broken places and revealing that part of us that can truly be awake like Jesus and can even be fully human like Jesus. And do "even greater things."[3]

I believe the centering pause practice that Jesus has taught us is a *sacrament* in the fullest sense of the Church's definition of one: it is "an outward and visible sign of an inward and invisible grace." This sacrament is nothing less than the key that can awaken us and equip us to live into our divine potential through the power and the love of God dwelling within us.

Since those first early days sitting in my living room chair with a big hardbound Bible in my lap and pencil in my hand, answering the monk's call to a deeper spiritual life, and then years later, sitting in my seminary's Eastern Christian spirituality class, enthralled with *metanoia* and *theosis* and the divine indwelling in each of us and in all things, I have wanted to find words that might somehow convince someone, anyone, everyone of the "secret beauty in their hearts,"[4] the light within that changes everything, the Love that will not let us go.

I do not know if the words in this book will fulfill that hope. But I do know there are some on this Earth who, when they do find a way to be quiet with God in their innermost selves, when they do find time to nurture the roots of their essence, they will discover their hidden wholeness. They will become truly awake and fully human, like Jesus.

As Thomas Merton says, "There is a hidden wholeness in all things."[5]

Always remember there is a hidden wholeness in *you.*

May we all be open to receive the grace to answer the call of the Divine within us—to be equipped to practice the centering pause of Jesus "so that we might become fully human" in the love of God.

Blessings, all.

Amen.

~ ~ ~

ACKNOWLEDGMENTS

I remember at the end of an especially full and exciting day of writing one of the chapters of *Practice the Pause*, I stood up from my desk, closed up my laptop, and said out loud, "Thanks, everybody!"

I laughed out loud at that unexpected exclamation, and I marveled at how it captured exactly how I felt on many days while writing *Practice the Pause*—that I was never really on my own here. So many people contributed to the writing of this book that there were some days I felt as though I was more the curator of this book than the writer of it.

So I would like to first express my gratitude to all the wisdom teachers who are a part of *Practice the Pause*—to those teachers who are here with us now and those who are beyond, those whose teachings are ancient and those whose teachings are fresh and new.

I am especially grateful for the intuition, hard work, confidence, and vision of Lisa Kloskin, my Broadleaf Books editor, and her remarkably talented Broadleaf Books team, who from the very start somehow knew this book was meant to be more than the short primer I had originally planned.

I am grateful for the many gifts of Christianne Squires, my book proposal "midwife," who gave me the confidence and assurance that I had a book in me and who enabled in both practical and perceptive ways a vision that had initially seemed impossible to be quite possible indeed.

I am grateful to Bridget Wingert, editor of the *Bucks County Herald*, who launched my writing vocation twelve years ago by saying yes to the vision of a bimonthly "*Mind & Spirit*" column in the *Herald*, and to Trent Gillis, former editor of *OnBeing.org*, along with the *On Being* team who published my first online essays and created an *On Being* author page for me that opened the way for future publications.

I am grateful to David Anderson, who dared the unorthodox hiring of this intentionally non-collared seminarian graduate to lead spiritual formation at Trinity Church, Solebury. It was when David looked at me and said the words "You are a writer" with such conviction and intention that I began to consider the possibility that such a thing might actually be true.

The seed for this book was initially planted at General Seminary in Professor Deirdre Good's class on the Gospel of Mark and in Professor David Keller's class on the Art of Contemplative Prayer. When I heard a presentation given by a fellow seminarian on the formative power of Jesus' presence in the lives of the disciples, I was inspired to write my thesis on the formative power of the practice of Presence in the life of Jesus himself. Professor Jonathan Linman suggested I follow up by writing a thesis-based book to spotlight "Jesus as a contemplative" to a greater audience. That nudge was a turning point, and I am very grateful.

I am grateful for Malika Cox, co-pastor of TheTableOKC, whose unquestioned belief in the power of what she herself describes as "Jesus' radically inclusive, self-giving love" fueled my confidence in speaking to the potential reconstructive power of *Practice the Pause* for those who are realigning their faith and understanding of the gospels while keeping Jesus of Nazareth as their mainstay.

I am grateful to Brian Allain, director of *Writing for Your Life*, for his devoted work to the success of writers of spiritual books. It is through Brian's *Writing for Your Life Spring 2021* conference that

I became aware of Broadleaf Books' vision of "expanding the mind, nourishing the soul, and cultivating the common good" and became hopeful that *Practice the Pause* might be a good fit.

I am grateful for the encouragement and care and editorial support of my friends Susan Wells and Henry Reath when the structure and vision of this book was in its earliest stages.

I am grateful for the love and inspiration of my soul friend Raymonde Djokic, one of the angels' own now, who is the closest to "being prayer" as anyone I have known. In her ninety-six years on this earth, Raymonde showed us through her inner joy, her constant prayer, and her love for all people what it looks like to live in Love itself.

I am beyond-words grateful to my husband, Reid, for his love and patience (and for those always-timely salted caramels) throughout this surprise year of writing and editing, and to my three daughters, Allie, Cat, and Susie, for their constant love and support (and our many met-the-deadline champagne & balloons celebrations); to Jack and Sue, my partners in joy throughout; to Kelly, who gave me the gift of telling me flat out, "Caroline, You Have To Write A Book About This"; to Aunt Sue, Cliff, Jeff, and Marion for their eternal and steadfast wing-mate belief in me; and to each one of my wonderfully close and "delight-full" family members—Margie, Wolfram, Jimmy and Jody, Jimmie, Tommy, Brendan, Ana, Sue and Brand, Malika, Marley, Sarah and David, Alisa and Don, Tysen and Julie, and Curt—who I treasure and who have given me steadfast affirmation and support in this extended writing adventure.

Finally, I am grateful for the love and support and encouragement of my dearest friends and for those souls in my life who have accompanied me in the *kairos* times and "thin places" that have opened the soul of me in ways I could never have imagined.

NOTES

Introduction

1. Walnut Street in Louisville, Kentucky, has since been named Muhammad Ali Boulevard.
2. Thomas Merton, *Conjectures of a Guilty Bystander* (New York, NY: Image Books, 1968), 155.
3. Matthew 13:16.
4. John 10:34.
5. Cynthia Bourgeault, *Wisdom Jesus: Transforming Heart and Mind* (Boston, MA: Shambhala, 2008), 19.
6. Bourgeault, *Wisdom Jesus,* chapter 62.
7. Philippians 2:5; it is notable that in an NRSV footnote this verse can read "let the same mind be in you that *you have* in Christ Jesus" and "have this mind among yourselves which is yours in Christ Jesus." https://www.biblegateway.com/passage/?search=Philippians+2&version=NRSV; accessed May 13, 2022.
8. Jim Forest, "Thomas Merton and Henri Nouwen: Western Explorers of the Christian East," Yale Divinity School Keynote Address, November 7, 2017. https://www.youtube.com/watch?v=dXNPEbrm7S8.
9. Merton, *Conjectures of a Guilty Bystander*, 153.
10. Bourgeault, *Wisdom Jesus,* 21.
11. The wisdom tradition is the perennial contemplative tradition in which are embedded the contemplative strands of the world's religious traditions. In Aldous Huxley's *The Perennial Philosophy*, vii, Huxley says the perennial tradition "may be found among the traditional lore of peoples in every region of the world, and in its fully developed forms it has a place in every one of the higher religions."

12. This sentence ending in "not only what I do but even greater things" is an imagined paraphrase of mine of the end of the John 14:12 verse—"will also do the works that I do and, in fact, will do greater works than these."
13. "See beyond your mind" is a closer translation of the original Greek *metanoia* than the mistranslated word "repent."
14. Mary Oliver, "Summer Day," in *House of Light: Poems*, ed. Mary Oliver (Boston, MA: Beacon Press, 1990), 60.
15. John 1:39.
16. Mindful Schools, Inc. transforms school communities by integrating mindfulness meditation into the everyday learning environment of K-12 schools: https://www.mindfulschools.org; accessed November 14, 2021.
17. Thomas Keating, *The Human Condition: Contemplation and Transformation* (New York, NY: Paulist Press, 1999), 23.
18. Thich Nhat Hanh, *Living Buddha, Living Christ* (New York, NY: Riverhead Books, 1995), 21.
19. Phileena Heuertz, "Contemplative Activism: Doing Good Better," *Gravity Center Newsletter*, December 2015.

Chapter 1: We Are Human, We Are Divine

1. Matthew 6:6.
2. Lawrence Cunningham, *Thomas Merton, Spiritual Master* (Mahwah, NJ: Paulist Press, 1992), 146.
3. Cynthia Bourgeault, *Centering Prayer and Inner Awakening* (New York: Cowley Publications, 2004), 13.
4. Richard Rohr, *Richard Rohr: Essential Teachings on Love* (Maryknoll, NY: Orbis Books, 2018), 71–72.
5. Bourgeault, *Wisdom Jesus*, 19.
6. John 8:12.
7. Matthew 5:14.
8. John Martin Sahajananda, *You Are the Light: Rediscovering the Eastern Jesus* (London: John Hunt Publishing, 2003), 157–158.
9. Bourgeault, *Wisdom Jesus*, 21.
10. Bourgeault, *Wisdom Jesus*, 21.
11. Acts 4:33.
12. Mitchell Clute, "Preface," in *Resurrecting Jesus: Embodying the Spirit of a Revolutionary Mystic*, ed. Adyashanti (Boulder, CO: Sounds True, 2016), xiii.

13. Adyashanti, *Resurrecting Jesus: Embodying the Spirit of a Revolutionary Mystic* (Boulder, CO: Sounds True, 2016), xviii.
14. Adyashanti, *Resurrecting Jesus: Embodying the Spirit of a Revolutionary Mystic*, xiv.
15. Bourgeault, *Wisdom Jesus*, 21.
16. Cynthia Bourgeault, *Wisdom Way of Knowing* (San Francisco: Jossey-Bass, 2003), 5.
17. Martin Luther King, Jr., "The Humanity and Divinity of Jesus," Stanford University, The Martin Luther King, Jr. Research and Education Institute, sourced from the Martin Luther King, Jr., Papers, 1954–1968, Howard Gottlieb Archival Research Center, Boston University, Boston, Massachusetts. https://kinginstitute.stanford.edu/king-papers/documents/humanity-and-divinity-jesus; accessed April 12, 2021.
18. King, Jr., "The Humanity and Divinity of Jesus."
19. Mark 1:35; Matthew 14:23; Mark 1:12–13.
20. Luke 22:39.
21. Luke 6:12.
22. Matthew 6:6, Bible Hub, Greek to English, *Biblos Interlinear Bible.* https://biblehub.com/greek/5009.htm; accessed November 14, 2021.
23. Ephesians 1:18.
24. Richard Rohr, "You Are the 'Imago Dei,'" *Center for Contemplation and Action Daily Meditations*, July 31, 2016.

Chapter 2: It's Not "Repent," It's *Metanoia*

1. Bourgeault, *Wisdom Jesus*, 41.
2. Robert N. Wilkin, "Repentance and Salvation," *Grace Evangelical Society* (Roanoke, TX: Biblical Studies Press, 1996). https://bibleresourceman.files.wordpress.com/2012/03/repentance-wilkin.pdf.
3. A. T. Robertson, *Word Pictures in the New Testament—2 Corinthians* (Grand Rapids, MO: Christian Classics Ethereal Library), November 14, 2014.
4. Robertson, *Word Pictures in the New Testament—Matthew.*
5. Bourgeault, *Wisdom Jesus*, 41.
6. Marcus Borg, *Listening for the Voice of God*, Lenten Noonday Preaching Series (Memphis, TN: Calvary Episcopal Church), March 17, 2003.
7. Edward J. Anton, *Repentance: A Cosmic Shift of Mind and Heart* (New York, NY: Discipleship Publications, 2005), 32–33.
8. *Luther's Works, Vol. 48, Letters* (May 30, 1518, Letter to John von Staupitz), 65–70.

9. Anton, *Repentance: A Cosmic Shift*, 32–33.
10. "Letter of John Staupitz Accompanying the 'Resolutions' to the XCV Theses by Dr. Martin Luther, 1518," *Works of Martin Luther*, ed. and trans. Adolph Spaeth, L. D. Reed, Henry Eyster Jacobs, et al. (Philadelphia, PA: A. J. Holman Company, 1915), volume 1, 39–43. https://en.wikipedia.org/wiki/Metanoia_(theology); accessed 1/14/22.
11. "Metanoia." *Merriam-Webster.com Dictionary*. https://www.merriam-webster.com/dictionary/metanoia; accessed March 16, 2021.
12. "Learn about the Orthodox Faith," *Introduction to Orthodoxy*, Greek Orthodox Church Archdiocese of America, August 19, 1995. https://www.goarch.org/-/repentance-and-confession-introduction.
13. Anton, *Repentance: A Cosmic Shift*, 33.
14. *BibleHub.com*; Interlinear Translation, English to Greek. https://biblehub.com/interlinear/matthew/3-2.htm; accessed May 13, 2022.
15. *BibleHub.com*; Interlinear Translation, English to Greek. https://biblehub.com/interlinear/mark/6-12.htm; accessed May 13, 2022.
16. *BibleHub.com*; Interlinear Translation, English to Greek. https://biblehub.com/interlinear/acts/17-30.htm; accessed May 13, 2022.
17. Petrushka Clarkson, *On Psychotherapy* (Lanham, MD: Jason Aaronson, Inc., 1993), 57.
18. R. Arp, *1001 Ideas That Changed the Way We Think* (New York, NY: Atria Books, 2013), 255.
19. Clarkson, *On Psychotherapy*, 56.
20. D. A. Leeming et al., *Encyclopedia of Psychology and Religion* (New York, NY: Springer, 3rd edition, 2020), 511.
21. Clarkson, *On Psychotherapy*, 63–64.
22. Bourgeault, *Wisdom Jesus*, 62–66.
23. Bourgeault, *Wisdom Jesus*, 41.
24. Bourgeault, *Wisdom Way of Knowing*, 5.

Chapter 3: The Jesus Formula: The Centering Pause Practice

1. Luke 22:39.
2. Thelma Hall, *Too Deep for Words: Rediscovering Lectio Divina* (New York, NY: Paulist Press, 1988), 13.
3. This well-known phrase is a reference to Paul's Philippians 2:5 directive to "Let the same mind be in you that is in Christ Jesus" and the Romans 13:14 directive to "Put on the Lord Jesus Christ."

4. Matthew 6:5–6.
5. Matthew 6:5–6.
6. Bible Hub, "Greek to English," *Biblos Interlinear Bible.* https://biblehub.com/greek/5009.htm.
7. Thomas Keating, *The Inner Room* (Sante Fe, NM: Center for Action and Contemplation, 2008), CD, disc 6.
8. Richard Rohr, *Dancing Standing Still: Healing the World from a Place of Prayer* (New York, NY: Paulist Press, 2014), 5–7.
9. Keating, *The Inner Room*, disc 6.
10. Richard Rohr, *Yes, and: Daily Meditations* (Cincinnati, OH: Franciscan Media, 2013), 407.
11. Richard Rohr, "Contemplation: A Life's Journey," *Contemplation and Action Daily Meditations: Contemplative Activists.* https://cac.org/contemplation-a-lifes-journey-2020-07-12; accessed July 12, 2020.
12. Rohr, "Contemplation."
13. Richard Rohr, "Joy in Contemplation," *Center for Contemplation and Action Daily Meditations: Joy and Hope.* https://cac.org/joy-in-contemplation-2018-11-28; accessed November 28, 2018.
14. Marsha Lucas, *Rewire Your Brain for Love: Creating Vibrant Relationships Using the Science of Mindfulness* (New York, NY: Hay House, Inc., 2012), 23.
15. Coleman Baker, "Between Stimulus and Response There Is a Space," *Medium.com*, January 24, 2018. https://medium.com/@colemanabaker/between-stimulus-and-response-there-is-a-space-ad5261e3c74.
16. John Parsons, "Be Still and Know I Am God," *Hebrew for Christians.* https://www.hebrew4christians.com/Meditations/Be_Still/be_still.html; accessed October 15, /2021.

Chapter 4: Wired for Transformation: Our Brain and Our Mind

1. Andrew Newberg and Mark Robert Waldman, *How God Changes Your Brain, Breakthrough Findings From a Leading Neuroscientist* (New York, NY: Ballantine Books, 2010), 34.
2. Paul MacLean, *The Triune Brain in Evolution: Role in Paleocerebral Functions* (New York, NY: Springer, 1990), 14.
3. Dan Siegel, *Mindsight, The New Science of Personal Transformation* (New York, NY: Bantam Books, 2010), 15.

4. Jaak Panksepps, *Affective Neuroscience: The Foundations of Human and Animal Emotions* (New York, NY: Oxford University Press, 1998), 43.
5. Newberg and Waldman, *How God Changes the Brain*, 17.
6. Michael J. Formica, "Neuroplasticity: The Revolution in Neuroscience and Psychology, Part I," *Psychology Today*, June 30, 2008.
7. Formica, "Neuroplasticity."
8. Karen Feldscher, "Training Your Mind to Improve Well-Being," *Harvard T. H. Chan School of Public Health News*, November 6, 2018.
9. Christina Congleton, Britta Hölzel, and Sara Lazar, "Mindfulness Can Literally Change Your Brain," *Harvard Business Review*, January 8, 2015.
10. Congleton, Hölzel, and Lazar, "Mindfulness."
11. Britta K. Hölzel, James Carmody, Mark Vangela, Christina Congleton, Sita M. Yerramsettia, Tim Gard, and Sara W. Lazar, "Mindfulness Practice Leads to Increases in Regional Brain Gray Matter Density," *Psychiatry Research: Neuroimaging* 191 (2011): 36–43.
12. Daniel J. Seigel, *The Mindful Brain: Reflection and Attunement in the Cultivation of Well-Being* (New York, NY: W.W. Norton and Company), 2007.
13. Lucas, *Rewire Your Brain*, 23.
14. Hölzel et al., "Mindfulness Practice Leads to Increases in Regional Brain Gray Matter Density."
15. Lucas, *Rewire Your Brain*, 23.
16. Lucas, *Rewire Your Brain*, 44.
17. Schwartz and Begley, *The Mind & The Brain*, 368.
18. Feldscher, *Harvard T. H. Chan School of Public Health News*.
19. J. A. Brefczynski-Lewis, Antoine Lutz, H. S. D. Schaefer, D. Levinson, and R. Davidson, "Neural Correlates of Attentional expertise in long-term meditation practitioners," *Proceedings of the National Academy of Sciences of the United States of America*, 2007.
20. Denise Ryan, "By 2050, Mental Exercise Will Be as Important as Physical: Neuroscientist," *National Post*, September 30, 2009.
21. Hugh Delehanty, "The Science of Meditation," *Mindful Magazine*, December 13, 2017.
22. Newberg and Waldman, *How God Changes Your Brain*, 17.
23. "An Interview with Thomas Keating," *Garrison Institute Newsletter*, 3.

Chapter 5: Flipping Your Lid: A Close-Up Look

1. Siegel, *Mindsight, The New Science of Personal Transformation*, 14.
2. Siegel, *Mindsight*, 21.
3. Siegel, *Mindsight*, 22.

4. Lucas, *Rewire Your Brain*, 24.
5. Siegel, *Mindsight*, 26. (Siegel's hand/brain model is fully explained between pages 14 and 22.)
6. Siegel, *Mindsight*, 22.
7. Marc Dingman, *Know Your Brain: Amygdala*. https://neuroscientificallychallenged.com/posts/know-your-brain-amygdala; accessed December 8, 2021.
8. Siegel, *Mindsight*, 18.
9. Seigel, *Mindsight*, 18.
10. Bourgeault, *Wisdom Jesus*, 62–66.
11. Seigel, *Mindsight*, 61.
12. Lucas, *Rewire Your Brain*, 96.
13. Lucas, *Rewire Your Brain*, 49.
14. Hölzel et al., "Mindfulness Practice Leads to Increases in Regional Brain Gray Matter Density."
15. Yi-Yuan Tang, Qilin Lu, Hongbo Feng, Rongxiang Tang, and Michael I. Posner, "Short-term meditation increases blood flow in anterior cingulate cortex and insula," *Frontier Psychology*, February 26, 2015. https://doi.org/10.3389/fpsyg.2015.00212.
16. Scott Seckel, "Meditation for a New You in the New Year," *ASU News* (Arizona State University, 2021). https://news.asu.edu/20211228-discoveries-meditation-new-you-new-year.
17. Lucas, *Rewire Your Brain*, 23.
18. Bourgeault, *Centering Prayer and Inner Awakening*, 23, 114.
19. Yi-Yuan Tang, "Body-Mind Meditation Can Boost Attention and Health, Lower Stress," *Newswise: Texas Tech University*, July 18, 2016. https://www.newswise.com/articles/body-mind-meditation-can-boost-attention-and-health-lower-stress.
20. Lucas, *Rewire Your Brain*, 49.
21. Lazar and Hölzel, 2011. Also: Britta K. Hölzel, James Carmody, Karleyton C. Evans, Elizabeth A. Hoge, Jeffery A. Dusek, Lucas Morgan, Roger K. Pitman, and Sara W. Lazar, "Stress Reduction Correlates with Structural Changes in the Amygdala," *Social Cognitive and Affective Neuroscience* 5 (2009): 11.
22. Lucas, *Rewire Your Brain*, 64.
23. Sara Panton, "This is Your Brain on Yoga," *Medium*, June 9, 2016.
24. Siegel, *Mindsight*, 61.
25. Siegel, *Mindsight*, 61.
26. Lucas, *Rewire Your Brain*, 84.

27. Jill Bolte Taylor, *Whole Brain Living: The Anatomy of Choice and the Four Characters That Drive Our Life* (Carlsbad, CA: Hay House, 2021), 264.
28. Lazar and Hölzel, "Mindfulness Practice Leads to Increases in Regional Brain Gray Matter Density."
29. Kabat-Zinn, Jon, *Full Catastrophe Living: Using the Wisdom of Your Body and Mind to Face Stress, Pain, and Illness* (New York, NY: Bantam Books), 2000, 2015. This book is an excellent source for more information about MBSR.
30. Lazar and Hölzel, 2011.
31. Congleton, Hölzel, Lazar, *Harvard Business Review*.
32. Congleton, Hölzel, Lazar, *Harvard Business Review*.

Chapter 6: Contemplative Neuroscience: Confessions of a Closet Meditator

1. Gates et al., "Interview with Richard Davidson."
2. Kathy Gilsinan, "The Buddhist and the Neuroscientist," *Atlantic Monthly*, July 4, 2015.
3. Barbara Gates, Margaret Cullen, and Wes Nisker, "Interview with Richard Davidson, Daniel Goleman & Jon Kabat-Zinn: Friends in Mind, Friends at Heart," *Inquiring Mind* 25, no. 2 (Spring 2009).
4. Gilsinan, "The Buddhist and the Neuroscientist."
5. Sharon Begley, *The Plastic Mind: New Science Reveals Our Extraordinary Potential to Transform Ourselves* (New York, NY: Ballantine Books, 2007), 11.
6. Daniel Goleman, "Preface," in Begley, *The Plastic Mind*, xii.
7. Goleman, "Preface," xiii.
8. Richard Davidson and Antoine Lutz, NCBI, "Buddha's Brain: Neuroplasticity and Meditation," *IEEE Signal Processing Magazine* 25, no. 1 (2008): 176–174.
9. Lutz, Brefczynski, Johnstone, and Davidson, 2008.
10. Ryan J. Foley, "Scientist Inspired by Dalai Lama Studies," *Associated Press*, May 14, 2010.
11. Lauren Effron, "Neuroscientist Richie Davidson Says Dalai Lama Gave Him 'a Total Wake-Up Call' That Changed His Research Forever," *ABC News*, July 27, 2016.
12. Effron, "Neuroscientist Richie Davidson."
13. Begley, *The Plastic Mind*, 316.

14. Michael Spezio, "Forming Identities in Grace: *Imitatio* and Habitus as Contemporary Categories for the Sciences of Mindfulness and Virtue," *Ex Auditu: An International Journal for the Theological Interpretation of Scripture: Science and Religion*, Volume 32, 2016, 128. Spezio is referencing these articles: Pieris, "Spirituality as Mindfulness"; Bernard McGinn, "Love, Knowledge, and Mystical Union in Western Christianity: Twelfth to Sixteenth Centuries," *Church History* 56 (1987), 7–24.
15. Spezio, "Forming Identities," 129.

Chapter 7: The Spiritual and the Secular: It's about Connection

1. Stephanie Derais and Daniel Gutierrez, "The Influence of Spiritual Transcendence on a Centering Meditation: A Growth Curve Analysis of Resilience," *Religions*, 2021.
2. Jesse Fox, Daniel Gutierrez, Jessica Haas, and Dinesh J. Braganza, "A Phenomenological Investigation of Centering Prayer Using Conventional Content Analysis," *Pastoral Psychology*, May 2015.
3. Fox et al., "A Phenomenological Investigation."
4. Fox et al., "A Phenomenological Investigation."
5. Denis Larrivee and Luis Echarte, "Contemplative Meditation and Neuroscience: Prospects for Mental Health," *Journal of Religion and Health* 57, no. 3 (2018), 960–978.
6. Gates et al., "Interview with Richard Davidson."
7. Jeffrey M. Schwartz and Rebecca Gladding, *You Are Not Your Brain: The 4-Step Solution for Changing Bad Habits, Ending Unhealthy Thinking, and Taking Control of Your Life* (New York, NY: Penguin Group, 2011).
8. Rev. Dr. John Polkinghorne, "Where God Meets Physics," Faraday Institute for Science and Religion, University of Cambridge, November 28, 2011. https://www.cam.ac.uk/research/discussion/where-god-meets-physics.
9. Polkinghorne, "Where God Meets Physics."
10. Goleman, "Preface," xii.
11. Jeffrey Schwartz, "Mindful Awareness and Self-Directed Neuroplasticity: Integrating Psychospiritual and Biological Approaches to Mental Health." *Jeffrey Schwartz Information Series* (2005), 3.
12. Schwartz, "Mindful Awareness and Self-Directed Neuroplasticity," 3.
13. Schwartz and Gladding, *You Are Not Your Brain*.

14. Jeffrey M. Schwartz, "Being Mindful and Changing Your Brain: Jeffrey Schwartz on Mindfulness," *Biola University Center for Christian Thought: The Table Conference,* January 2014.
15. Karen Armstrong, *Muhammad: A Biography of the Prophet,* Harper One, April 1992, p. 224.

Chapter 8: Jesus the Rabbi: First-Century Jewish Spirituality

1. Bourgeault, *Wisdom Way of Knowing,* 5.
2. Elizabeth Palmer, "Knowing and Preaching the Jewish Jesus: Elizabeth Palmer Interviews Amy Jill-Levine," *Christian Century,* March 13, 2019. https://www.christiancentury.org/article/interview/knowing-and-preaching-jewish-jesus; accessed 1.11.2021.
3. Mark 12:29.
4. Rabbi Wayne Dosick, *Living Judaism: The Complete Guide to Jewish Belief, Tradition, and Practice* (New York, NY: HarperCollins Publishers, 1995), 228.
5. Deuteronomy 6:4–9.
6. Lev Gillet, *Communion in the Messiah: Studies in the Relationship between Judaism and Christianity* (Cambridge, England: Lutterworth Press, 2002), 132.
7. Mark 12:31.
8. "Matthew Henry's Commentary on the Whole Bible—Matthew 22," Mhcw.biblecommenter.com. Archived from the original on 2013-03-11. Retrieved 2013-03-28.
9. Matthew 22:39–40.
10. Julian of Norwich, *Showings* (Mahwah, NJ: Paulist Press, 1978), 309. and Richard Rohr, *Oneing: The Perennial Tradition,* ed. Vanessa Guerin (Albequerque, NM: Franciscan Media, 2014), i.
11. J. S. Banks, "Jesus at Prayer," in *The Expository Times, Volume 11,* ed. James Hastings (Edinburgh: T.T. Clark, 1900), 270.
12. Nissan Mindel, "The Three Daily Prayers," *Chabad.org* (Kehot Publication Society). https://www.chabad.org/library/article_cdo/aid/682091/jewish/The-Three-Daily-Prayers.htm; accessed 1.4.2021.
13. Mindel, "The Three Daily Prayers."
14. Numbers 6:24–26.
15. Gillet, *Communion in the Messiah,* 133.

16. W. Corswant, *A Dictionary of Life in Bible Times* (New York, NY: Oxford University Press, 1960), 218.
17. Banks, "Jesus at Prayer," 270.
18. Thomas Kelly Cheyne and John Sutherland Black, *Encyclopaedia Biblica* (London: MacMillan Company, 2003), 2996.
19. Louis Jacobs, *The Jewish Religion: A Companion* (New York: Oxford University Press, 1995), 198.
20. Cheyne and Black, *Encyclopaedia Biblica*, 2996.
21. Berakhot, 31a.
22. Asher Finkel, "Prayer in Jewish Life of the First Century as Background to Early Christianity," in *Into God's Presence: Prayer in the New Testament*, ed. Richard N. Longenecker (Grand Rapids, MI: William B. Eerdmans Publishing Company, 2002), 47.
23. DovBer Pinson, *Meditation and Judaism: Exploring the Jewish Meditative Paths* (Lanham, MD: Rowman & Littlefield Publishers, 2004), 4.
24. Bourgeault, *Centering Prayer and Inner Awakening*, 13.
25. David Anderson, *Breakfast Epiphanies: Finding Wonder in the Everyday* (New York: NY, Beacon Press, 2002).
26. Frost and Hirsch, *The Shaping of Things to Come: Innovation and Mission for the 21st Century Church* (Grand Rapids, MI: Baker Books, 2013), 130.
27. Rabbi Rachel Barenblat, "A Short History of Jewish Meditation," *Velveteen Rabbi*, February 10, 2014. https://velveteenrabbi.blogs.com/blog/2014/02/jewish-meditation.html; accessed 11/14/2021.
28. Barenblat, "A Short History of Jewish Meditation."
29. Berakhot 5:1.

Chapter 9: The Call of the Natural World in Jesus' Time and Now

1. Loorz, 89.
2. James D. G. Dunn, *Christology in the Making: A New Testament Inquiry Into the Origins of the Incarnation* (Grand Rapids, MI: Wm B. Eerdmans Publishing Company, 2003), 136.
3. Victoria Loorz, *Church of the Wild: How Nature Invites Us into the Sacred* (Minneapolis, MN: Broadleaf Books, 2012), 114.
4. Loorz, *Church of the Wild*, 118.
5. Loorz, *Church of the Wild*, 61.
6. Loorz, *Church of the Wild*, 61.

7. Loorz, *Church of the Wild*, 61.
8. Loorz, *Church of the Wild*.
9. Leah Rampy and Carole Crumley, "Thin Places: Openings to the Sacred," *Shalem Institute Newsletter*, October 2021.
10. Eric Weiner, "Where Heaven and Earth Come Closer," *New York Times*, March 9, 2012.
11. Weiner, "Where Heaven and Earth Come Closer."
12. Dunn, *Christology in the Making*, 136.
13. Daniel J. Harrington and John R. Donahue, *Sacra Pagina Series, Volume 2, The Gospel of Mark* (Collegeville, MN: The Liturgical Press, 2002), 212.
14. Dunn, *Christology in the Making*, 317.
15. Exodus 40.35, Genesis 9:27, 14:13, Psalm 37:3, Jeremiah 33:16.
16. Lea Sestieri, "The Jewish Roots of the Holy Spirit," *Jubilee Magazine* (a Vatican document), 2000. https://www.vatican.va/jubilee_2000/magazine/documents/ju_mag_01021998_p-24_en.html; accessed 11/14/2021.
17. Michael E. Lodahl, *Shekhinah Spirit: Divine Presence in Jewish and Christian Religion* (Mahwah, NJ: Paulist Press, 1992), 51.
18. Johann Jakob Herzog and Philip Schaff, *The New Schaff-Herzog Encyclopedia of Religious Thought* (Funk and Wagnalls, 1911), 389.
19. "Guide For a Correct Presentation of Jews and the Jewish Religion in the Preaching and Catechesis of the Catholic Church," *Catechism of the Catholic Church*, Vatican City, 1994.
20. Sestieri, *Jubilee Magazine*, 2000.
21. Mark 6:30–32.
22. Matthew 6:33.

Chapter 10: Time Alone with God: Jesus Practicing the Pause

1. Barbara Brown Taylor, *The Luminous Web: Essays on Science and Religion* (New York, NY: Cowley Publications, 2000), 51.
2. Taylor, *The Luminous Web*, 73–74.
3. John 14:12.
4. Annie Lamott, "viral" Facebook post, posted April 8, 2015; www. facebook.com/AnneLamott.
5. Greek Concordance, *BibleHub.com*. https://biblehub.com/greek/2048.htm; accessed 1/11/21.
6. Victoria Loorz, *Church of the Wild: How Nature Invites Us into the Sacred* (Minneapolis, MN: Broadleaf Books, 2012), 62–63.

7. Loorz, *Church of the Wild*, 65.
8. Matthew 1:14.
9. Mark 1:32.
10. BibleStudyTools.com. https://www.biblestudytools.com/lexicons/greek/nas/proi.html; accessed 1/10/21.
11. BibleStudyTools.com.
12. Matthew 14:13.
13. Matthew 6:6.
14. Luke 21:37–38.
15. Dunn, *Christology in the Making*, 136.
16. Harrington and Donahue, *Sacra Pagina Series—Mark*, 212.
17. Luke 6:12–13.
18. Luke 5:15–16.
19. Luke 50.
20. Matthew 26:38.
21. Mark 14:35.
22. Luke 22:44.

Chapter 11: Contemplation in Action: Jesus Practicing off the Mat

1. Acts 1:12–14.
2. Luke 24:33.
3. Howard Thurman, *Meditations of the Heart* (Boston, MA: Beacon Press, 1999), 173–174.
4. Harrington and Donahue, *Sacra Pagina Series*, 87.
5. Matthew 18:20.
6. Howard Marshall, "Jesus—Example and Teacher of Prayer in the Synoptic Gospels," *Into God's Presence: Prayer in the New Testament*, ed. Richard N. Longenecker (Grand Rapids, MI: William B. Eerdmans Publishing Company, 2002), 116.
7. Louis Jacobs, *The Jewish Religion: A Companion* (New York: Oxford University Press, 1995), 198.
8. John 6:23.
9. This is a reference to a quote by an anonymous third-century monk, quoted by Keith Kristich in a *Closer Than Breath* group discussion.
10. Richard Rohr, *The Universal Christ: How a Forgotten Reality Can Change Everything We See, Hope For and Believe* (New York, NY: Convergent Books, 2021), 5.

11. Thich Nhat Hanh, *Living Buddha, Living Christ* (New York, NY: Riverhead Books, 2007), 31.
12. Douay-Rheims Bible, 1 Corinthians 11:25.
13. Patrick D. Miller, *They Cried to the Lord: The Form and Theology of Biblical Prayer* (Minneapolis, MN: Fortress Press, 1994), 47.
14. Psalm 22:24.
15. Psalm 31.5.
16. Luke 23:34.

Chapter 12: Between Fight and Flight: The Revolutionary Third Way of Jesus

1. Luke 11:1.
2. Marshall, "Jesus—Example and Teacher," 116.
3. Ched Myers, *Binding the Strong Man: A Political Reading of Mark's Story of Jesus* (Maryknoll, NY: Orbis Books 2006), 256.
4. Matthew 26:40.
5. Luke 21:44.
6. Matthew 26:41 NCV.
7. Acts 1:14.
8. Lynn C. Bauman, *Luminous Gospels: Thomas, Mary Magdalene and Philip* (Praxis, 2008).
9. Cynthia Bourgeault, *The Meaning of Mary Magdalene: Discovering the Woman at the Heart of Christianity* (Boston, MA: Shambhala Publications, 2010), 55.
10. Walter Wink, *Jesus and Nonviolence: A Third Way* (Minneapolis, MN: Augsburg Fortress: 2003).
11. Matthew 5:44; Luke 6:27.
12. Matthew 5:39; Luke 6:29.
13. Matthew 18:22.
14. John 8:7.
15. Matthew 6:28.
16. Matthew 7:3.
17. Luke 5:10, 8:50, 12:7, 12:32.
18. Bourgeault, *Wisdom Jesus*, 63.
19. Acts 9:13.
20. Acts 9:18.
21. Jewel Kilcher, "Standing Still," *This Way*, album release October 2001.
22. Luke 24:36.

23. Matthew 28:10.
24. Walter Wink, *The Powers That Be: Theology for a New Millennium* (New York, NY: Doubleday, 1999), 99.
25. John Lewis, US Congressman, Twitter, June 2018, two years before he died.
26. Martin Luther King, Jr., sermon delivered at Dexter Avenue Baptist Church in Montgomery, Alabama (Christmas 1957), written in the Montgomery jail during the bus boycott. Reprinted in the A. J. Muste Essay Series, number 1 (A. J. Muste Memorial Institute, 339 Lafayette St., New York, NY 10012).
27. Richard Rohr, "The Third Way," *Center for Action and Contemplation Daily Meditations*, August 20, 2019.
28. Matthew 7:14.
29. Walter Wink, *Jesus and Nonviolence: A Third Way* (Minneapolis, MN: Augsburg Fortress, 2003), chapter 5.
30. 1 Thessalonians 5:16.
31. Center for Action and Contemplation website. https://cac.org/about/who-we-are/; accessed March 15, 2022.
32. Lori Deschene, *Tiny Buddha: Simple Wisdom for Life's Hard Questions* (San Francisco, CA: Conari Press, 2011).
33. Matthew 6:33.
34. Cynthia Bourgeault, *Contemplative Prayer and Inner Awakening* (New York, NY: Cowley Publications, 2004), 82.
35. Bourgeault, *Contemplative Prayer*, 94.
36. Bourgeault, *Contemplative Prayer*, 96.
37. Bourgeault, *Contemplative Prayer*, 122.
38. Brian C. Taylor, "Changing Your Mind: Contemplative Prayer and Personal Transformation," in *Spirituality, Contemplation & Transformation: Writings on Centering Prayer* (New York, NY: Lantern Books, 2008), 286.

Chapter 13: Ancient/New Teachers: The Desert Mothers and Fathers

1. Roberta Bondi, *To Love as God Loves: Conversations with the Early Church* (Minneapolis, MN: Fortress Press, 1987).
2. Douglas Burton-Christie, *Word in the Desert: Scripture and the Quest for Holiness in Early Christian Monasticism* (New York, NY: Oxford University Press, 1993), 261.
3. Laura Swan, *The Forgotten Desert Mothers: Sayings, Lives, and Stories of Early Christian Women* (New York, NY: Paulist Press, 2001), 10.

4. This description of Jesus was inspired by Rev. Nancy Dilliplane's 8/15/21 sermon, offered here with her permission.
5. This presentation of Jesus was inspired by a Sunday sermon by Rev. Nancy R. Dilliplane, offered at Trinity Buckingham Church, Doylestown, PA, 8/15/21, printed here with permission.
6. Luke 17:21.
7. Bondi, *To Love as God Loves*, 17.
8. Ephesians 4:22.
9. Thomas Merton, *The Wisdom of the Desert* (New York, NY: New Directions Publishing Corporation 1970), 30.
10. Kallistos Ware, *The Inner Kingdom* (Crestwood, NY: St Vladimir's Seminary Press, 2000), 101.
11. John Cassian, *John Cassian: Conferences (Classics of Western Spirituality)* (New York, NY: Paulist Press, 1985), 131.
12. Henri Nouwen and Yushi Nomura, *Desert Wisdom: Sayings from the Desert Fathers* (Maryknoll, NY: Orbis Books, 2000), 114–115.
13. Merton, *The Wisdom of the Desert*, 8.
14. Ephesians 4:14–24.
15. Evagrius Ponticus, trans. John Eudes Bamburger OCSO, *The Praktikos & Chapters on Prayer* (Kalamazoo, MI: Cistercian Publications, 1981), lxxxi.
16. William Harmless, *Mystics* (Oxford: Oxford University Press, 2008), 149.
17. Ponticus, *The Praktikos: Chapters on Prayer*, lxxxiii.
18. Harmless, *Mystics*, 148.
19. Bourgeault, *Centering Prayer and Inner Awakening*, 166.

Chapter 14: Just Being with God

1. Ephesians 4:1.
2. Jane Woods, "Waking House," Instagram post, January 11, 2022.
3. Thomas Keating, "The Process of Awakening," *Contemplative Outreach News* 38, no. 2 (June 2021), a republished article from June 2016.
4. Kristich, *Closer Than Breath*.
5. The version of this Rumi quote that we most often see is "You are not a drop in the ocean. You are the entire ocean in a drop." There is no available citation for that version. This more correct version can be found here: Lassaâd Metoui, *Love: The Joy That Wounds: The Love Poems of Rumi* (London: Profile Books, 2017), 27.
6. I am indebted to Jill Benet, a leader in the contemplative prayer community, for this insight, as presented in the Centering Prayer Summit on

January 15, 2022, hosted by Keith Kristich, founder of the online *Closer Than Breath* community.

Chapter 15: Reading with God: When Scripture Shimmers

1. Cynthia Bourgeault offered this observation at the January 15, 2022, *Closer Than Breath* online summit.
2. Rev. Dr. Virginia Sheay, Trinity Church, Solebury, PA.
3. Kristich, *Closer Than Breath*. https://closerthanbreath.com.
4. Maria Popova, "Waking Up: David Whyte and the Power of Poetry and Silence as a Portal to Presence," *Marginalian*, April 30, 2021. https://www.themarginalian.org/2021/04/30/david-whyte-silence-poetry-waking-up.
5. Marjorie Thompson, "Praying the Scriptures," *The Meeting God Bible: Growing in Intimacy with God through Scripture* (Nashville, TN: Upper Room Books, 2013); *SoulFeast: An Invitation to the Christian Spiritual Life* (Louisville, KY: Westminster Knox, 1999).
6. Christine Valters Paintner, "Monks in Our Midst: Christine Valters Paintner on Lectio Divina As a Lived Practice," *Monasteries of the Heart: An Online Movement Sharing Benedictine Spirituality With Contemporary Seekers*. https://www.monasteriesoftheheart.org/monks-our-midst/christine-valters-paintner-lectio-divina-life-practice.
7. Jonathan Linman, *Holy Conversation: Spirituality for Worship* (Minneapolis, MN: Fortress Press, 2010).
8. James Ford, "Of Richard Hooker, His Three-Legged Stool, and a Dream for a Progressive Zen Buddhist," *Patheos: Monkey Mind, Easily Distracted*, November 3, 2021. https://www.patheos.com/blogs/monkeymind/2021/11/of-richard-hooker-his-three-legged-stool-and-a-dream-for-a-progressive-zen-buddhism.html.
9. Ford, "Of Richard Hooker."

Chapter 16: The New *Lectio*: Noticing and the Seven-Second Pause

1. Deborah Arca, "Seeing with the Eyes of the Heart: A Q&A with Christine Valters Paintner," *Patheos*, May 31, 2013.
2. Arca, "Seeing with the Eyes of the Heart."

3. Paintner, "Monks in Our Midst."
4. Paintner, "Monks in Our Midst."
5. Paintner, "Monks in Our Midst."
6. Chade-Meng Tan, "Just Six Seconds of Mindfulness Can Make You More Effective," *Harvard Business Review: Emotional Intelligence*, December 30, 2015.
7. A suggestion I recall Cynthia Bourgeault offering at one of her Wisdom Schools.
8. Carmen Acevedo Butcher, *Practice of the Presence: A Revolutionary Translation* (Minneapolis, MN: Broadleaf Books, 2022), 11.
9. "Listen carefully, my son, and listen to the master's instructions, and attend to them with the ear of your heart" is the first line of the Rule of St. Benedict.

   Timothy Fry, OSB, ed., *The Rule of St. Benedict* (New York, NY: Vintage Books), 3.
10. Thomas Keating, Centering Prayer and Lectio Divina with Thomas Keating, Part 1, Lectio Divina Institute Conference, Benedictine Center, Beech Grove, Indiana, January 1997. https://www.youtube.com/watch?v=q7igrkA8OCw&t=0s.

Chapter 17: The Centering Pause: Nourishing the Roots of Our Essence

1. *The Book of Common Prayer and Administration of the Sacraments of the Church* (New York, NY: Church Publishing, 1979), 832.
2. We can sometimes sense that same full and centering pause between spoken words, often in poetry, and between certain notes of music. I've noticed this also happens in music. Listen to the pause just before the final "Amen" of Handel's *Messiah*. You will see what I mean!
3. Keating, *Open Mind, Open Heart*, 44.
4. Psalm 78:39.
5. *Church of the Wild.*
6. Barbara Crafton, "Retreats: How to Lead Them," *General Theological Seminary* coursework, 2010.
7. Naomi Shihab Nye, "Rising to Your Best Self: Naomi Shihab Nye with Krista Tippett," *On Being Wisdom App* "Hope Is a Muscle, I" course. https://onbeing.org/wisdom; accessed April 20, 2022.

8. Krista Tippett, "Write Things Down: Guided by Krista," *On Being Wisdom App* pause ritual. https://onbeing.org/wisdom/; accessed April 20, 2022.
9. David Frenette, *The Path of Centering Prayer: Deepening Your Experience of God* (Boulder, CO: Sounds True, 2012), xix.
10. Kristich, "*Closer Than Breath* course." https://closerthanbreath.com.
11. David Whyte, "Silence," *Consolations: The Solace, Nourishment, and Underlying Meaning of Everyday Words* (Langley, WA: Many Rivers Press, 2014), 156.
12. Whyte, "Silence," 156.
13. Susan Cole, Spiritual Director, Chestnut Hill, PA.
14. Henri Nouwen, *Walking With Henri Nouwen: A Reflective Journey* (New York, NY: Paulist Press, 2003), 40.
15. Thomas Keating, *Human Condition*, 33.
16. Joseph G. Sandman, "Centering Prayer: A Treasure for the Soul," *America: The Jesuit Review*, September 9, 2000.
17. Sandman, "Centering Prayer."
18. Andrew Travers, "How Thomas Keating Launched a Global Interfaith Movement from a Snowmass Monastery," *Aspen Times*, October 31, 2019.
19. Sandman, "Centering Prayer."
20. Daniel P. Horan, "Why Should Anyone Care About Thomas Merton Today?" *National Catholic Reporter*, December 10, 2018.
21. For the conceptual formatting of this section on Thomas Merton, I am indebted to Sandman of "Centering Prayer."
22. Andrew Travers, "How Thomas Keating Launched a Global Interfaith Movement from a Snowmass Monastery," *Aspen Times*, October 31, 2019.
23. Sandman, "Centering Prayer."
24. Sandman, "Centering Prayer."
25. Keating, *Open Mind, Open Heart*, 127.
26. Sandman, "Centering Prayer."
27. Phileena Heuertz, *Mindful Silence: The Heart of Christian Contemplation* (Downers Grove, IL: Intervarsity Press, 2018), 14.
28. Thomas Keating, Centering Prayer and Lectio Divina with Thomas Keating, Part 1, Lectio Divina Institute Conference, Benedictine Center, Beech Grove, Indiana, January 1997. https://www.youtube.com/watch?v=q7igrkA8OCw&t=0s.
29. Cynthia Bourgeault, *The Heart of Centering Prayer: Nondual Christianity in Theory and in Practice* (Boulder, CO: Shambhala), 38.

30. Sandman, "Centering Prayer."
31. Keating, *Open Mind, Open Heart*, 58.
32. Chris Ravendal, Pendle Hill instructor of "Prayer with No Strings Attached," 1995.
33. Bourgeault, *Centering Prayer and Inner Awakening*, 39–40, 119.
34. Spiritual director and bereavement counselor Inez Bing, Bucks County, PA.
35. Thomas Keating, "Centering Prayer and Lectio Divina with Thomas Keating, Part 1," Lectio Divina Institute Conference, Benedictine Center, Beech Grove, Indiana, January 1997. https://www.youtube.com/watch?v=q7igrkA8OCw&t=0s.

Chapter 18: Centering Prayer: Divine Therapy for the Human Condition

1. This is a phrase from Thomas Merton's epic poem "Hagia Sophia" published in 1962—There is in all visible things an invisible fecundity, a dimmed light, a meek namelessness, a hidden wholeness. This mysterious Unity and Integrity is Wisdom, the Mother of all, Natura naturans. There is in all things an inexhaustible sweetness and purity, a silence that is a fountain of action and of joy. It rises up in wordless gentleness and flows out to me from the unseen roots of all created being. . . ." Christopher Pramuck, *Sophia: The Hidden Christ of Thomas Merton* (Collegeville, MN: Liturgical Press, 2009), 193.
2. Parker Palmer, *Hidden Wholeness: The Journey Toward an Undivided Life* (San Francisco, CA: Jossey-Bass, 2009), 2.
3. Thomas Keating, *Intimacy With God* (New York, NY: Crossroad Publishing, 2009), chapter 9.
4. Keating, *The Human Condition*, 29.
5. Richard Rohr, "The Unconscious," *Center for Contemplation and Action*, December 14, 2018. https://cac.org/the-unconscious-2018-12-14.
6. Fr. Thomas Keating, "The Beatitudes: Healing the Emotional Programs, Part 1," *The Spiritual Journey Part 4, Contemplation: The Divine Therapy*. https://www.contemplativeoutreach.org/course/61-the-beatitudes-healing-the-emotional-programs-part-1; accessed May 13, 2022.
7. I am indebted to contemplative leader Tia Norman and her presentation on Keating's psychological model at the January 2022 *Closer than Breath* Centering Prayer Summit which refreshed my memory and my

conference notes from 2006. Tia Norman serves as pastor of the Awakenings Movement and curator of the Life Design Academy in Houston, Texas. She is the author of *Giving Up Mediocrity: A 40-Day Fast Toward Living a Crazy Fulfilled Life.*

8. Thomas Keating, *Fruits and Gifts of the Spirit* (New York, NY: Lantern Books, 2000), 26.
9. Fr. Thomas Keating, "The Beatitudes: Healing the Emotional Programs, Part 1," *The Spiritual Journey Part 4, Contemplation: The Divine Therapy.* https://www.contemplativeoutreach.org/course/61-the-beatitudes-healing-the-emotional-programs-part-1.
10. Keating, *Human Condition*, 25.
11. Keating, *Human Condition*, 25.
12. Richard Rohr, "Transforming Pain," *Contemplation and Action Daily Meditations*, October 17, 2018. https://cac.org/transforming-pain-2018-10-17.
13. Richard Rohr, "The Unconscious," *Center for Contemplation and Action*, December 14, 2018.
14. Thomas Keating, "Dismantling the Emotional Programs, Part 2, with Thomas Keating," *Contemplative Outreach YouTube Channel*, April 13, 2018. https://www.youtube.com/watch?v=uRFK8H-eiDM.
15. Keating, *Human Condition*, 32.
16. Keating, "Dismantling the Emotional Programs."
17. Thomas Keating, *Invitation to Love: The Way of Christian Contemplation* (New York, NY: Continuum Publishing, 1994), 128.
18. Thomas Keating, *On Divine Therapy* (New York, NY: Lantern Books, 2012), Kindle Edition.
19. "An Interview with Thomas Keating," *Garrison Institute Newsletter*, November 2008, 3–5.
20. Thomas Keating, *Divine Therapy and Addiction: Centering Prayer and the Twelve Steps* (New York, NY: Lantern Books, 2009), 106.
21. Keating, *Divine Therapy and Addiction*, 106.
22. Keating, *Human Condition*, 36.
23. Sandra L. Logan, author of *Sophia's Way: Wisdom's Dance With the Feminine Soul*, 2021.
24. Fr. Thomas Keating, "The Beatitudes: Healing the Emotional Programs, Part 1," *The Spiritual Journey Part 4, Contemplation: The Divine Therapy.* https://www.contemplativeoutreach.org/course/61-the-beatitudes-healing-the-emotional-programs-part-1.
25. Rev. David R. Anderson, Trinity Church, Solebury, PA, May 2003.

Epilogue

1. Baptismal Covenant, *The Book of Common Prayer* (New York, NY: Church Publishing, 1979), 305.
2. Kristich, *Closer Than Breath* coursework. https://closerthanbreath.com; accessed 1.10.2022.
3. John 14:12.
4. Merton, *Conjectures of a Guilty Bystander*, 153.
5. Pramuck, *Sophia*, 193.

INDEX